Law's Limits

The Rule of Law and the Supply and Demand of Rights

What law is, can be, or ought to be is determined by the character of those institutions that make, interpret, and enforce law. The interaction of these institutions molds the supply of and demand for law. Focusing on this interaction in the context of U.S. property law and global debates about private property and the Rule of Law, this book paints an unconventional picture of law and rights. Law and rights shift and cycle as systemic factors, such as increasing numbers and complexity, strain both supply and demand. This strain produces tough institutional choices and unexpected combinations of goals and institutions, such as private property best protected by the unconstrained political process and communitarian values best achieved through exit and atomistic markets. It also frustrates the hopes for courts, rights, and law embodied in notions such as the Rule of Law and constitutionalism. Although there may be an important role for law, rights, and courts both in the United States and abroad, it can not be facilely defined. This book proposes a way to define that role and to reform legal education and legal analysis.

Neil Komesar is the Burris-Bascom Professor of Law at the University of Wisconsin. He has been a Woodrow Wilson, National Science Foundation, and Smongeski Fellow. Professor Komesar has written on a wide variety of subjects including constitutional theory, tort reform, land use, damages, criminal victimization, public interest law, property rights, landlord-tenant law, and class actions. He is the author of *Imperfect Alternatives – Choosing Institutions in Law, Economics and Public Policy* (1994) and coauthor of *Public Interest Law: An Economic and Institutional Analysis* (with Burton Weisbrod and Joel F. Handler, 1978). Professor Komesar teaches or has taught courses on torts, property, land use, constitutional law, and law and economics.

Law's Limits

The Rule of Law and the Supply and Demand of Rights

NEIL K. KOMESAR

University of Wisconsin, Madison

CAMBRIDGE UNIVERSITY PRESS

PUBLISHED BY THE PRESS SYNDICATE OF THE UNIVERSITY OF CAMBRIDGE
The Pitt Building, Trumpington Street, Cambridge, United Kingdom

CAMBRIDGE UNIVERSITY PRESS
The Edinburgh Building, Cambridge CB2 2RU, UK
40 West 20th Street, New York, NY 10011-4211, USA
10 Stamford Road, Oakleigh, VIC 3166, Australia
Ruiz de Alarcón 13, 28014 Madrid, Spain
Dock House, The Waterfront, Cape Town 8001, South Africa

http://www.cambridge.org

First published 2001

Printed in the United States of America

Typeface Times Ten Roman 10/13 pt.   *System* QuarkXPress 4.04 [AG]

A catalog library for this book is available from the British Library.

Library of Congress Cataloging in Publication Data
Komesar, Neil K.
Law's limits : the rule of law and and the supply and demand of rights / Neil Komesar.
p. cm.
Includes bibliographical references and index.
ISBN 0-521-80629-1 (hardback) – ISBN 0-521-00086-6 (pbk.)
1. Right of property – United States. 2. Land use – Law and legislation – United States.
3. Rule of law – United States. 4. Law – Methodology. I. Title.
KF562 .K65 2001
346.7304'32–dc21
2001022307

ISBN 0 521 80629 1 hardback
ISBN 0 521 00086 6 paperback

To Rose, Eve, and Justin

Contents

Preface

Writing is a great teacher. This book began as an application of the analytical framework set out in my first book on institutional choice, *Imperfect Alternatives*,[1] to property law and property rights. But it quickly grew in several directions, carrying its author with it. First, the scope of application expanded. It became evident that what could be said about property law and rights could be said about law and rights in general. In turn, this brought me to the provocative topics of the Rule of Law and constitutionalism. Without losing its interest in property law, this book became a book about the legal process in general and about law and rights around the world.

Second, law and rights took on shapes I had not fully expected and was certainly different from what I had foreseen in the first book. In particular, law and rights shift and cycle. As systemic variables like numbers and complexity increase, there is increased cycling between basic judicial strategies such as cycling between individual and class actions and between rules and standards, as well as a long-term shift toward rules of abdication as courts abandon entire areas of social decision making.

Third, the analytical framework deepened and changed. I had to reconsider and rework the analytical framework presented in the first book. In particular, I needed to explore the implications of systemic factors like numbers and complexity for institutional choice and institutional comparison. In *Imperfect Alternatives,* I suggested that institutions moved together, but I did not explain why. Numbers and complexity are readily understandable and universally relevant variables that tell us why institutions move together and dramatically expose the common fallacy

[1] Komesar (1994).

ix

of generating critique in one context and reform in another. Focusing on numbers and complexity deepens comparative institutional analysis and gives familiar institutional choices new meaning. In addition, as I wrote this book, I saw the importance of examining communities as an institutional alternative and I saw the connections between communities and their informal norms and the institutions with which I was more familiar.

Fourth, the role of the participation-centered approach I suggested in the first book grew in importance. In *Imperfect Alternatives,* I argued for comparative institutional analysis in general and downplayed the particular strategy I employed. But, as this book evolved, I began to understand the central place of participation not only in understanding institutions, but also in understanding social goals and values. Many prominent goals are defined by basic notions of participation and, therefore, a participation-centered approach provides a way to cut across goals as seemingly diverse as resource allocation efficiency and equality and to link goal choice and institutional choice.

My growth through writing was aided by many. A number of friends and colleagues read drafts of this book and some even read several drafts. I owe a great debt to Vicki Been, Jill Fisch, Yash Ghai, David Goldberger, Michael Heise, Kathryn Hendley, Jane Larson, Victoria Nourse, Paul Olzowka, Tom Palay, Boa Santos, David Schwartz, Greg Shaffer, and Bill Whitford for their insights. I owe a particularly great debt to Miguel Poiares Maduro, my friend and sojourner in comparative institutional analysis. Miguel read and commented on drafts beyond count. His insights, so kindly and enthusiastically given, advanced my thinking immensely. I am fortunate to have such a friend and ally.

I was aided by the excellent research of David Northcutt, Ed Pardon, and Jake Blavat and by the tireless and resourceful efforts of Theresa Dougherty who saw me from scrawled pages and muttered dictation to word processing. I am indebted to the editors at Cambridge University Press, in particular Scott Parris and Laura Lawrie, for all their efforts on behalf of this book. I owe thanks to Quarles and Brady and various law school funds for providing me with the time to write. I owe special thanks to Allen Fitchen for his counsel and support. I also owe more than I can count to my wife, Shelley Safer, for her wisdom, love, and laughter.

PART I

THE BASIC FRAMEWORK

1

Supply and Demand

The essence of law does not lie in disembodied principles and abstract values. What law is, can be, or ought to be is determined by the character of those processes that make, interpret, and enforce law. The interaction of these processes molds the supply of and demand for law. When U.S. lawyers and legal scholars use the term "law," they commonly mean court-made law. Here law is the product of a process – the adjudicative process – filled with limits and trade-offs. This process has elaborate procedures that raise the cost of participation and reduce access to information. It has limited physical resources and is constrained by the bottleneck of an appellate system that restricts its growth. Defining a role for law – at least the U.S. sense of law – means defining a role for this adjudicative process, and that requires recognizing its limits. This is the supply side of law.

Allocating these judicial resources appropriately, however, means considering demand as well as supply, and that necessitates looking at more than courts. Courts are most needed where alternative decision makers such as political processes, markets, and informal communities work least well. If we focus solely on questions of supply and, therefore, solely on the characteristics of the courts, we will often waste the courts by using them where they are least needed. By contrast, if we focus solely on demand and, therefore, on the failings of these other decision-making institutions, we will set tasks for law and courts that far exceed their capacity. To understand what law is or ought to be, we must consider both supply and demand. We must understand both the ability of courts to deliver legal protections and the need for these protections and that means understanding and choosing among alternative decision makers such as courts, markets, communities, and political processes.

This book focuses primarily on court-based law and legal rights. A significant emphasis on courts and rights is by no means exclusively associated with the United States. It has developed in various forms in many Western democracies. In fact, the influence of this vision of law and rights extends beyond the confines of the United States and the other Western democracies. It is exported under labels like the Rule of Law and constitutionalism. Many believe that a strong judicial presence and strong legal rights will provide the protection of property and the individual that will allow markets and democracies to flourish.[1]

As this book shows, however, systemic forces operating through supply and demand are bound to frustrate these hopes for courts, rights, and law, both at home and abroad. The same forces that produce the call for law and rights cause a deterioration in their functioning. The same forces that increase the demand for law and rights diminish their supply. These forces require us to reexamine the role of law and rights and the associated role of courts. There may be an important role for law, rights, and courts, but it cannot be facilely defined.

Analyzing law, rights, and the role of courts by joining supply and demand means coping with the reality of institutional behavior. Courts, political processes, markets, and informal communities all function well when the number of people affected by the relevant decision is small and the complexity of the decision is low. Ideal types ranging from civic republics and informal communities to minimal states and the Rule of Law are conceived in this setting. But all these ideal types deteriorate as numbers and complexity increase. Moreover, numbers and complexity are high and increasing. Reality is a long way – an increasingly long way – from ideal types.

This book paints a picture of law and rights unlike that commonly portrayed. Increasing numbers and complexity strain courts as the demand for law and rights increases and the capacity to supply them decreases. Law and rights shift and cycle. There is increased cycling between basic judicial strategies, such as cycling between individual and class actions and between rules and standards. There will be long-term trends toward rules of abdication as courts abandon entire areas of social decision making. On a normative level, there will be unexpected combinations of goals and responses – private property best protected by the political process and communitarian values best achieved through exit and atomistic markets.

In this portrayal, legal rights are forged by the forces of supply and demand; they are quintessential institutional choices. Rights mark those instances in which courts have significant decision-making responsibility.

---

[1] Ackerman (1997); Franck (1992); Sunstein (1993).

The strongest legal rights involve significant judicial activism but not necessarily significant judicial activity. Although, on one level, strong legal rights mean the substitution of courts for other institutions, on another level, courts deflect most of this decision-making responsibility. Thus, for example, the strongest First Amendment rights see courts substituting their decisions for legislative or political process determinations, while at the same time allocating much of the decision about the content of speech to the individual or the marketplace.

This distinction between judicial activism and judicial activity interacts with the traditional dichotomy between rules and standards. Moderate rights involve standards and judicial balancing and, therefore, require the most judicial activity. But both the strongest and weakest judicial activism are found in rules that involve limited judicial activity. These rules allocate significant responsibility away from courts to other institutions such as the market or the political process. Systemic forces – such as increasing numbers and complexity – make these shifts of responsibility to other institutions both increasingly necessary and increasingly difficult. Here lie the dynamics of shifts and cycles between rules and standards and between judicial philosophies. Systemic forces and institutional choices determine these shifts and cycles and mold rights in surprising ways. In turn, they confound icons like minimal states and informal communities.

In order to establish and elaborate this vision of law and rights, I begin by exploring law, rights, and the role of the courts in the context of U.S. property law and property rights. The Rule of Law being promoted around the world often relies on a vision of strong property rights apparently modeled on the U.S. system. But the reality of U.S. property law and property rights is inconsistent with the strong judicial presence supposed in the Rule of Law. U.S. courts mostly decide not to decide, leaving the protection of property to other institutions. These anointed institutions often are highly imperfect – biased, corrupt, insensitive, or worse – and these imperfections are likely to increase over time. Yet, the allocation to these other institutions is increasingly necessary, even as these alternatives deteriorate in ability. Exploring U.S. property law with its emphasis on local decision making also allows us to assess the communitarian position commonly counterposed to the Rule of Law. As we shall see, informal communities and norms are no more a cure-all than courts and the Rule of Law.

Cosmic ideological debates rage around the subject of property: communitarians versus liberals; civic republicans versus individualists; the market-oriented versus the government-oriented, and so forth. These debates focus on the virtues and vices of what is referred to as the "institution of property" – usually meaning the institution of private property. In this book, however, I am interested in the institutions of the institution of property – those processes in society that define, monitor, protect, and allocate property. There is a variety of these institutions, ranging from informal communities operating through norms to complex market transactions to governmental regulatory programs to courts operating in a variety of roles.

The workings of these institutions of property are central, whether the property in question is called private, public, common, communal, or republican. Choice among and comparison of these institutions provides us with an intriguing and even startling picture of property law and rights and of law and rights in general. Everything from the Coase Theorem to the role of communities and norms takes on new meaning, and the very definitions of private and common property are called into question.

I will allocate three chapters to U.S. land use regulation and the property rights associated with its judicial review. Much is at stake here. The battle over U.S. land use regulation concerns the environment, housing, racial and economic integration, public education, and community values. Here, the controversy over property rights is a controversy over basic human rights.

Examining the reality of U.S. land use law exposes the problems facing the globalization of the Rule of Law and allows us to identify those moments where courts will work well enough to make the Rule of Law more than a slogan. Institutional choices and comparison determined by systemic factors like numbers and complexity are essential in understanding all institutions and all legal systems. Although the structures of law clearly differ across nations, these basic systemic variables and difficult institutional trade-offs are universal.[2]

The first two parts of this book explore the central issue of U.S. property law – the resolution of conflicting land uses. Part I presents the basic framework in the context of traditional common law doctrines. Chapter

---

[2] Similarly, the insights about institutional choice and comparison revealed in the exploration of land use regulation and real property discussed in this book – what might be considered traditional property – should be equally applicable to newer forms of property involving telecommunications and cyberspace. See, generally, Lessig (1999); Laffont and Tirole (1999); Sidak and Spulber (1997). Indeed, this world of explosive increases in numbers and complexity will demand a strong grasp of the insights gleaned here. This is a setting in which the institutions meant to define, monitor, and enforce property rights will be severely tested. As a general matter, the same basic issues of institutional choice and comparative institutional analysis confront any form of law and right.

2, " The Spectrum of Rights," shows that even these traditional, court-centered doctrines exhibit continuous shifts in the role of courts and significant allocations of decision-making responsibility away from courts to the market and the political process. In order to understand the dynamics of these shifts and the systemic factors that produce them, I present a comparative institutional approach that integrates supply and demand. I then contrast this approach with the demand-side approaches of standard law and economics and conventional legal analysis. I discuss the central role that institutional choice must play in both institutional and neoclassical economics. Chapter 3, "The Supply Side – The Little Engine of Law and Rights," examines the adjudicative process. It uses systemic factors to analyze the performance of the courts and basic issues of adjudication such as the choice between individual and class action.

Part II examines the sorts of constitutional rights and serious constitutional judicial review that are thought to be the essence of property rights and, more broadly, of constitutionalism and the Rule of Law. Chapter 4, "Zoning and its Discontents – Political Malfunction and the Demand for Rights," focuses primarily on the demand for these rights. It analyzes various forms of political malfunction and shows the necessity of employing a two-force model of the political process rather than the one-force model that characterizes the interest group theory of politics and the economic theory of regulation. This two-force model recognizes the possibility of both over- and underrepresentation of the majority – majoritarian and minoritarian bias – and sets out the conditions that make one or the other more likely. This approach proves crucial in understanding local community decision making like that involved in zoning. The chapter evaluates several strategies to deal with these political malfunctions. Chapter 5, "Just Compensation – The Problems of Judicial Pricing," explores the Takings Clause and the United States Supreme Court's recent regulatory takings cases, considered the foundation of a revolution in property rights. It shows the systemic limits of these ambitious attempts to construct strong property rights. In Chapter 6, "High Stakes Players and Hidden Markets," I propose a strategy for judicial review of land use regulation that promotes an unorthodox combination of no rights and market pricing.

Utilizing the lessons from U.S. property law, Part III explores the role of the same basic systemic forces in two broad legal settings. Chapter 7, "Theories of Property – From Coase to Communitarianism," analyzes the debates about private property. It examines the economic theory of private property as well as theories of communal or civic republican property and shows how systemic forces and institutional choice dissolve ideological positions on property and draw into question the definitions of private and common property. Chapter 8, "Numbers, Complexity, and the Rule of Law," analyzes the role of the courts and of law and rights as societies become massive and complex. It focuses attention on the forces that produce shifts and cycles in law and rights and, thereby, undermine the stability and certainty sought by the proponents of the Rule of Law. Here I evaluate the positions of both the advocates of the Rule of Law and its communitarian opponents. The last chapter, "Changes," sets out needed reforms in legal analysis, economic analysis, legal education, and judicial decision making.

There are basic lessons here for the establishment of the Rule of Law around the world. We are most likely to hear cries for a stable, clear, evenly applied Rule of Law in those situations in which it will be most difficult to achieve this Rule of Law. Where numbers and complexity are high, the Rule of Law will be most demanded, but it also will be in the shortest supply. This does not mean that the adjudicative process cannot play a meaningful role in dealing with these tough conditions, but it may mean that it can do so on a broad basis for only a short time, and that any long-term role for serious judicial intervention will require severely narrowing the band of societal issues allocated to the courts.

In turn, there are basic lessons about the attractive images of the judicial and political processes that seem to carry the debate about judicial review and the Rule of Law. This imagery – such as notions of deliberation, consensus, and community – fits neatly into the easy world of low numbers and complexity. But this is not where courts, judicial review, and the Rule of Law are most needed. They are needed where numbers and complexity are high and, therefore, where deliberation, consensus, and community are strained and distorted. The resulting tensions require that any meaningful analysis of the role of the courts eschew attractive imagery and easy answers. These problems promise to haunt analyses of courts both in Western democracies and developing nations.

From a distance – and in the throes of nostalgia – laws, rights, and decision-making institutions seem to work simply and well. But especially at high numbers and complexity, a closer look yields a different picture. Institutions will function far more imperfectly and the institutional choices will be both more difficult and less attractive. As a poignant example of the lessons of a closer look, one only needs to reflect on what we have learned about the U.S. political processes and courts during the 2000 presidential election.

This is a book about the legal process and the laws and rights it produces. More exactly, it is a book about reforming the way we think about the legal process, law, and rights. Law and rights cannot be understood by methods of legal analysis that focus attention solely on goals and values or at most discuss the horrors of present systems. The first is totally indeterminate, and the second leaves us in continuous and costly cycling among highly imperfect alternatives. Different tools must be employed – different questions asked – to understand what law and rights are, what they can be, and what they ought to be.

If law and rights are the product of tough institutional choices impacted by systemic variables such as the costs of participation and numbers and complexity, then we need a conception of law and rights that reflects these tough institutional choices and models of the various decision-making institutions that embody these systemic variables. We need a vision of the adjudicative process that reflects the dynamics of litigation and the severe constraints on resources as well as the competence of judges and juries and a vision of the political process that reflects and integrates both the power of the few and the power of the many. This means serious reform in the way we analyze and teach law.

These propositions hold no matter how we define law. In this book, I focus primarily on court-made law. This is a narrow definition of law. Even in the U.S. context, law is the product of societal institutions such as legislatures, bureaucracies, and informal communities as well as courts. My use of this narrow definition does not mean that I believe that law and public policy should be court centered. Quite the opposite. The limits of the courts and, hence, the limits of court-made law are central tenets of this book. Nor does it mean that I discuss and focus exclusively or even primarily on the characteristics of the adjudicative process. My approach to law requires an understanding of both the adjudicative process and its substitutes or alternatives such as legislatures, bureaucracies, and informal communities. I spend much of the book discussing the roles of these alternative societal institutions and, therefore, exploring broader definitions of law.

The analytical framework employed here to study court-made law is equally applicable to other definitions of law or, more broadly, to law and public policy in general. Whether seen as the product of courts, legislatures, bureaucracies, or informal communities, the meaning and efficacy of law will be determined by the abilities of the institution or institutions meant to deliver legal protections. Under alternative definitions of law, courts might be considered as substitute decision makers with legislatures, bureaucracies, or informal communities now considered primary. But the same issues of supply and demand will surface everywhere.

The analysis presented here warns against attaching normative significance to any definition of law. As this book shows, deciding whether and to what extent law produced outside the courts is superior to court-made law is a tricky business. The same sort of challenging systemic or institutional quandaries raised in this book remain, no matter how one rearranges the institutional alignment. All forms of law depend on imperfect structures and involve difficult institutional choices. No matter how it is defined, law has limits.

2

The Spectrum of Rights

In one form or another, judges are asked to decide who will decide basic substantive decisions. Rather than directly addressing these substantive decisions, courts funnel most of them elsewhere – to markets or to the political process. They allocate only a very limited and often shifting range of these substantive decisions to themselves. The role of courts and the character of law and legal rights are determined by these allocations of decision making.

This chapter and the next use several traditional common law property issues to explore these institutional choices and the systemic factors that underlie them and to examine the role of these choices in shaping law and rights. This chapter focuses primarily on the common law doctrines of nuisance and trespass and employs a case popular among legal scholars and casebook authors, *Boomer v. Atlantic Cement Company*.[1] I use *Boomer* and its simple and familiar setting to introduce most of the themes and analytical tools I will employ in this book. I show the shifts and changes in law and rights associated with variation in systemic factors such as numbers and complexity, introduce a simple analytical model for institutional choice and comparison – the participation-centered model – and show its use across the three alternative institutions at play in *Boomer* – the courts, the market, and the political process.

Boomer involves two levels of institutional choice – the choice between the market and the courts that so often characterizes private law such as torts and contracts – and the choice between the courts and the political process, which is more commonly seen in public law areas such as constitutional law. These institutional choices produce property rights that take on unexpected shapes. Property owners injured in much the

[1] 26 NY2d 219, 309 NYS2d 312, 257 NE2d 870 (1970).

same way or to much the same extent receive different protection from the courts – different property rights. Systemic factors rather than the merits of the individual dispute determine rights and legal protection.

I. *BOOMER* – THE COMMON LAW AND INSTITUTIONAL CHOICE

The *Boomer* case arose from private litigation by seven neighbors against a large cement plant near Albany, New York. The seven neighbors brought an action in the state courts of New York arguing that the dirt, smoke, and vibration emanating from the plant constituted a common law nuisance and, therefore, violated their private property rights. They sought the traditional remedy for violation of these rights – an injunction against continuation of this injurious activity. The trial court found that the defendant was maintaining a nuisance, but, contrary to precedent, refused the plaintiffs' request for an injunction, offering them damages instead. The New York Court of Appeals reviewed this unorthodox response and, with slight modification, upheld it. A strong dissent called for imposition of the injunction.

A. The Market versus the Courts

Under the older rule changed in *Boomer,* the *Boomer* plaintiffs only needed to show that the defendant's activities constituted a nuisance and that the plaintiffs suffered significant injury. Whether or not that injury exceeded the value of the use enjoined – the cost to the defendant of the injunction – was not relevant. Under this older rule, the plaintiffs had a simple and powerful property right. But, under the new rule, the plaintiffs would receive an injunction only if they established that their injury exceeded the value of the offending use. Without such a showing, the plaintiffs could at most receive damages. Under the new rule, in order to issue an injunction, the courts must make a more complex determination about the relative value of the uses.

The majority's logic for the new rule and for refusing an injunction in the circumstances of this case is simple. The majority of the appellate judges refused the injunction because they believed that the harm to the plaintiffs caused by the defendant's cement plant was far less than the value of the plant. The trial court estimated the total loss to the seven plaintiffs at $185,000. The value of the defendant's plant was described as involving an investment of roughly $45 million as well as employing over three hundred people.[2]

The *Boomer* court's concern with the relative impact of the remedy – the rough balance between social benefits and costs – corresponds to the goal of resource allocation efficiency so central to the economic approach to law.[3] In more common legal vernacular, these are concerns about the highest and best use of the resource. Whether called highest and best use or resource allocation efficiency, it seems virtually impossible to deal with conflicting uses without serious concern for their relative impact or relative merits. But this is hardly the only goal that competes for attention. In *Boomer,* for example, we can see concern not only about whether the cement plant should move but also about how the benefits and costs of this locational decision should be distributed. The decision to grant permanent damages in the case can be seen as an attempt to achieve not only the highest and best use, but also distributional fairness.

As the book progresses, I will consider several goals primarily to show that the connection between goals, values, or ideologies and law and rights depends on institutional choice. Considering resource allocation efficiency here allows me to make this point in the context of an important societal goal and it allows me to show the import of institutional choice for a significant approach to legal analysis – law and economics. We can see the equivocal nature of the connection between goals and law in general and between resource allocation efficiency and the refusal of the injunction in *Boomer,* by briefly considering traditional property law.

As a general rule, awarding injunctions without judicial balancing is a quite common response to property rights violations. In common law trespass actions, courts award an injunction for the violation of a property right without ever hearing or being willing to hear arguments about the relative merits or values of the particular offending and protected uses. If I construct a building on your land, you can enjoin my intrusion without regard to the value of my use relative to yours. I cannot offer a "relative impact" defense. There is no place in this litigation for the balancing of

---

[2] Technically, the figures are not comparable. The loss to society of closing the defendant's plant might be less than $45 million, depending on the value of the plant (and the land on which it was located) for other purposes. Similarly, the loss to the employees from cessation of business would depend on their alternative employment opportunities. Nevertheless, the figures used by the court roughly relate to the losses that would be associated with a cessation of the defendant's operation.

[3] For a more formal definition of resource allocation efficiency, see Komesar (1994) at 30–4.

competing uses found in the *Boomer* case. Unconditionally awarding an injunction to prevent a trespass is a basic tenet of Anglo-American property law.

The very existence of this simple, unconditional enforcement of property rights seems, at first blush, to conflict with a concern for resource allocation efficiency because it resists judicial comparison of social benefits and costs. If judicial balancing of social benefits and costs like that in *Boomer* exemplifies concern for resource allocation efficiency, then a refusal to carry out such a balance seems to disprove this concern.

Law and economics scholars have offered a way around this apparent conflict by arguing that the courts will not and should not balance benefits and costs when this balance can be accomplished by market transactions.[4] In particular, in the simple case of injunctions for trespass, if the offending use is more valuable, then the offending user, precluded by injunction from simply imposing his or her use, will purchase that right to use from its owner. The market transaction manifests in a straightforward manner that the benefits of the use are greater than its costs. Since the market resolves relative impact, courts do not have to do so.[5]

From this standpoint, however, the majority position in *Boomer* no longer seems so obvious. It would seem that enjoining the use need not force the cement company to cease socially beneficial production. If the benefits to the cement company of continuing the offending use exceed the detriments to the plaintiffs, the cement company, once it has been enjoined, can acquire the right to continue its use by purchasing that right from its owners, the plaintiffs. Contrary to the fears of the *Boomer* majority, the traditional injunction asked for by the plaintiffs would not stand in the way of the best use. We are now left to wonder why we ever see courts in the business of comparing benefits and costs as they did in the majority opinion in *Boomer* and as they do in many areas of law.

---

[4] See R. Posner (1992) at 56–61. Posner's analysis reflects an earlier analysis by Guido Calabresi, a founder of law and economics. See Calabresi and Melamed (1972).

There exists a rich and sophisticated law and economics literature on this general question. See, e.g., Kaplow and Shavell (1996); Krier and Schwab (1995); Levmore (1997); Merrill (1985).

Many of these works see the issue as a choice between injunctions and damages. But there is a more basic issue inherent in cases like *Boomer* – the choice between injunctions with and without judicial balancing or, more broadly, the choice between rules and standards. This is the issue addressed in this chapter.

[5] R. Posner (1992) at 56.

Law and economics scholars, however, are not at a loss to explain this institutional choice. Where the difficulty of transacting increases and, therefore, the likelihood of a beneficial transaction decreases, it is less likely that the market will correctly balance costs and benefits in the context of an injunction. The simple injunctive response of trespass law makes less sense and the greater role of courts in balancing benefits and costs makes more sense as the cost of transacting increases. As Richard Posner puts it, where the market works, the courts allocate the efficiency decision (the balancing of costs and benefits) to the market; where the market does not work, the courts make the efficiency determination themselves.[6]

From this perspective, one can see an important difference between the standard two-person setting of trespass cases and the setting in *Boomer,* where the company would have to deal with seven parties. A larger number of parties results in higher costs of transaction simply because more transactions (six more) must be accomplished. More important, the presence of seven neighbors each of whose rights must be purchased means that the defendant faces seven parties each of whom holds veto power over the project. If each neighbor tries to push the defendant to its limit, the defendant could be faced with a cost significantly (as much as seven times) in excess of the value of its use. Under these conditions, it is entirely possible that no transaction would take place and, therefore, the unattractive result envisioned by the majority – the closing of a far more valuable plant – would occur.[7]

If the transaction fails, everyone is worse off. The cement plant must close at appreciable cost and the neighbors have missed a chance to sell their $185,000 interest for several times its value. But, in order for the neighbors to sell their interest, they must cooperate. The transaction is endangered when each neighbor tries to extract the maximum. If they can cooperate, they can each reap a sizeable gain. The transaction costs here include the costs of achieving cooperation among the neighbors. Here is our first glimpse of the most pervasive barrier to many institutional

---

[6] Id. at 62–3.

[7] There are transaction costs even in two-party situations especially where the parties can only deal with each other. Here we have bilateral monopoly problems. These issues have been much discussed in the law and economics literature. See, e.g., Polinsky (1980), Sterk (1987), and the sources cited in note 4, supra. A recent study casts some doubt on the possibility of bargaining around an injunction. Farnsworth (1999).

I will return to this subject in greater detail in Chapter 3. For present purposes, the point remains that variation in factors such as numbers and complexity can affect the chance of transacting.

responses – collective action problems.[8] The tendency to cheat or act opportunistically and the costs of arranging and policing a collective arrangement in the face of cheating often raises transaction costs and explains why arrangements involving fewer people are usually more successful than arrangements with more people. More people – larger numbers – are involved in the *Boomer* setting than in the standard trespass setting and, therefore, according to the conventional law and economics analysis, the market will work less well.

Thus, institutional choice is central to the conventional economics analysis of law. Only by adding important institutional insights can law and economics scholars provide their creative explanation for the difference between property and liability rules. Concern for resource allocation efficiency standing alone does not help to resolve the legal decision – the choice of property law response.

In this account, property law and rights depend on institutional choice. As institutional choice changes, property rights change. The injured party's rights grow weaker as we move from the institutional choice of the market in trespass to the institutional choice of the courts in nuisance. The injured party must now prove more or show more in order to receive the same remedy. This change in institutional choice and, therefore, in law and rights is related to a simple set of variables. Transaction costs increase as the number of transacting parties – or, more exactly, the number of parties relevant to a transaction – and the complexity of the transaction increase. Numbers and complexity affect institutional performance and institutional performance affects property remedies and rights.[9]

B. The Political Process versus the Courts

These same points apply to another institutional choice in *Boomer*. This institutional choice is the basis for the difference between the positions

---

[8] The classic work on the problems of collective action is Olson (1965) and its classic application to property rights is G. Hardin (1968).

[9] This institutional rendition of the difference between trespass and nuisance will seem at odds with the traditional legal analysis based on distinctions between interference with the right to exclusive possession and interference with use and enjoyment and more particularly with the concept of physical invasion. Upon closer inspection, however, these distinctions and constructs are largely empty and depend for substance on the sort of analysis proposed in this book. I will return to this subject at the end of this chapter.

of the majority and the dissent. The dissent wanted an injunction in this case. The dissent's position, however, did not stem from a belief in the older and simpler property rules with their market determination of relative impact. Like the majority, the dissent believed in judicial determination of relative impact. In fact, the dissent was far more ambitious for this judicial determination than the majority. The dissent wanted to expand the scope of this determination to include not just the seven plaintiffs in the case but also the other victims of the defendant's pollution – the residents of the Hudson River Valley. Thus, the dissent, like the majority, was interested in the goal of highest and best use or resource allocation efficiency. The dissent, however, saw these goals in more global terms.

According to the dissent, an injunction should be issued because of the adverse impacts of the defendant's activities not only on the seven plaintiffs but also on the citizens of the Hudson River Valley. Pointing to studies and broad social concerns about air pollution, the dissent wanted the defendant and similarly situated polluters to have sufficient incentives to find means to abate the nuisance. Since such technology did not exist and it was by no means certain that it would be found in time, the dissent was willing to risk plant closure apparently seeing it as superior to the continuing pollution of the Hudson River Valley. For the dissent, the adjudicative process must consider the full range of impacts and address the important problem of pollution on a more general level. Here the dissent and the majority disagree.

The issue that separated the majority and the dissent was not whether the appropriate property remedy was an injunction issued without judicial balancing of relative impacts rather than one that required such balancing. They did not differ over the choice to substitute the courts for the market – the institutional choice we just discussed. Both believed that the relative impact issue in *Boomer* should be decided by the courts. The question that separated them was how large a range of relative impacts the courts would consider and how much they would leave to other decision makers. From the perspective of rights and remedies, the issue became not whether property owners in the Hudson River Valley injured by pollution would receive judicial protection more or less easily, but whether they would receive judicial protection at all. Another important institutional choice lurks. Here the majority's response to the dissent's position is telling.

The majority, also aware of the general problems of pollution, justified its more modest adjudicative role by placing greater reliance on yet another institution – the political process:

Effective control of air pollution is a problem presently far from solution even with the full public and financial powers of government. In large measure adequate technical procedures are yet to be developed and some that appear possible may be economically impracticable.

It seems apparent that the amelioration of air pollution will depend on technical research in great depth; on a carefully balanced consideration of the economic impact of close regulation; and of the actual effect on public health. It is likely to require massive public expenditure and to demand more than any local community can accomplish and to depend on regional and interstate controls.

A court should not try to do this on its own as a by-product of private litigation and it seems manifest that the judicial establishment is neither equipped in the limited nature of any judgment it can pronounce nor prepared to lay down and implement an effective policy for the elimination of air pollution. This is an area beyond the circumference of one private law suit. It is a direct responsibility for government and should not thus be undertaken as an incident to solving a dispute between property owners and a single cement plant – one of many – in the Hudson River Valley.[10]

At least at first blush, the majority's position on this issue again seems sensible. Pollution in the Hudson River Valley is a far-flung, complex phenomenon. The political process with its wide range of investigative, regulatory, and taxing alternatives seems preferable to an adjudicative process strained by such determinations. Allocating such global and complex issues to the political process is a response commonly found in judicial opinions from all areas of the law. If the citizens in the Hudson River Valley want property protection, they must get it from the legislature. To the majority, this ended the issue.

As we shall see, the resolution of this essential issue is far from obvious. Before turning to this issue, however, there are several important points to emphasize. First, the issue that separates the majority and the dissent is an issue of institutional choice. Both the majority and dissent agree on the importance of relative impact. They differ about who will resolve this issue. Second, the institutional choice has changed from the earlier one inherent in trespass versus nuisance. The choice is no longer between the market and the courts. The choice now is between the courts and the government – or, as I shall call it, the political process. Third, al-

---

[10] 257 N.E.2d 870, 871 (1970).

though these two institutional choices are different, the same or very similar factors seem to be driving both. The majority explains its decision in terms of numbers and complexity. Pollution in the Hudson River Valley involves very large numbers of potential victims and even a sizeable number of polluters. In the majority's view, the issue is so complex both in its causes and its solutions that it is a job for the political process with its broader scope of inquiry, remedy, and resources. These are the same factors that Posner employed to explain the difference between trespass and nuisance and the choice between markets and courts. Fourth, property remedies and property rights again vary with institutional choice and they vary dramatically. There is now the distinct possibility that property owners in the Hudson River Valley injured in much the same way as those in *Boomer* (and, as a group, to a much greater extent) may be without judicial protection and, therefore, without any property right. We will return to this issue in the next chapter when we consider the dynamics of litigation and class actions.

C. Generating the Spectrum – The Need for Institutional Comparison

Joining the insights from both these institutional choices, we can see a spectrum of property rights generated solely by variation in systemic factors and, in particular, by increases in numbers and complexity. The analysis suggests a predictable shift in the choice of institution as numbers and complexity increase. When numbers and complexity are low, courts can make simple judgments – employ simple rules – that send the tougher issues of balancing to markets. This is a world of strong rights and certain remedies – the world of trespass. We have significant judicial activism, but limited judicial activity. Courts decide that markets or transactions will evaluate relative impact.

As numbers and complexity continue to grow, disputes reaching courts force greater judicial activity. As transactions become more difficult and costly, courts consider themselves to be better determiners of relative impact than existing markets. Courts must now do much more, but the property rights of the injured parties are weaker and property law is less clear. Judicial activism decreases but judicial activity increases. We have moved from clear rules to fuzzier standards.

In turn, as high numbers and complexity continue to grow, courts, recognizing their own limitations, send matters to the political process. Here we again have a simple rule, but no court-produced rights or remedies at all. Now both judicial activism and judicial activity have reached their nadir.

As we proceed through the book and add institutional possibilities, this sort of spectrum will reappear in several forms. One basic attribute, however, will remain the same – variation in institutional choice dictates variation in law and rights. But a sophisticated understanding of institutional choice will require more than we have seen thus far. Unfortunately, the framework for institutional choice generated by combining the analyses of law and economics and the *Boomer* judges is inadequate. We need more.

The analysis of institutional choice employed by law and economics scholars like Richard Posner asks how one institution – the market – works in two different settings and bases its vision of law on the variation of market performance in these two settings. These law and economics scholars are following the maxims of welfare economics that connect public policy to imperfections in the market – called "market failures." This law and economics approach associates simple injunctions with instances in which transaction costs are low or the market works well and complex injunctions with higher transaction costs or instances in which the market does not work well.

This conventional analysis seems straightforward. But something quite basic is missing. The legal issue of simple versus complex injunctions confronted by the judges in the *Boomer* case involves two institutions not one. The issue is whether it will be the courts or the market that balances the cost and benefits. Where the market is the preferred balancer, we have simple property rules; where the courts are the preferred balancers, we have more complex property rules. If the issue involves a choice between two institutions – the market and the courts – then why do law and economics scholars focus their analysis only on variation in the ability of the market? Something needs to be said or at least assumed about the other institution – the courts. The analysis must be comparative institutional not single institutional. We must ask about supply as well as demand.

Analysts like Richard Posner implicitly assume that, where transaction costs are "low" or the market "works," it makes the allocation decision better than the courts. A hidden comparative institutional judgment lies buried in this single institutional formulation – that where transaction costs are low, the market is always superior to the courts as the balancer of costs and benefits. Although this judgment is hidden, it seems plausible.

Follow what happens to the Posnerian analysis, however, as we move from the simple setting of low transaction costs and market dominance to the world of high transaction costs. According to Posner, we change legal outcomes. We move from simple property rules to more complex property rules and the judiciary becomes the balancer of benefits and costs. Again we have the peculiar outcome that a greater role for the judiciary is based solely on variation in the characteristics of the market with no explicit consideration of variation in the ability of the judiciary. More important, here the implicit assumption of judicial superiority is subject to serious doubt or at least serious qualification.

As with the market, the courts' ability decreases as the number of parties and the complexity of the issues increases. As the number of potential plaintiffs or defendants increases, the costs of bringing actions increase and the dynamics of litigation become more complex. Larger numbers of parties mean higher litigation costs such as service of process, notice of motions, depositions, and other forms of trial preparation. Larger numbers also mean that negotiations over settlement are more complicated and less likely to reach a value-enhancing result. The problems of collective action that plague market transactions as numbers increase also plague adjudication: larger numbers mean more hold-outs and greater likelihood of a failed settlement.

In addition, the task of comparing benefits and costs or of setting damages becomes more difficult for the courts as the number of parties and the complexity of the interaction of their land uses increases. The courts must now listen to and balance a larger number of impacts and a larger number of views on these impacts. Both the ability of courts to make accurate assessments and the likelihood that the issue will be brought to court and sufficiently contested are likely to decrease. Like the market process, the adjudicative process becomes less effective as numbers and complexity increase.

For an argument supporting the view that the ability of the courts deteriorates with higher numbers and complexity, we need go no further than the majority's opinion in *Boomer*. As we saw, the majority argued for allocating more global air pollution issues to the political process based on the fact that the adjudicative process decreases in ability as numbers and complexity increase. These quite valid assertions reveal a common concern about judicial ability in the face of increasing numbers and complexity. We will see it repeated throughout the book.

Unfortunately, these observations – however valid – do not provide a sufficient basis for the majority's position. Like the law and economics analysis, the majority's analysis is largely single institutional. If the issue is the choice between the courts and the political process, then we must also seriously examine the ability of the political process in this same context of large numbers and complexity. It will not do to compare a real world, highly imperfect adjudicative process with a frictionless political process. Like the frictionless market and the frictionless adjudicative process, a frictionless political process is an obvious solution. But it is also an unavailable solution. Like all real-world institutions, the political process is never frictionless.

On the simplest level, time and other resources are needed to investigate, legislate, and implement. The more complex the issue and the larger the number of people involved, the higher these costs. More important, the large numbers, great complexity, and widely dispersed stakes associated with regional air pollution cause problems for the political process by distorting the political participation of various constituent interests in such activities as lobbying and voting. These distortions of the political process are dramatic enough to be captured in two traditional but polar opposite perceptions of political malfunction – minoritarian bias, which is the overrepresentation of concentrated interests (special interest legislation), and majoritarian bias, which is the overrepresentation of dispersed larger interests (the tyranny of the majority).

In the pollution setting, the familiar scenario involves a large but mostly dormant majority that is basically unaware of the problem or unwilling to bear the expense of fighting against better-organized special interests. The outcome is minoritarian bias and special interest legislation. The likelihood of minoritarian versus majoritarian bias and the workings of the two-force model of politics used to understand it are subjects we will consider in depth in Part II of this book. It is sufficient at this juncture to see that the political process, like the market and adjudicative processes, also functions worse as numbers and complexity increase and as the distribution of stakes becomes more complex and more dispersed. Thus, although it is quite sensible for the majority in the *Boomer* case to see the political process as a viable alternative to adjudication for the general environmental issue, it is also quite sensible for the dissent to have been far less optimistic about this alternative. The essential issue separating the judges is institutional choice and it is not an easy choice.

II. SOME GENERAL LESSONS

Although we have only begun to examine the institutional alternatives and choices, certain generalizations or lessons can be drawn. First, identifying a goal – in this instance, resource allocation efficiency – tells us virtually nothing about law and rights. In the *Boomer* setting, a judge ardently devoted to resource allocation efficiency has at least three choices: stand by the simple property rule and impose an injunction without considering the relative merits of the uses, consider the relative merits of the uses and impose an injunction (the dissent's position), or consider the relative merits of the uses and refuse an injunction (the majority's position). The choice depends on the outcome of an essential and nontrivial set of institutional comparisons. The importance of resource allocation efficiency alone tells us nothing about *Boomer* and the property law concepts underlying it unless we address the difficult but central question of which institution will determine and work out resource allocation efficiency – who will balance the costs and benefits. Second, this analysis cannot be carried out through single institutional analysis no matter how careful or creative. All institutions are imperfect and choice between alternatives can be sensibly made only by considering their relative merits.

Third, we have seen an attribute of institutional choice that makes single institutional analysis obsolete and comparative institutional analysis both essential and difficult. *Institutions tend to move together.* The same factors that cause one institution to vary often similarly affect alternative institutions. In particular, we have seen a link between institutional performance and variation in numbers and complexity. Increases in the number of relevant participants and the complexity of the controversies adversely impact all the institutional alternatives.

Numbers and complexity are variables of great import. They generate shifts and cycles in law and rights. Viewed through the lense of comparative institutional analysis, it is a pattern of shifts and cycles more compelling and intriguing than that generated by single institutional analysis. This pattern will become more evident as we proceed through the book. But we have seen enough to offer some preliminary generalizations about the connection between numbers and complexity, institutional choice, and law and rights.

First, if all institutions deteriorate in ability as numbers and complexity increase, then we must be careful about the context (the level of numbers and complexity) from which we draw generalizations or judgments about any of these institutions. Comparability is fundamental. Drawing observations about one alternative from a context in which numbers and complexity are low and applying them in comparison with an institution operating at large numbers and complexity invalidates the analysis. Single institutional analysis is an extreme form of this failure of adequate comparison. The implicit assumption is that a perfect or idealized institution is waiting in the wings.

Second, because institutions move together, analysis of law and rights will usually involve a series of close institutional choices. Institutional choices at low numbers and complexity as well as institutional choices at high numbers and complexity will often be close calls. But, because all institutions tend to deteriorate as numbers and complexity increase, these are likely to be close calls of quite different types. At low numbers and complexity, we will often have the pleasant task of choosing the best of good or attractive alternatives. But, at high numbers and complexity, we are more likely to be choosing the best of bad or unattractive alternatives.

These close calls suggest that we often may see a wide variety of judicial reactions to the same general legal issue. Nuisance law – and even trespass law – are examples. Courts vary in how they treat the *Boomer* issue. Some follow *Boomer* and require balancing. Others issue an injunction without regard to balancing.[11] Some jurisdictions employ a strict liability approach to damages, like that in *Boomer,* while others require judicial balancing on this issue as well.[12] Even the world of trespass has been invaded by balancing as some courts and legal authorities have allowed the "balancing of hardships" to condition the issuance of injunctions even given a clear physical trespass.[13]

This pattern of conflicting results could be taken as a rejection of the law and economics proposition that the pattern of the common law can be explained by the goal of resource allocation efficiency. But that does not follow. As the discussion of *Boomer* showed, for example, both the positions of the majority and the dissent are consistent with resource allocation efficiency depending on the outcome of difficult institutional choices. The complex pattern of results commonly found in the law only

---

[11] See *Crushed Stone Co. v. Moore,* 369 P.2d 811 (Okla. 1962).

[12] Compare *Waschak v. Moffat,* 379 Pa. 441, 109 A.2d 310 (1954) with *Jost v. Dairyland Power Cooperative,* 45 Wis.2d 164, 172 N.W.2d 647 (1969).

[13] See *Urban Site Venture v. Levering Associates,* 340 Md. 223, 665 A2d 1062 (1995). Restatement (Second) of Torts, section 941.

rejects a law and economics analysis that is single institutional. It is consistent with a comparative institutional, law and economics analysis.

I have given significant play to the role of numbers and complexity. Throughout this book, I associate increasing numbers and complexity with decreasing institutional performance. This assertion is sensitive to the definition of "numbers." For example, markets work better as numbers rise in the sense that greater numbers of competitors mean a greater likelihood of competition. The "miracle of the market" lies in the ability of the atomistic forces of competition to deliver goods and services from many to many. But this is a different meaning of numbers than I am using. These are large numbers of actors acting largely independent of one another. The miracle of the market involves many *independent* transactions. It is when these transactions have serious effects on others not party to the transaction that nonmiraculous elements like air pollution show up.

It is also important not to equate complexity just with technical difficulty and technological innovation. Complexity can be associated with quite mundane and common issues. Thus, for example, concerns about aesthetics or community values have been with us for a long time and are understandable to everyone at a general level. But, because they are amorphous and hard to measure and define in the particular, they can create the same sort of difficulties as newer, higher tech issues. These amorphous interests and goals provide leeway for free riding in transactions and subterfuge both in political activities and adjudication. We will see examples of the impact of these amorphous concerns in the discussion of U.S. land use regulation in Part II.

My critique of single institutionalism has focused primarily on economic analysis of law and the goal of resource allocation efficiency. But the critique and its importance to law go far beyond law and economics and the goal of resource allocation efficiency. For example, there are those who see a significant role for the courts in common law adjudication in pursuit of nonresource allocation efficiency goals such as altruism or equality.[14] Like the economic analysis of law, this role is based on problems in the market. Both are demand-side arguments. Although these noneconomic analysts emphasize different goals and, presumably, see more and different problems with the market than does Posner,[15] they

---

[14] See, for example, Kennedy (1976).

[15] For example, there are concerns with commodification and alienation emphasized by commentators like Margaret Radin. I discuss these in Chapter 7.

must confront the same issues of institutional comparison as the economic analysts of law. Anyone interested in promoting altruism and equality – like anyone interested in promoting resource allocation efficiency – must seriously address institutional choice or risk undercutting the goals that they seek.

The tendency to define the role of law and rights – and, therefore, the role of the courts – from perceived problems in other institutions is pervasive. From contract law to constitutional law, from corporate law to administrative law, legal commentators call upon courts to step in when markets, legislatures, administrative agencies, and corporate boards malfunction. The failure of these demand-side analyses to scrutinize the parallel functioning of the adjudicative process is quite astounding coming from legal scholars who ought to and indeed do understand the courts better than any of the other institutions.

It is especially remarkable for economic analysts of law to construct analyses based on demand without parallel considerations of supply. Such an approach ignores the most basic canons of economics. In general, such single institutional analysis violates the notion of rational choice that underlies most economic analysis. Rational people do not make choices by considering only one alternative. The choice among alternatives underlies such central notions of economics as opportunity costs and the role of substitutes and complements.

The failure of many legal analysts to systematically consider the supply side of law – the courts – is especially troubling given the severe constraints on the adjudicative process. When compared to either the political process or the market, the adjudicative process has always been a relatively small institution. More important, it is an institution whose ability to grow is far outstripped by the other institutions. The relatively small adjudicative process has, over time, become even smaller relative to the institutions it is called upon to scrutinize.[16] Under these circumstances, a single institutional focus, mistaken in conception, becomes useless in execution. For all these reasons, it is essential to consider the supply side of law – the adjudicative process – as well as the demand side. And that is the subject of the next chapter.

---

[16] See Komesar (1994), 250–2.

III. COMMUNITIES, MARKETS, PARTICIPATION, AND METHODOLOGY

Before leaving this chapter, I want to provide a more robust view of the market as a decision-making institution by focusing on informal communities and relationships. The property rights and property law literature is replete with valuable work showing the ability of people to resolve the sort of conflicts and controversies that arose in *Boomer* without recourse to the courts or to formal law at all. Informal relationships and informal communities, operating in myriad ways, work things out. We used this ability to make decisions outside of formal law earlier to justify simple property rules. The balancing of benefits and costs via market transactions allowed courts to employ simple property rules without worrying about the allocation of resources.

But "market transactions" come in a wide variety. As many have shown us, people work out their differences in myriad and mysterious ways without recourse to or even consideration of their formal legal rights. If what is going on is bargaining in the shadow of the law, that shadow is very faint. In fact, these informal modes of working things out may not even involve transacting in any straightforward sense. Norms with the associated fear of ostracism and shame may simply dictate or at least affect behavior.[17]

This informal world can be seen in Shasta County as described by Robert Ellickson where stable communities of neighbors operating through informal social norms solve conflicts over property without recourse to law.[18] It can be seen in continuing relationships described by Stewart Macaulay in which sophisticated commercial arrangements are established and governed without detailed formal contracts or recourse to litigation.[19] It is also the world described by Elinor Ostrom in which common property resources are communally and informally governed without bureaucracies or individual property rights and without the disasters associated with the tragedy of the commons.[20]

There is much to love about this world of informal relationships and communities. Many different intellectual traditions and ideologies can claim an affinity for this world. Pro-market proponents can claim this informal world as their own because it shows that individuals can

---

[17] See E. Posner (1996).   [18] Ellickson (1991).
[19] Macaulay (1963).   [20] Ostrom (1990).

imaginatively and creatively operate outside of legislatures, bureaucracies, and courts. Others, more dubious about the world of markets and commercial transactions, can see these informal settings as indicative of the power of cooperation and the real possibility of communitarian activity.

On closer inspection, it is easy both to see why this informal world works so well and to spot its limits. The most attractive of these informal episodes are always found in the context of small numbers and low complexity. But this is a context in which all institutional alternatives work well. Where knowledge is easily accessible and largely equal, where the relevant parties can be determined and their positions easily known, measured, and monitored, everything works well. Informal arrangements may be the best, but, as our earlier analysis of *Boomer* showed, even formal institutions like courts or political process are at their best in the smaller, simpler world. Here we have choices among very attractive alternatives.

Our previous analysis, however, warns us of a less attractive world – a world of high and growing numbers and complexity. Much of the rest of this book concerns what happens when we must leave the largely frictionless world of low numbers and complexity and journey to a world of high numbers and complexity. But there are already inklings of the problems and paradoxes to come. As we move away from the world of low numbers and complexity, property rights may be more important, but they will be weaker. Paradoxically, if we take *Boomer* seriously, private property protection should eventually find its home in the hands of big government and the regulatory state. As numbers and complexity increase, the pleasant world of informal communities becomes more strained, less attractive, and less available. Formal institutions may become more attractive, but only in a relative sense. They are the best of deteriorating alternatives.

As numbers and complexity increase, cooperative or transactional activity becomes less frequent and when it occurs it may even be socially unattractive. Real communities increasingly differ from ideal communities. People seriously affected by the decisions of the real community are excluded from decisional processes and institutional participation becomes skewed and unequal. This incomplete or unequal participation produces well-established evils in the market, the political process, and even the courts. In the market, differential participation can be the source of everything from collusion – cartels – to unconscionable transactions. In the political process, these evils can range from special interest legislation to ethnic cleansing.[21] In the courts, we can get either the absence of litigation or distorted litigation.

I do not mean to claim that informal arrangements or communities are bad. Like other institutional alternatives, however, their goodness or badness depends on the context in which they are envisioned. Informal communities work well where the setting is simple and numbers are small. There they may be the best choice. All the affection for them points in that direction. Indeed, all institutions become largely informal and look much the same. In a frictionless or even low-friction world, all markets might well be ongoing informal relationships and all political processes might well be consensual communal determinations. As complexity and numbers increase, however, the formal institutional alternatives become more necessary and, at the same time, more imperfect and the role of informal relationships and communities is no longer so easy or so beneficent.

I will return to the role of informal arrangements and, in particular, informal communities many times throughout this book. But, like the other institutional alternatives raised here, the role of informal communities cannot be resolved by simple formulations or nostalgic imagery. Like the other institutional alternatives, their place and validity must be forged via institutional comparison and that comparison must occur in parallel settings.

The relationship between informal arrangements and markets raises the subject of the categorization of institutions – the first of two general methodological issues that need to be addressed. I tend to speak of three institutional alternatives – the market, the political process, and the courts or adjudicative process. But, this categorization of institutions will vary depending on the subject studied and the inclinations of the investigator. The political process is not homogeneous. At various times, I have broken out the administrative process (the bureaucracy) from the legislative process.[22] In Part II, I will divide the political process by jurisdictional size into local, state, and federal. As we have just seen, informal arrangements and communities deserve special attention either as a separate alternative or as distinct parts of the market and political processes.

More important than the categorization of institutions, however, is the approach to their behavior. My analytical strategy or framework is

---

[21] For a chilling examination of communities gone wrong, see R. Hardin (1995).

[22] See Komesar (1994) at 90–7 and the discussion of administrative agencies in land use regulation in Chapters 4 and 5.

already evident in my examination of *Boomer* and my discussion of informal communities. Institutional performance and behavior are tied to the pattern of participation of important institutional actors common to all the institutions. I emphasize the activities of consumers, producers, voters, lobbyists, and litigants. At least initially, official actors in the political process and the judiciary – legislators and judges – play a secondary role. Mine is primarily a bottom-up perception of institutions.

This participation-centered approach identifies the actions of the mass of participants as the factor that, in general, best accounts for how institutions function. In this view, the adjudicative and political processes are like the market with its myriad buyers and sellers. As with analyses of the market, the interaction of these many actors rather than the will of a few officials receives central attention. The importance of officials vis-à-vis other actors varies across institutions and across issues, and this variation provides an important aspect of institutional comparison and choice. This participation-centered approach seems particularly applicable to the analysis of informal communities, which, by their nature, are based on interactive group behavior.

The basic model of institutional participation is conceptually simple. The character of institutional participation is determined by the interaction between the benefits of that participation and the costs of that participation. The benefit side focuses on the characteristics of the distribution of benefits or stakes across the relevant populations. The central determinants are the average per capita stakes and the extent to which per capita stakes vary within the population. The cost side focuses on the costs of participating in the institutions – transaction costs, litigation costs, political participation costs. These costs generally fall into one of two broad categories – the cost of information and the cost of organizing collective action. The cost of information is the more important category – in good measure, organization is highly dependent on information. The central determinants of the cost of participation include the complexity of the issue in question, the number of people on one side or the other of the issue, and the costs of access associated with institutional rules and procedures.[23] As I show throughout this book, participation is a central

---

[23] Nothing is new or startling about the participation-centered approach. Ronald Coase's transaction cost approach to the organization of production emphasized the cost of information in understanding institutional activity in general and transacting in particular. Coase (1937); Coase (1960). The emphasis on the distribution of stakes can be traced to Mancur Olson's work on collective action. Olson (1965).

theme not just in the behavior of institutions but also in defining the social values and goals that underlie law.

My use of the term "institution" and the connection between my approach and those of institutional and neoclassical economics also deserve comment. Institutions for me are large-scale social decision-making processes – markets, communities, political processes, and courts. I use the choice among these institutional processes to clarify basic issues such as the roles of regulation, rights, governments, and capitalism. These processes are alternative mechanisms by which societies carry out their goals.

But institutional economists and many other social scientists use the term institution to denote laws, rules, and customs. These laws, rules, and customs often are used to explain the behavior of decision-making processes. In particular, institutional economists emphasize laws, rules, and customs as the determinants of market and economic activity. Put simply, institutional economists believe that economic activity is a function of transaction costs and that transaction costs are a function of laws, rules, and customs.[24] Consistent with the coverage of this book, these economists place special emphasis on the institution of private property – property laws and rights.

The relationship between institutions as laws, rules, and customs and institutions as decision-making processes is both complicated and important. As institutional economists suggest, the behavior of decision-making processes is a function of laws, rules, and customs. The costs of participating in these processes – such as transaction costs (the costs of participating in the market) – are determined in part by these laws, rules, and customs.

But the relationship works both ways. Decision-making processes, such as courts, political processes, communities, and markets, produce the laws, rules, and customs that interest institutional economists. Laws and rules are the product of the political process and the adjudicative process. Customs and informal arrangements are the product of communities and markets. Because the outcomes of these decision-making processes are a function of the costs of participation, the basic causal relationship operates in reverse: Laws, rules, and customs are a function of the costs of institutional (in my sense) participation such as transaction costs, litigation costs, and lobbying costs.

---

[24] This position is nicely articulated in North (1990).

Moreover, using a participation-centered approach to study institutional choice and comparative institutional analysis provides important analytic advantages. In institutional economics, laws, rules, and customs are largely external or exogenous to the analysis. They are taken as givens or parameters. But, in the conception of institutional choice and comparative institutional analysis used in this book, laws, rules, and customs are the product of decision-making processes that are internal to the analysis. They are endogenous. The interaction between institutions as laws, rules, and customs, and institutions as decision-making processes is built into the participation-centered model employed in this book.

When one sees laws, rules, and customs as endogenous, it is easier to understand the sources of variation in the costs of enforcement and measurement that interest institutional economists and analysts in general. But something more powerful – if disturbing – also follows. Rather than remaining fixed, parameters of laws, rules, and customs change, fluctuate, and cycle. The rules of the game are not fixed and the participation-centered model lets us see the basic tension between demand and supply that produces these fluctuations. We will return to this subject often throughout this book.

There is a long-standing debate between institutional economists and the more prevalent neoclassical economists about the role and necessity of laws, rules, and customs in understanding economics. Neoclassical economists stress the parsimony of the basic tools of economics and their analytical power. I like parsimony. The participation-centered models I present are simple and spare. If the correct simple conception or model is employed, it asks the important first questions and provides an analytical framework valuable in organizing and evaluating other factors.

But I am asking neoclassical economic analysts of law and public policy to complicate their analysis in quite a different way. Moreover, although – in the name of parsimony and power – neoclassical economists might resist the complications proposed by institutional economics, they cannot resist the necessities of both institutional choice and comparative institutional analysis. Institutional choice defines the most basic issues posed by these economists, and only a comparative institutional approach to understanding these issues is consistent with the basic precepts of economics. I will return to the reform of economic analysis this portends in the last chapter of this book.

IV. CONCLUSION

This chapter shows property law and rights determined by institutional and systemic considerations. Property rights vary in strength and type depending on institutional choice. In turn, institutional choice depends on systemic variables like the number of relevant participants and the complexity of the substantive issues. Law and rights take on unexpected shapes. Property rights appear qualified, variable, and even weak. Property owners injured in much the same way or to much the same extent receive different protection from the courts – different property rights – depending on systemic factors like numbers and complexity that are beyond their control and are not usually visualized in connection with a term like "property right." That systemic rather than individual differences determine the extent to which someone receives the protection of the law seems in tension with at least the more straightforward senses of the Rule of Law.

Either as a matter of description or prescription, cases like *Boomer,* legal doctrines like nuisance and trespass, and law and rights in general cannot be understood without giving serious attention to these systemic considerations. Thus, for example, the difference between trespass and nuisance is supposedly based on distinctions between interference with the right to exclusive possession and interference with use and enjoyment and, more particularly, on the concept of physical invasion. If there is a physical invasion, then there is an interference with the right to exclusive possession and the injured party can seek redress for trespass with the associated stronger remedies and rights. If there is no physical invasion and, therefore, only an interference with use and enjoyment, the injured party has the lesser rights and remedies associated with nuisance. This all seems neat and sensible and does not seem to require recourse to institutional analysis.

Upon close inspection, however, these distinctions and constructs are largely empty and depend for substance on institutional considerations. The problem can be seen in the central concept of physical invasion. Understood in its most straightforward manner, this term does not distinguish between trespass and nuisance. The events associated with nuisance such as the pollution in *Boomer* also involve physical invasion. The particles of cement and even the vibrations and noises caused by the neighboring cement plant are physical phenomena; they constitute a physical invasion just like rocks or cattle let loose by neighbors – classic cases of "physical invasion" for purposes of trespass. Courts can of course define a construct in any way they wish. But when their definitions exclude significant potential coverage, these constructs raise rather than answer legal questions. Why should the courts choose to define physical invasion to include some physical invasions and not others? Why are straying cattle an interference with the right to exclusive possession and straying particles only an interference with use and enjoyment?

The traditional constructs and traditional legal analysis do not answer these questions. But comparative institutional analysis can. The narrow definition of physical invasion employed in property law aligns with institutional analysis by treating those physical invasions involving small numbers and low complexity as physical invasions for legal purposes. It sends more far-flung and complex physical invasions to nuisance by excluding them from the legal definition and thereby subjecting them to the judicial balancing of nuisance law.

This pattern roughly reflects the institutional factors we discussed in our analysis of *Boomer*. The shifts and cycles in the definitions of physical invasion and, therefore, trespass and nuisance can be understood from a comparative institutional perspective.[25] Institutional choices like the role of courts versus markets define the terms of legal analysis not the other way around. As we shall see, the central constructs of law in general are often just rough proxies for institutional choice and can best be understood through comparative institutional analysis.

At base, the issue of who decides defines the character of law and rights. In *Boomer,* we saw that property rights will be strong, weak, or nonexistent depending on whether the market, the courts, or the political process are chosen to decide substantive issues like relative merit of the uses. As we shall see, what is true for common law property rights is true for rights and law in general.

As we have already seen, however, this central question of institutional choice is too often addressed in the legal literature as though one could make a choice by examining only one alternative and the unexamined institution is often the courts. These demand-side arguments are used to generate enormous tasks for the courts. But where one considers demand, one must consider supply: Any analysis of law and rights must give careful consideration to the characteristics and abilities of the courts. It is time now to look more closely at the supply side.

---

[25] For an analysis of trespass and nuisance that reflects comparative institutional ideas, see Merrill (1985).

3

The Supply Side – The Little Engine
of Law and Rights

We have seen law and rights defined by systemic variables and institutional choices – by the forces of supply and demand. Court-made law and rights are supplied by the adjudicative process. The adjudicative process is the engine of law and rights (property or otherwise), but it is a tiny engine that faces increasing strains on both its substantive abilities and physical capacity. In this chapter, I focus on this supply side of law and rights – the adjudicative process, its limitations, and its strengths.

I. THE ADJUDICATIVE PROCESS

The working of the adjudicative process raises three broad institutional considerations: the competence or substantive ability of adjudicative decision makers such as judges and juries, the dynamics of litigation, and the physical capacity of the adjudicative process. These three considerations interact with each other and with factors such as numbers and complexity to determine the performance of the courts and the character of law and rights.

These interactions are played out against the background of the structure of the adjudicative process. Compared to the political process and the market, the judicial or adjudicative process exhibits three distinctive systemic elements. First, the adjudicative process is more formally defined and has more formal requirements for participation than do the other two institutions. Second, the adjudicative process is much smaller – its physical resources and personnel are far fewer – than the political or market processes. More important, it is far more difficult to increase in size. Third, judges, the central officials of the judicial process, are more independent from the general population than either their market or political counterparts. These three basic characteristics – higher threshold access cost, limited scale, and judicial independence – are related.

The independence of judges stems primarily from their terms of employment. The connection can be seen most dramatically in the U.S. federal judiciary. Federal judges serve for life and cannot be removed except by the cumbersome impeachment process. Compensation is set for judges as a class, and Congress cannot single out individual judges.[1] In addition, federal judges traditionally come to the bench as a final vocation. The longevity and high average age of federal judges attest to a limited interest in job mobility. Although judges are not completely indifferent to alternative job opportunities, the range of alternatives attractive to judges appears to be more limited than for political and market actors. Job security and the general disinterest in other positions makes it difficult to influence judges by replacement or inducement. Replacing judges is a longer term strategy than replacing legislators. Financial inducement of judges is more difficult to arrange than with elected officials both because elected officials have a more pressing need for campaign contributions and because contributions to elected officials carry fewer sanctions.

Juries are similarly walled off from outside influence. They are chosen at random from the population and serve for only short periods – in general, for only a few trials or indictments. Their anonymity and continuous turnover as well as the difficulty of predicting which case any individual juror may hear makes them a difficult target for influence. Unlike bureaucrats who hear many cases of a specialized type, a given juror will hear only one or two cases. Any long-term or subtle efforts aimed at gaining favor with jurors – such as educating them to favor a given position – would have to be aimed at the general population. Jurors are a vast, diffuse, and moving target.

Independence, or at least insulation from unequal influence, is also increased by the manner in which information comes to judges and juries. Information reaching both judge and jury is largely funneled through the courtroom and the adversarial process. Obviously, neither judge nor jury is immune to pretrial sources of information; they were not born on the day of trial. But informal, ex parte discussion is, at least formally, precluded and is, in reality, much more difficult to accomplish than in the less formal political process let alone in the highly informal market. The re-

---

[1] Even state court judges serve for longer terms and are otherwise more insulated from the general electorate than are comparable legislative and executive officials.

quirements of written complaints, service, and notice along with pretrial discovery and the rules of evidence are designed to give all parties to a lawsuit equal access both to information and to official decision makers.

These features of the adjudicative process lend support to the popular image that the judicial process is more evenhanded and its officials more independent than political officials. However, the same structural elements and safeguards that produce independence and evenhandedness raise the cost of participation – the costs of litigation – in several ways. Before any trial is held, litigants can expect contests before judges testing the sufficiency of the complaint or of its service as well as raising issues such as standing, jurisdiction, choice of law, justiciability, and ripeness.[2] Litigants can also expect to spend a long period before trial in a process of discovery used to elicit information and evidence. Unlike fact gathering in the political process, this factual investigation is funded primarily by the parties, not the public. If trial follows, the arguments and the evidence presented to judges and juries must fulfill extensive rules of procedure and evidence. These rules are complex and, therefore, expensive to understand and fulfill. This expensive presentation is again made and funded primarily by the litigating parties.

The costs of participation in the adjudicative process, like the costs of participation in the market and political processes, are largely information costs. In the adjudicative process, the formalities and complexities of the process itself require such a significant accumulation of knowledge and experience that the virtually universal manner of dealing with them is to hire an expert – the lawyer. Thus, although litigants can, in theory, represent themselves in court, few litigate their interests without the significant, often dominating, presence of a hired lawyer with expertise in the particular area of law. Lawyers are hired as the least expensive (but certainly not inexpensive) way to deal with the daunting information costs of litigation.[3]

From a social standpoint, the greater insulation of judges from the various pressures, produced in part by the presence of all these procedures and formalities, provides an important comparative advantage for the

---

[2] Standing determines who can bring action based on a given wrong. Jurisdiction determines which court can hear the action. Justiciability and ripeness determine when wrongdoing can come to the courts. Justiciability focuses the courts on cases presented in an adversary context and capable of resolution through the judicial process. Ripeness limits court involvement until a controversy is sufficiently immediate and developed.

[3] For a sophisticated examination of the lawyer's role, see Gilson (1984).

adjudicative process. This independence provides judges with the opportunity to shape social decisions without some of the systemic pressures
that distort other institutions. It also creates a greater formal equality in
which all litigants are forced to influence the decision in the controlled
environment of the courtroom. But the costs of litigation, interacting with
the distribution of stakes, can keep the courts from given social issues and
even from large sets of social issues. Moreover, the dynamics of participation in litigation can produce serious inequality as low stakes players
and those with limited experience with adjudication are systematically
disadvantaged.

The high threshold costs associated with the formal requirements of
the adjudicative process will not preclude all issues nor do they mean that
the cost of participation in the adjudicative process will necessarily be
higher than the cost of participation in other institutions. That depends on
the setting. The point here is that the judicial independence that distinguishes the adjudicative process from other institutions comes at a significant cost that will affect the number and type of issues handled by the
judiciary.

The dynamics of litigation is the feature of the adjudicative process
that is linked most directly to the participation-centered model of institutional behavior discussed in Chapter 2. I will spend much of the rest of
this chapter exploring its implications for law and rights. Before I do so,
however, I want to briefly consider the related issues of competence and
scale. By competence, I mean the ability of trials (the adversarial process)
and of triers (judges and juries) to investigate, understand, and make the
substantive social decisions that may come to them. By scale, I mean the
resources or budget available to the judiciary and the constraints on the
expansion of the size of the adjudicative process. Scale and competence
interact with each other and with the determinants of litigation (stakes
and costs) to determine the institutional ability of the adjudicative
process.

Various concerns have been raised about the competence of judges
and juries as decision makers: concerns about the ability of juries to understand highly technical issues and evidence in complex, large-scale litigation;[4] concerns about the ability of judges to handle complex and sen-

---

[4] Serious criticism of juries has been around for a long time. See Frank (1936). For more recent discussions concerning jury competence, see Luneberg and Nordenberg (1981); Huber (1988), 41–4, 50–1; Committee on the Federal Courts of the New York State Bar Association (1988); Symposium (1989).

sitive issues concerning subjects such as foreign affairs or national defense;[5] and concerns about the ability of the courts to deal with large-scale social policy issues where there are many conflicting interests and a continuing need for implementation and oversight.[6] There is little doubt that juries have limited technical expertise. Jurors are randomly chosen from the general population, and individual jurors are often chosen in the voir dire explicitly to avoid expertise in the specific issues of the case. These inexpert juries are then often asked to listen to the technical and complex testimony of conflicting expert witnesses and decide difficult substantive issues. Similarly, trial and appellate judges formally trained only as lawyers and coming from a wide variety of practice backgrounds must fashion rules and remedies for a comprehensive range of social issues. These judges, both trial and appellate, usually are not asked to specialize in one type of controversy and, therefore, do not obtain the expertise that such frequent exposure would bring.

Juries and judges can easily be unfavorably contrasted with the technically more expert bureaucrats of administrative agencies who, like juries and judges, serve as fact-finders and implementers of rules and standards but who, unlike judges and juries, have acquired specialized expertise. Similarly, recent suggestions for specialized courts and for limitations on large-scale interventions into political process decision making are reactions to the limited technical ability of generalist judges.[7] As I have shown elsewhere, these various proposals and concerns raise institutional choices more difficult than their proponents suppose.[8] Greater substantive competence is often purchased by increased systemic bias. Inevitably, this institutional choice like all institutional choices involves difficult trade-offs. In making these tough judgments, however, the issue of adjudicative competence is significant.

In theory, the implications of increasing or decreasing the physical capacity (the scale) of any institution are significant in determining the ability of that institution. However, considerations of size, in particular the

---

[5] See the discussion of the *Pentagon Papers* case in Chapter 2 of Komesar (1994). See also Scharpf (1966).

[6] See Horowitz (1977).

[7] For suggestions concerning specialized courts, see Revesz (1990); Jordan (1981); Meador (1983). For a thorough discussion of the differing views concerning specialized courts, see R. Posner (1985), 147–60; Currie and Goodman (1975), 63–85; Carrington et al. (1976), 168–72.

[8] See Komesar (1994), 140–2.

implications of severe constraints on growth, play such an important role in the adjudicative process and so strongly affect interinstitutional choices that they require special consideration. The constraints on the size of the adjudicative process and the implications of these constraints on judicial choices are more obvious and dramatic than any comparable constraints on the size of the market and political processes. In fact, it is the relative ease with which the market and political processes expand that creates the demands that strain the physical capacity of the adjudicative process. As we shall see throughout the book, as numbers and complexity increase and these alternative institutions deteriorate, demand on the courts will increase.[9]

The most important constraint on the expansion of the adjudicative process stems from the central role of judges, particularly of appellate judges. Independence and competence make substitution of nonjudges for judges difficult. To some degree, such substitution does occur. Judicial clerks and, to some degree, clerical help ease the load of judges. Trial judges call upon masters and magistrates for help. Various "managerial" judges have created helpers such as plaintiffs' committees or community advisors to aid when large-scale litigation requires an ongoing role for the trial court in the oversight of important public functions.[10] Whatever these successes, however, the central role of the independent judge makes it doubtful that adjudicative capacity – the size or scale of the courts – can be expanded as easily as the capacities of the market and the political process without seriously changing the character of the adjudicative process.

The main bottleneck here is the appellate court structure. Each judicial system within the United States has at its apex a supreme court meant to articulate the rules under which adjudication takes place and to define the rights that trigger litigation. These courts are staffed by a small set of judges.[11] The most obvious reform, increasing the number of judges on these high courts, does not easily or even necessarily increase the output of this court. Although an increase in judges would decrease the per judge

---

[9] As a reminder, "numbers" here refers to the number of persons impacted by and relevant to the societal decision in issue. See the discussion in Chapter 2.

[10] There was an extensive and creative use of masters and specialized trial courts in the *Mt. Laurel* case discussed in the next chapter.

[11] Twenty-six state supreme courts have seven judges; eighteen states have five; seven have nine; one has eight (total includes DC and Puerto Rico). BNA (2000).

load of opinion writing, increasing the numbers of judges would also make collective appellate decision making more difficult and time consuming.[12]

Judiciaries grow. The U.S. judiciary has grown significantly. But, as the U.S. experience indicates, this growth is far less rapid than the growth in the alternative institutions. Judiciaries cannot grow at the same rate as other societal institutions without eradicating most of the attributes we associate with the adjudicative process. Thus, judicial independence – an essential attribute of the adjudicative process especially for Rule of Law functions – is linked both to higher costs of access and constraints on the ability to expand. Because judges are given so much power without the discipline of lost profits or lost office, we constrain this power by more formality and require many layers of review. Formality means increased cost and the hierarchy of review both increases costs and constrains growth.

We can now explore the workings of the adjudicative process by returning to *Boomer*. Although all three institutional issues – competence, scale, and dynamics of litigation – will be considered in this chapter, dynamics of litigation will hold center stage. These dynamics mold the character of rights often producing strange and surprising results.

II. NUMBERS, COMPLEXITY, AND THE DYNAMICS OF LITIGATION

We can see the importance of the dynamics of litigation by returning to *Boomer* and the dissent's view that the permanent damage remedy is inadequate to handle the larger problems inherent in particle pollution in the Hudson River Valley. The dissent's concerns would disappear if the adjudicative process worked frictionlessly. If all the victims foreseen by the dissent brought actions (or there was a serious threat that they would bring actions), the pollution problem that worried the dissent would be solved by the damage remedy suggested by the majority. Faced with the

---

[12] See R. Posner (1985), 14. Increasing the number of intermediate courts of appeals can serve to decrease the strain on these supreme courts. At some stage, however, conflicts among the views taken by these separate courts create greater uncertainty and greater demands for resolution by the higher supreme court. The adjudicative process depends on hierarchical review and formal procedure as a means to ensure that judges do not abuse their independence. These needs make the resolution of conflicts and errors by higher courts a necessary component of the adjudicative process.

threat of paying damages to all the citizens injured by the pollution, polluting cement companies would have the incentive to reach the correct locational and abatement solutions. Like the transaction-costless world where market transactions internalize everything, the frictionless adjudicative world would send the correct signals.

Alas, like the real-world market, the real-world adjudicative process is neither frictionless nor costless. More important, its frictions and costs increase as numbers of litigants, size of individual damages, disparity of interests, and the complexity of the substantive issues increase. Air pollution in an area like the Hudson River Valley is likely to be characterized by a large social loss dispersed over many victims each of whom suffers relatively low loss and, therefore, has relatively low stakes in any subsequent litigation. These impacts, as well as the sources of pollution, are complex, subtle, and difficult to recognize. Even if victims recognize these losses and their cause, the low stakes may not justify the significant threshold costs of litigation. Litigation has significant economies of scale – one does not buy any serious lawyering for the expenditure of $100, $1,000, or even $10,000. Because of these limitations on litigation, the *Boomer* judges could not reasonably expect all or even a significant fraction of the people in the Hudson River Valley to bring or credibly threaten to bring permanent damage actions against Atlantic Cement or other local polluters.

Thus, a legal regime that depended on the permanent damage remedy would send a signal to potential polluters that underpriced locational impacts. The point is simple and familiar but important: The strength of judicial protection of property and, therefore, of property rights depends on the reality of adjudicative remedies, these remedies depend on the dynamics of litigation and, in turn, the dynamics of litigation depend on the factors of the participation-centered model – in particular, numbers and complexity.

Even if judges and juries with the aid of the adversarial process were good at estimating loss – pricing the impact – the signal sent and, therefore, the possibility of robust protection of property would be distorted by problems in the dynamics of litigation. Depending on factors such as the distribution of social losses (per capita impact, numbers, variance in distribution) and the cost of litigation, the deterrence impacts of court pricing through the damage remedy can be severely impaired. In turn, the protection accorded property rights from the negative impact of neighbors like Atlantic Cement is diminished severely. Plants will locate where they should not and injuries will go uncompensated when they do. As we shall see, the resulting locational decisions may be quite perverse. Taken to its extreme the analysis suggests that future Atlantic Cements might even locate in areas that are highly developed and land use is quite dense.

Similar problems with the dynamics of litigation also haunt injunctive property remedies (both complex and simple). Large numbers, dispersed interests, and costly litigation mean injured parties will not even recognize the injury or the availability of legal remedy and, if they do, will wait for others to bear the costs of organizing or promoting that litigation. The larger the numbers, the more complex the issue, the more dispersed the interests, and the more costly the litigation, the more problematic will be the dynamics of litigation.

Upon closer inspection, *Boomer* itself reveals an intriguing and vexing dynamics of litigation and institutional participation that raise questions about the positions of both the *Boomer* majority and dissent. Viewed carefully, there may have been little reason to abandon the precedent of simple property rules in this case because an injunction issued under the old rule is unlikely to have closed the cement plant. Although there may be considerably more difficulty in reaching a negotiated solution when there are seven parties to bargain with than when there is one, the defendant spurred on by the dire results of plant closing would likely have found a way to overcome the holdouts and collective action problems associated with dealing with seven parties. Put differently, the high returns associated with the potential of extracting millions would provide significant incentive to the seven plaintiffs to overcome whatever problems of collective action confronted them. If the number was seventy or seven hundred, then the point of no return would have more obviously been reached. Given the small number of parties in *Boomer* combined with the high stakes involved for the defendant, it seems likely that we would have seen the plant in place even had the court issued an injunction.[13]

---

[13] Recent work by Ward Farnsworth showing an absence of postjudgment bargaining in nuisance cases might cast doubt on my assertion of a postjudgment buyout by Atlantic Cement. Farnsworth (1999). But the vast difference in stakes – even allowing for significant uncounted nonpecuniary stakes for the plaintiffs – strongly suggests that Atlantic Cement would have continued to operate even given the awarding of an injunction. I am supposing that even the litigation animosity identified by Farnsworth has its price and that several million 1970 dollars would suffice. That the parties did not reach a financial settlement before judgment is likely to be the product of a significant difference in perception of the applicable law and, therefore, the terms of trade. Recall that *Boomer* changes the existing law.

It is not random or accidental, however, that *Boomer* involved a relative impact balance that might well have been resolved by market transaction. The same factors that determine the propensity to transact determine the propensity to litigate. As the number of parties increases, the incentive to litigate decreases because greater numbers mean greater costs of litigation and a greater possibility of collective action problems. Each party is more likely to wait for others to bring action and it is more difficult to overcome this free-rider problem via negotiation. Thus, those situations in which parties can bargain around an injunction are also likely to be those situations in which parties will litigate. Both activities are more likely at low numbers and complexity.

Thus, paradoxically, the dynamics of litigation make it likely that the *Boomer* majority would have had as its vehicle for moving from a simple to a complex property rule a case in which market transactions were in fact feasible and, therefore, a complex property rule was less needed. As numbers and complexity increase, the chance of litigation decreases. The dynamics of this decrease in litigation can have perverse effects on locational choice. Here the paradox returns us to an ominous possiblity.

If we have a simple injunction rule *with thorough enforcement,* we can expect that a knowledgeable and sophisticated potential polluter will avoid any litigation by purchasing the neighbors' permission. This potential polluter might well locate in such a manner as to minimize transaction costs. If such a plant were to locate without the protection of this permission, its significant investment would enhance the possibility of injunctions against it.[14] But such an analysis depends heavily on enforcement and, therefore, on the dynamics of litigation. As numbers increase, we get greater dispersion of loss, lower per capita victims, and a decreased prospect of enforcement via litigation.

This analysis suggests that potential polluters will choose either of two extreme location strategies. They will move to an area in which land ownership is as undivided as possible so as to increase the prospect of successful transactions *ex ante.* Or they will move to an area in which land

---

[14] This would be true, of course, only so long as courts before *Boomer* really closed down such plants. Despite the version of the law presented by the *Boomer* court, it may well have been that many courts manipulated the facts so as to avoid such results. If that were the case, then sophisticated plant owners may have located without prior arrangements and depended on courts to finesse injunctions. None of this, however, alters the basic analytical points in the text.

ownership is divided as much as possible to decrease the prospect of anyone seeking to enforce simple property rules *ex post.*

The latter strategy is socially perverse because it would mean locating in highly populated areas where the *total* societal negative impacts of pollution are largest because this larger loss would be so dispersed or divided as to decrease the chance for litigation.[15] Whether such a strategy would be followed depends on a number of factors including the chance of political responses. We will consider the likelihood of such a response in Part II. But strictly from the viewpoint of court-provided property rights, inadequacies in protection of these rights due to problems with the dynamics of litigation can produce socially perverse results. Once again, the character of law and rights and their implications for the welfare of society are determined by institutional and systemic factors.

III. NUMBERS, COMPLEXITY, AND CLASS ACTIONS

I have been skirting the edges of the important subject of class actions. Class actions provide a potential cure for the difficulties in the dynamics of litigation we just discussed. Where there are dispersed potential plaintiffs, the class action mechanism can increase the chance of adjudication. It promotes litigation by providing a way to cover litigation expenses from a source other than the pocket of a single member of the plaintiff group. Thus, all those in the Hudson River Valley injured by the air pollution created by Atlantic Cement could bring one action, represented by one set of lawyers paid from one pot of damages. The expenses of the class action are paid from the collective award before the remaining amount is distributed to the larger group. Even where there is only injunctive relief, the courts are often empowered to order the losing defendant to pay the plaintiffs' litigation expenses.

Although in theory the class action mechanism could solve the problems in individual litigation caused by the dispersion of stakes, there are severe problems within the existing class action system and these

---

[15] The environmental justice literature indicates that polluters do not tend to locate in highly dense areas. See Been and Gupta (1997), 25. But nothing in this literature negates the tendency of the dynamics of litigation – in this case, the dynamics of nonlitigation – to promote these perverse locational results. These results also may be associated with population characteristics more familiar to this literature: Polluters may want to locate where the people suffer difficulties in litigating because of discrimination, poverty, and illegal immigration status in addition to dispersed low stakes.

problems, like the problems with individual litigation, increase as numbers and complexity increase. We have a familiar story. Institutions move together. The result is that class actions may function least well when they are most needed and best where they are least needed.

The class action mechanism tends to improve the dynamics of litigation at the expense of degrading the substantive competence of the adjudicative process. In individual litigation, judges and juries are informed by a contest between two opposing viewpoints. Each one-sided view is tempered by an opposing one-sided view. Although hardly perfect, this competition of views has value as a truth-finding device. It is a far less credible system if judges and juries hear only one side.

The standard configuration of interests in class action situations offers a greater possibility of a one-sided or at least distorted representation than would be the case with most individual litigations and this possibility again increases as numbers and complexity increase. The issue is representation and the problems with representation relate to differences in the incentives of various parties on the dispersed plaintiff side. We may have active plaintiffs and passive plaintiffs. Their claims may differ in amount and legal sufficiency. Frequently, passive plaintiffs may be those who have been exposed to a danger, but whose injury has not yet manifested. There are reasons to worry about whether the active plaintiffs will adequately represent the needs of future victims (the passive plaintiffs). Active plaintiffs may accept awards for their damages and allow less tangible or less manifested injuries to be far less completely compensated. Active plaintiffs may not care about preventative measures if they are no longer exposed to danger even though a significant portion of the passive plaintiffs are still in harm's way.

As the number of victims (potential class members) increases and the substantive issues become increasingly complex, even named plaintiffs may have little role in determining what is litigated. Here the class-action lawyer takes center stage. Even in individual litigation, lawyers can control the course of litigation. But there the prospect of client monitoring creates a realistic expectation of convergence in client and lawyer interests. As numbers and complexity increase, we move into the realm of class actions, and the prospect of client monitoring decreases. The very problems that make individual litigation unlikely make client monitoring unlikely.

The adversarial system here adds a perverse wrinkle. The active client-lawyer team will be on the defendant side. Defendants are able to exploit the passivity on the plaintiff's side by offering settlements favorable to active plaintiffs but unfavorable to passive plaintiffs' or favorable to plaintiffs' lawyers but unfavorable to plaintiffs as a whole.[16] A few active plaintiffs may receive large recoveries while agreeing to little, if any, recovery for future victims. Class lawyers may receive significant fees as part of a settlement in which the class may receive far less than it might have gained with less conflicted representation.[17] There apparently are a number of increasingly successful strategies in which defendants have been able to choose the plaintiff's counsel most amenable to settlement on the defendant's terms.[18] There is even the possibility of fraudulent actions in which a would-be defendant manufactures a plaintiff class that generously settles the action in the defendant's favor and precludes real plaintiffs from subsequent action. Sadly, this analysis suggests that defendants will tend to attack the classes that are most socially useful – where interests are least likely to be otherwise litigated – and overlook problems with classes that are really only substitutes for individual actions that would likely have been brought anyway and would have been less manageable or malleable, from the defendant's viewpoint, in the form of individual actions.[19]

Courts have responded to these distortions in representation by scrutinizing class actions more carefully than individual litigation. Much of this scrutiny centers on the certification of the class where courts address the sometimes overlapping issues of representativeness, numerosity, commonality, and typicality. Without going into unnecessary detail here, these are all attempts to establish the correlation between the interests of active and passive members of the class before the litigation begins. Courts

---

[16] For example, in reviewing the settlement in the General Motors "sidesaddle" fuel tank case, the Third Circuit was concerned with the possibility of an inequitable distribution that primarily benefitted major car fleet owners – the only class members with economic interests large enough to undertake to monitor the litigation. *In re General Motors Corp. Pickup Truck Fuel Tank Prods. Liab. Litig.,* 55 F.3d 768, 780–1, 806–10 (3d Cir. 1995).

[17] See Macey and Miller (1991), 22–5.

[18] See Coffee (1995a), 1370–1. Those plaintiffs' attorneys unwilling to cooperate are frozen out. By strategically expending resources in opposition to certification, concentrated defendant groups may be able to select opposing counsel with an eye to those who will be most amiable in producing these long-run settlement arrangements. See Coffee (1995a), 1371–3.

[19] See Macey and Miller (1991), 63. See also *Umbriac v. American Snacks, Inc.,* 338 F. Supp. 265, 275 (E.D. Pa. 1975); *Eggleston v. Chicago Journeymen Plumbers' Local Union,* 367 F.2d 80, 895 (7th Cir. 1981).

also can impose extensive notice requirements on the class representatives, again as an attempt to protect passive plaintiffs.[20]

Even if these various devices help to cure concerns about the competence of class representation, however, they do so only by raising the costs and difficulty of bringing class actions which, in turn, has adverse effects on the dynamics of litigation. Sadly, the factors that raise costs are also the factors that create greater need for class actions – increasing numbers and complexity. Greater numbers increase the likelihood of heterogeneity in the class and, therefore, increase the chance of problems with representativeness which, in turn, increase the expenses of litigation to deal with these problems.[21] In addition to increasing the costs of defending the validity of the class, concerns about representativeness and fair treatment for passive plaintiffs increase the likelihood that judges will require individual notice to each of these inactive members. This notice, whatever its importance, increases the costs of litigation at a rate that increases with the number in the class.[22] The significant and increasing expenses associated with notice and certification make the adjudication of highly dispersed claims unlikely. The much trumpeted decline of class actions in general seems to indicate an increasing deterioration in the representation of highly dispersed interests in private adjudication.[23] With the exception of occasional "public interest" actions, widely dispersed interests seem largely absent from the courts.

All of these elements are played out against the backdrop of the sort of judicial discomfort with massive and complex societal issues we saw in *Boomer*. Expanding the class action mechanism would bring the courts the complex and profound problems of air pollution that the *Boomer* majority felt were the job of the political process. Cases involving larger groups are likely to be more complex. This complexity is heightened when

---

[20] There is a significant literature debating the efficacy of these various devices. See Koniak and Cohen (1996); Coffee (1995a, 1995b, and 1987); Macey and Miller (1991).

[21] For a discussion of the impact of increasingly restrictive representativeness requirements on class actions in the employment discrimination area, see Johnson (1987).

[22] The Supreme Court of the United States seriously restricted class actions, especially for highly dispersed interests, in three central cases, *Snyder v. Harris,* 394 U.S. 332 (1969), *Zahn v. International Paper Co.,* 414 U.S. 291 (1974), and *Eisen v. Carlisle & Jacquelin,* 417 U.S. 156 (1974). For a discussion of the status of class actions following these decisions, see American Bar Association Section of Litigation (1977).

[23] See Martin (1988), quoting remarks of Paul Carrington, official reporter of the Federal Rules of Civil Procedure, that "class actions had their day in the sun and kind of petered out." See also Johnson (1987) and Donohue and Siegelman (1991).

most of the plaintiffs are not present or even known. Problems of representativeness correlate with complexity and, therefore, with strains on judicial competence and resources and all of these correlate with increasing concerns about the trustworthiness of the adversarial process.

Although class actions can be a powerful device to allow court access to cases and parties that could not otherwise participate in the adjudicative process, they do not remove the worries about complexity and fear of mistakes that seem to haunt the *Boomer* majority. They increase them. Courts are likely to translate these concerns into greater requirements of notice and certification that, no matter how justified, impose a major tax on the use of class actions. The size of this tax will depend, in part, on the extent to which courts feel that some other institution, such as the political process, should be resolving the substantive issue. If class actions promise too great a strain on court resources and competence, the courts are in position to tighten the parameters of class actions and decrease the chances of litigation.[24]

Present tendencies in the expansion and contraction of class action tend to reflect this picture and to spell trouble for active adjudication of widely dispersed interests and, in turn, for judicial protection of potentially important property interests. Expansion in class actions has occurred primarily on the "supply side" rather than the "demand side."[25] The emphasis by the courts seems to be on the cost-effective management of cases that would often have been brought into the adjudicative process

[24] Similar reactions can be expected for other adjudicative access issues such as standing and justiciability. See, e.g., *Diamond v. General Motors Corp.,* 97 Cal.Rptr. 639 (Cal.Ct. App. 1971).

[25] The mass tort class action, often involving the consolidation of a series of smaller traditionally adjudicated cases, is an example of "supply-side" class actions. The typical class action today is more likely to be a mass-tort case rather than the public law reform invoked by earlier class action cases involving school desegregation, constitutional rights of prisoners, or poor treatment of mental health patients, which can be thought of as "demand-side" class actions. See Mullenix (1994), 581. Many symposia and articles dealing with the topic of class actions focus on mass torts. See, e.g., Crampton (1995); Hricik (1998); Symposium (1997).

A recent study for the Advisory Committee on the Rules of Civil Procedure scanned five major legal databases in an initial effort to "describe the class litigation landscape." The largest categories of class actions were securities and consumer litigation, with lesser numbers of cases identified as torts, employment, civil rights, and "benefits, taxes, [and] other governmental" issues. The study's authors conclude that there has been a shift from "class action as a representative action with absent plaintiffs" to "representative actions that are, in reality, aggregations of individual plaintiffs' claims, as well as some cases that involve both absent plaintiffs and aggregated claims." Hensler, et al. (1997), 16.

as individual litigation rather than on increasing the ability to bring cases that would otherwise not have been brought. The class action mechanism has been creatively expanded in mass torts involving a large number of sizeable per capita personal injuries. Given the per capita stakes, many of these actions would likely be adjudicated even without consolidation in class actions. By lowering costs of litigation, this expansion of class actions has no doubt increased litigation (the number of cases) brought. But it is doubtful that that is either the primary purpose or effect. At the same time, class actions concerning issues involving significant but very widespread injury like the air pollution in *Boomer* have met a much colder welcome. Courts have commonly refused to certify air pollution cases and the *Boomer* court's concerns about broader-based pollution contexts have surfaced in these decisions.[26]

Once again, rights are dependent on systemic factors. The dynamics of litigation largely forecloses individual litigation of significant but highly dispersed property injuries and, therefore, any effective protection of the legal rights of these property owners. Class action seems the magic wand to remove these difficulties. But this seemingly easy answer is subject to its own difficulties and these difficulties are a function of the same factors that cause problems with individual claims. We have a familiar problem to which there is no easy answer.

---

[26] See, e.g., *Diamond v. General Motors Corp.,* 97 Cal.Rptr. 639 (Cal.Ct. App. 1971) (affirming denial of class certification for air pollution suit on behalf of 7,119,184 residents of Los Angeles against 1,293 named and unnamed alleged polluters); *Reader v. Magna-Superior Copper Co.,* 515 P.2d 860 (Ariz. 1973) (denying class treatment for air pollution action by 700,000 residents against seven local smelter companies); *Boring v. Medusa Portland Cement Co.,* 63 F.R.D. 78 (M.D. Pa. 1974) (class certification denied for air pollution suit on behalf of over one thousand residents of York County, Pennsylvania against two alleged polluters); *RSR Co. v. Hayes,* 673 S.W.2d 928 (Tex. Ct. App. 1984) (reversing lower court order certifying class of residential property owners within two-mile radius of lead smelter). But see *McCastle v. Rolling Envtl. Services of Louisiana,* 456 So.2d 612 (La. 1984) (reversing denial of class certification for air pollution suit on behalf of four thousand plaintiffs on grounds that small-stakes class members could employ no reasonable alternative mechanism to collect their due).

In contrast, water pollution class actions have generally received a warmer reception in the courts. See *Ouellette v. Int'l Paper Co.,* 86 F.R.D. 476 (D. Vt. 1980) (certifying class of four hundred lakeshore property owners for water pollution claims against local paper mill, but denying class certification of area residents for air pollution claims against same defendant); *Pruitt v. Allied Chemical Corp.,* 85 F.R.D. 100 (E.D. Va. 1980) (judicially creating six subclasses of plaintiffs in order to grant certification of water pollution class action). This disparate treatment appears to be grounded in the tendency of water pollution to produce a more geographically discrete class of plaintiffs than does air pollution.

The class action mechanism seems an easy answer but only if we focus solely on the problems with individual actions – a standard single institutional response. However, the same increases in numbers and complexity that create problems for individual litigation also cause a deterioration in the ability of the class action mechanism and create a parade of horribles there as well. Many scholars have demonstrated these horribles and contemplated significant limitations on class actions.[27] Unfortunately, however, these responses also are largely single institutional. It is no more valid to limit the class action mechanism based on its revealed imperfections than it was to anoint it based on imperfections in the alternative. Two "wrongs" (single institutional analyses) do not make a "right" (a comparative institutional analysis). Here, as elsewhere, the quality and meaning of law and rights depends on close choices between imperfect alternatives.

IV. CONCLUSION

Close examination of the legal process reveals a fascinating if somewhat disturbing picture of law and rights. As increasing numbers and complexity distort the dynamics of litigation and strain both the substantive competence of judicial decision makers and limited judicial resources, we get an increasing divergence between idealized and actual property rights and remedies. Rights in general and common law property rights in particular are complex and conditional. Property rights and remedies shift depending on such mundane factors as the number of parties involved.

Where there are only a few parties, the simple and powerful remedy of automatic injunction prevails and we have strong property rights. As the number of parties rises, the remedy becomes more complex and more qualified, ranging from property rights conditioned on the relative impact defense (as in *Boomer*) to abandonment of any judicial protection in lieu of political process regulation. Here property rights weaken and eventually disappear. Tough institutional choices define both substantive constructs like trespass and nuisance and procedural constructs like class action.

Common law property rights are forged and reforged in an adjudicative process defined by the dynamics of litigation, by constraints on its

---

[27] See e.g., Coffee (1995b), 856–7; Henderson (1995); Koniak (1995), 1048–9; Menkel-Meadow (1995), 1213–19.

physical resources and by variations in the competence of judges and juries. Much depends on systemic variables like numbers and complexity.
The adjudicative process has always allocated decisions to other institutions and that trend must of necessity accelerate – a topic we will consider
throughout the rest of this book. The dynamics of litigation keep important issues from the courts unless the courts are willing to take radical
steps in aggregating claims. The reluctance on the part of the courts to
open themselves to large and difficult cases – especially without the normal protections of the adversarial process – is understandable when one
considers limits on the competence and scale of the courts. But that this
response is understandable does not come close to answering the question of whether it is correct.

The issue of expanding or contracting class actions is a microcosm of
the broader issue of defining the role of courts and of rights and law in
general. Courts are severely limited in significant ways and there are no
easy and sweeping reforms that will remove these limitations. That does
not mean that courts should do nothing or that they should do only what
will minimize their errors and limitations. Courts may be and at least
sometimes are the best decision makers. But at high numbers and complexity that means that they will be the best of highly imperfect alternatives. The perfectionist images of courts that crowd the legal literature
have no value in determining where and when courts should decide. The
role of courts must be forged from an appreciation of their limitations relative to their alternatives such as political processes, markets, and communities. Defining that role requires careful consideration of demand as
well as supply.

This task means confronting the basic quandary that we saw in the discussion of class actions. Courts are most comfortable where numbers and
complexity are low – where remedies can be easily provided and rights
are strong and clear. But it is here that these judicial protections are generally least needed. The opposite is also true. Where the protections of
courts are most needed, courts may be the most uncomfortable and least
competent. This quandary, the task of confronting the supply and demand
of law and the various lessons of *Boomer* are just as central in the world
beyond common law property. We will now begin to explore this larger
world.

PART II

LAND USE AND RIGHTS

4

Zoning and Its Discontents – Political Malfunction and the Demand for Rights

As we saw in Part I, the role of courts and the character of law and rights are determined by systemic factors. Rights wax and wane with variation in numbers and complexity. Faced with the strains of land use decisions at high numbers and complexity, the *Boomer* majority argued that complex and widespread land use conflicts are the business of the political process not the courts. This argument suggests that, at high numbers and complexity, courts and legal rights disappear. To a great extent, U.S. law reflects this picture. Public regulation of land use conflict and, in particular, local zoning are both pervasive and important influencing, among other things, where people live and how their children are raised and educated.

But these regulations are also highly controversial. Serious distrust of land use regulation and zoning is common across the ideological spectrum. Zoning impacts a wide range of social concerns including preserving liberty, maximizing resource allocation efficiency, protecting the environment, providing affordable housing, and minimizing income and racial segregation. This amalgam of dramatic concerns produces a range of critiques. Those adversely affected by zoning often turn to constitutions and, therefore, to courts – both state and federal – for relief.

There are important tensions here. In *Boomer,* we saw the desire of common law courts to allocate complex land use issues to the political process. This desire accompanied a decrease in judicial role and a diminution and even disappearance of rights. Now we see a push for an increased judicial role in reviewing the political process resolution of these complex land use issues and with it the promise of significant rights. This ambivalence about law, rights, and the relative roles of the courts and the political process reflects strong and conflicting institutional choices embodied in the need for protection both *by* and *from* the political process. These difficult and conflicting institutional choices complicate the picture of law and rights. In order to understand this picture and to choose between the various judicial strategies to reform zoning, we must examine the workings of the regulatory process and its would-be substitute, the courts.

I begin by examining the demand for judicial protection against political malfunction. The task is made both difficult and interesting by the presence of two quite different forms of political malfunction. Understanding these two forms of malfunction is crucial in assessing the role of rights and the form of judicial response. Responding to the wrong malfunction not only wastes judicial resources; it can aggravate the existing malfunction in the political process. In this chapter, we will explore these two forms of political malfunction in the zoning context and consider several judicial responses, leaving one, judicial review of just compensation, for the next chapter.

Land use regulation and its judicial review are important subjects. But there is far more at issue here than land use regulation. The Rule of Law is meant to control the excesses of government in general. Controlling these excesses requires understanding and assessing them. Fears of the few and fears of the many haunt virtually all political settings. The tension between these two forms of political malfunction and the judicial response to them are fundamental to the workings of constitutionalism and the Rule of Law everywhere. The necessity of understanding political malfunction and the possibilities of judicial response to it goes far beyond issues of property and land use. The same analysis applied to property rights applies to human rights in general. Because the conflicting perceptions of political malfunction are so close to the surface and because judicial solutions are so difficult, U.S. land use law provides an exceptional vehicle to explore global issues like the Rule of Law and the role of courts and, because we will be dealing with local determinations, to explore the interaction between courts and communities.

I. CONFLICTING VISIONS OF UNDER- AND OVERREGULATION

Informal communities and markets can and do respond to land use conflicts without recourse to law in any formal sense. Communities can operate through informal sanctions, such as shunning and gossip, to enforce norms about land use. There is also prevention by transaction and more formalized private planning. Contractual arrangements, usually in the form of developer-imposed covenants, create elaborate private land use plans. The developer of a large parcel attempts to minimize land use conflict by a series of interrelated restrictions on use. These plans are quite common in modern residential subdivisions. Even operating extremely well, however, such private planning will hardly prevent all land use conflict. There are conflicts between these large parcels and other uses; much land has been developed without such restrictions and sources of conflict arise that are not envisioned in such plans.

Governmental regulation is a device to deal with the larger, more complex land use conflicts that escape private plans. The most pervasive regulatory response to land use conflict has been local zoning. In the United States, zoning by local authorities (cities, towns, and counties) leaves little land within touch of populations unregulated or unrestricted. Add to these restrictions those imposed by extensive state and national land use programs and land use regulation is pervasive. The issues dealt with in these regulations are both complex and important. Land use regulations emanate from a wide range of possible concerns including congestion, pollution, safety, community preservation, aesthetics, fiscal impacts, crime, class, and race. The result is a system of regulation that is controversial as well as pervasive.

Although there is widespread dissatisfaction with public land use regulation, it reflects two widely diverse, even opposite, perceptions of malfunction in the political process and, therefore, quite different perceptions of the resulting evils in zoning. In one perception, concentrated interests, usually in the form of land developers, are overrepresented and, therefore, there is a tendency to underzone or underrestrict. In the other perception, the same developers are viewed as underrepresented relative to surrounding homeowner majorities and the tendency is to overzone or overrestrict. In the vernacular of the field, underzoning is often characterized as "spot zoning" and overzoning is often characterized as "exclusionary zoning."

These quite different and conflicting perspectives of the underlying malfunction in the political process, not surprisingly, imply quite different types of legal responses. In fact, legal responses that ameliorate or correct one of these malfunctions or biases can aggravate the other. Thus, questions of institutional choice in the land use setting require us not only to identify the extent of political malfunction but also its form. In this section, I will introduce these different forms of political malfunction as perceived by courts in two cases. In the next section, I will address the analytical underpinnings of these two forms in greater depth.

A strong fear of underzoning and the overrepresentation of the concentrated few animates *Fasano v. Board of County Commissioners of
Washington County*.[1] In 1970, the A.G.S. Development Company, owner
of a thirty-two-acre parcel, sought and received from the local zoning authorities a loosening of the single-family residential zoning restrictions in
order to construct a mobile home park. This change was opposed by
homeowners in the vicinity of the proposed mobile home park. Despite
this opposition, the Board of County Commissioners granted the change.
The neighboring homeowners then brought action in the Oregon courts
to invalidate the zoning change. The trial court ruled in favor of the plain-
tiff-homeowners and invalidated the change and the Oregon Supreme
Court in the opinion considered here affirmed.

In theory, the rezoning process gives zoning authorities the flexibility
and discretion to deal with the ever-changing circumstances that confront
the use of land. Any increased judicial review and invalidation of these
changes runs the risk of interfering with legitimate planning. The *Fasano*
court understood this risk, but perceived a greater countervailing risk:

> However, having weighed the dangers of making desirable change more difficult
> against the dangers of the almost irresistible pressures that can be asserted by pri-
> vate economic interests on local government, we believe that the latter dangers
> are more to be feared.[2]

The Oregon court believed that special interests, in the form of land
developers, have disproportionate influence on the rezoning process. The
source of this influence is certainly not the greater number of votes held
by developers. The surrounding homeowners are more numerous. Instead,
it is the perception that concentrated interests – especially where pecuniary stakes are involved – are overrepresented in the rezoning process by
such means as campaign contributions, lobbying, or even plain old bribery.

This is hardly an outlandish or unusual perception. The power of the
concentrated few, reflected in phrases like "special interest legislation," is
a pervasive perception and has been embodied in the interest group theory of politics and the economic theory of regulation. Because dispersed
majorities face problems in information and organization, the more numerous, but dispersed majority remains dormant and the more active concentrated minority is the only position represented. I have termed this

---

[1] 264 Or. 574, 507 P.2d 23 (1973).
[2] 264 Or. 574, 507 P.2d 23, 30 (1973).

overrepresentation of concentrated minorities "minoritarian bias." Minoritarian bias is a common view of malfunction in local zoning and in the political process in general. But it is not the only view.

There is an opposite perception in which the problem is overzoning. Here the lower per capita stakes homeowners of the jurisdiction are an active majority and the developers with few if any votes are the victims of underrepresentation. I have termed this underrepresentation of the concentrated minority "majoritarian bias."

This vision of overzoning and majoritarian bias underlies *Construction Industry Association of Sonoma County v. City of Petaluma.*[3] In 1971, the City of Petaluma established a plan meant to control growth and development. The complex plan controlled the number of permits for new construction and the extension of the city's borders and its services "in order to protect the small town character and surrounding open spaces." The plaintiffs, an association of developers, attacked the Petaluma Plan for unreasonably constraining development and, thereby, depreciating the value of their enterprises and seriously harming those who would want to move to Petaluma and the general San Francisco area. In a decision later reversed on appeal, the District Court struck down the Petaluma Plan.

As we move from *Fasano* to *Petaluma,* we see a dramatic change in casting. Developers are now the victims. Homeowners, viewed as underrepresented in *Fasano,* are now overrepresented. Just as the court in *Fasano* believed that the local zoning authorities had ignored or undervalued the interests of existing homeowners and overemphasized the interest of the high-stakes developer, the court in *Petaluma* sees the local zoning authority as ignoring or undervaluing the interests and concerns of the developers (and the potential consumers of their housing) and overvaluing the interests of existing homeowners.

The effects of overzoning can be quite serious. The developer represents many would-be home buyers who are now shut out of the City of Petaluma.[4] Even more broadly, overzoning can create serious impacts on

---

[3] 375 F. Supp. 574 (N.D. Cal. 1974), reversed 522 F.2d 897 (9th Cir. 1975), cert. denied, 424 U.S. 934 (1976).

[4] In this sense, this political malfunction can be seen as another American classic: spillover effects. As the court in *Petaluma* saw it, the city of Petaluma is imposing costs on people far beyond its borders – people who are not voters in the locale. A deep concern for the inability of a jurisdiction to consider effects outside its boundaries animates much of the U.S. constitution. It was the concern for the impediments to commerce caused by state

consumers of housing across the region. As the district court's opinion shows, growth control ordinances like that in *Petaluma* when projected across a region like the San Francisco Bay area can have drastic, detrimental effects outside the jurisdiction itself. Impacts on the regional housing supply can be severe, resulting in income and racial segregation as well as adverse effects on the poor. Whether the malfunction is viewed as an underrepresentation of the concentrated interest (developers) in favor of the local majority (homeowners) or as the failure to consider the cost imposed on those outside the jurisdiction, the malfunction and its effects are serious.

Fasano and *Petaluma* are two important attempts by courts to review and oversee local zoning determinations. They are, however, based on two very different – virtually diametrically opposite – conceptions of the problems in the political process. The same sort of legislation (local zoning), the same basic cast of characters (developers of housing versus established homeowners), and the same sort of basic issue (density of housing) can quite plausibly be seen as subject to either minoritarian or majoritarian bias.

The correct characterization of the political malfunction is central to any serious attempt to deal with the evils of zoning. If in *Fasano* the surrounding neighbors rather than the developer were overrepresented, the resulting decision in favor of the underrepresented party would hardly be subject to deep suspicion and, therefore, would not need judicial intervention. Similarly, if in *Petaluma* developers in general were overrepresented in the political process making the zoning decision, the resulting decision against them again would not be subject to much fear of bias or distortion or need judicial review. Worse yet, as we shall see, the wrong perception and the wrong remedies can aggravate the true malfunction and create even worse problems.

II. THE TWO-FORCE MODEL OF POLITICS: FEAR OF THE FEW AND FEAR OF THE MANY

As the correct understanding of the political process under challenge is both essential and complex, we need to examine majoritarian and mi-

---

regulations and tariffs of out-of-state merchandise that motivated the calling of the Constitutional Convention. Thus, the general structure of the federal government, the Privileges and Immunities Clause of Article IV, and a number of judicial doctrines such as the dormant Commerce Clause all reflect concern about the ability of smaller jurisdictions to decide issues when there are significant effects beyond its borders.

noritarian bias and their interaction carefully. Minoritarian bias and majoritarian bias, their determinants, trade-offs, and interactions are part of what I have termed the "two-force model" of politics. To understand these versions of political malfunction, we again turn to the participation-centered approach – the distribution of per capita stakes and the costs of political participation. Employing these factors, we can determine which version of political behavior is likely to be most relevant.

Participation in the political process can be costly. These costs depend largely on the cost of information, which in turn depends on the complexity of the substantive issues and the complexity of the political process involved. The complexity of the political process depends on the size and intricacy of the legislative or administrative agendas. In addition, for larger groups, the cost of participation depends heavily on the cost of organization, which in turn depends on both the size of the group to be organized and the difficulty of identifying and convincing potential allies. The cost of organization is again a function of the cost of information.

In the face of these costs, the strength of minoritarian bias, most often associated with the interest group theory of politics, lies in the distribution of the benefits of political action.[5] Interest groups with small numbers but high per capita stakes have sizeable advantages in political action over interest groups with larger numbers and smaller per capita stakes, because higher per capita stakes mean that the members of the interest group will have greater incentive to expend the effort necessary to recognize and understand the issues. In the extreme but not uncommon case, the members of the low per capita stakes losing majority (often consumers or taxpayers) do not even have the incentive to recognize that they are being harmed. In some instances, they may even be convinced that they are being aided. The majority is not stupid or innately passive. In most instances, the majority is us. The per capita impact on each member of the majority is just too low to justify the expenditure of resources necessary to recognize the issue involved.[6]

---

[5] I explore the intellectual underpinnings of the interest group theory of politics in Komesar (1994), 55–8.

[6] Legislation that effectively excludes competition and, therefore, harms consumers, is often cast in terms of consumer health and safety. A classic example is the legislation involved in the *Carolene Products* case, *United States v. Carolene Products Company*, 304 U.S. 144 (1938), whose famous footnote is an important moment in U.S. constitutional jurisprudence. I explore both the footnote and the case in Komesar (1994), Chapter 7.

Even if a member of an affected group recognizes the impact of the legislation and his or her per capita benefit exceeds the allocated share of costs of political participation, we may still observe no willingness to contribute from this member and, more importantly, no collective action from this group. Whatever benefits an individual might gain by producing the collective action through his or her contribution, the net benefits to that individual would be even greater if he or she did not have to contribute. There is, therefore, an incentive to refuse to contribute and allow others to bear the costs of political participation; there is an incentive to free ride.

The severity of the shortfall in the representation of a group depends on the degree or extent to which members of the group free ride. At one extreme, if only a few free ride and the efforts of others take up the slack, there is no underrepresentation. At the other extreme, if all free ride, they will have no political representation and everyone in the group will lose.

When one considers this interaction between the costs and benefits of political participation, it is relatively easy to see why the dominant image of the political process and its biases is minoritarian. The concentrated few with their substantial per capita stakes have the incentive to understand their interests, organize for political activity, and determine the correct channels of influence in a complex political process. Their small numbers make organization and collective action easier. From this vantage, it is easy to see why the few are active and the many are dormant and why minoritarian bias is the prevailing perception of the political process.[7]

There is, however, significant variation in each of the factors we have discussed; consequently, there are significant sources of variation or gradation in the dominance of the few and the dormancy of the many. These factors and, therefore, the likelihood that the majority will be dormant vary across political issues and political jurisdictions. As the *absolute* per capita stakes for the majority increase (even holding constant the ratio between majoritarian and minoritarian per capita stakes), members of the majority will more likely spend the resources and effort necessary to understand an issue and recognize their interests. In turn, variation within the distribution of the per capita benefits of political action – the degree of heterogeneity – affects the probability of collective action on behalf of the majority by subgroups of higher stakes individuals. This collective ac-

---

[7] For a more extensive discussion of the interaction between constituent participation and political outcomes, see Komesar (1994), Chapter 3.

tion can take the form of informing and organizing lower per capita stakes members of the majority, thereby increasing the chance that an otherwise dormant majority will act. In these instances, those with higher stakes operate as a catalytic subgroup, activating the more dormant members.[8]

On the cost side, the probability of majoritarian response varies as the costs of political action vary. These costs depend on the rules, structure, and demography of the political process such as the size and population of the jurisdiction, the size of the legislature (number of legislators), the frequency of election, and the size and scope of the legislative agenda. Smaller numbers of voters are easier to organize and it is easier to prevent free riding and therefore, the probability of majoritarian activity increases. Smaller legislatures with fewer legislators make it easier to understand the position of any legislator and, therefore, it is easier to discipline unwanted action at the ballot box and to make the threat of such voting known and credible.

Complexity and, therefore, the cost of information also vary with the subject matter of the issue in question. The degree to which someone understands any issue also depends on that person's stock or endowment of general information. This stock is determined by culture, formal education, and the coverage of the press and media. Each culture has certain subjects such as religion or ethnicity that are part of the common experience of the members of that culture. This stock of "simple symbols" provides certain issues with easy recognition. Because the press and the media provide cheap and accessible information, press and media response is a central element in determining the degree of majoritarian influence.

Thus, the political influence of concentrated minorities varies depending on the complexity of the issue involved, the absolute level of the average per capita stakes of the larger group, the heterogeneity of this distribution of stakes, and the availability of free or low cost information. In other words, the prospect of majoritarian activity and majoritarian influence and, therefore, the majority's ability to offset minoritarian influence are determined by variation in the same factors employed by the interest group theory of politics to generate its conclusion of minoritarian

---

[8] Representation by these concentrated subgroups can suffer from all the ills of representation we saw in connection with class action representation in the adjudicative process. Since the dormant, dispersed group will not have the incentives (or even the knowledge) to monitor, the extent to which any subgroup will be a true representative will depend on just how closely the interests of the smaller and larger group converge.

dominance. I have simply broadened the scope of the factors to cover majoritarian as well as minoritarian participation.[9]

Taken to its logical conclusion, this analysis suggests not just that the relative advantage of the concentrated group will vary, but that there may be instances in which the larger group can dominate and even be overrepresented. This potential for domination stems from the simplest dimension of the difference between larger and smaller groups – the number of members in the two groups. In the most straightforward sense, larger numbers of members translates to political power via voting.[10] Voting provides large groups with a form of political action that, in the right circumstances, can be a powerful substitute for the organizational advantages of special interest groups. However haltingly and awkwardly, the power of the majority and their threat at the ballot box are felt. The fear of majority influence has a long history, and its imprint can be found in present day politics in many ways – most obviously in the tremendous effort public figures expend on public and press relations.

A few words on good and evil seem necessary here. The extent to which either majoritarian or minoritarian dominance is a social evil and, therefore, associated with terms like majoritarian or minoritarian bias depends on the goal in question. For example, those who value a more equal distribution of wealth may have a different conception of majoritarian bias than those who value resource allocation efficiency. Where votes are more equally distributed than wealth, a political process characterized by one person, one vote may be more attractive to those devoted to greater equality than to those devoted to resource allocation efficiency. Majoritarian influence might be seen less often as majoritarian bias.[11]

As a general matter, the intuitions that underlie the concepts of minoritarian and majoritarian bias relate to a broad sense of social goals – much broader than just resource allocation efficiency. The excesses of ma-

---

[9] For a more extensive exploration of the two-force model, see Chapter 3 of Komesar (1994).

[10] Voting is not the only way in which numbers translate into political influence. Even in political systems without effective elections, large numbers may be important. Revolts, mobs, demonstrations, passive resistance, and sabotage allow political costs to be imposed by large numbers on a government otherwise ruled by the few.

[11] The correlation between majoritarian dominance and such goals as equality, progressive redistribution, and racial and ethnic integration is by no means always so straightforward and attractive. As we shall see throughout this book, the relationship between majoritarian dominance and these laudable goals can be quite perverse.

joritarianism captured in phrases like "tyranny of the majority" are not the product of economists or other devotees of resource allocation efficiency. Similarly, antipathy to the overrepresentation of concentrated interests does not require any special allegiance to resource allocation efficiency. The common vocabulary and the popular media regularly reflect concern about the excessive power of special interests. This concern predates any formal articulation of the interest group theory of politics or of resource allocation efficiency. The concepts of majoritarian and minoritarian bias capture the pervasive sense that both counting noses without considering the degree or extent of impacts and ministering to the desires of the active few can create injustice.

This general sense reflects the normative importance of participation. Majoritarian bias and minoritarian bias, like the other basic concepts I use throughout the book, reflect an attraction to broad-based participation. This attraction, however, is to a notion of complete or equal participation. Increasing participation in a seriously incomplete or unequal way can create rather than alleviate societal problems.[12]

Many seemingly diverse views or philosophies stress the importance of participation and the detriments of inadequate, incomplete or unequal participation. Civic republicans stress greater and more equal participation as the core of the goals they seek. The amount, pattern, and quality of participation define communitarian notions.[13] Resource allocation efficiency, a seemingly quite different societal goal, is also defined in terms of the completeness of participation. Ask any economist whether a result is "efficient" and he or she will speak in terms of participation. The central issues of "externality" and transaction costs are about the extent and quality of participation in the market; an allocation decision is inefficient if an impact on someone is not represented in the transaction. Market failures are failures of participation. The world of zero transaction costs defines efficiency precisely because all costs and benefits are represented through

---

[12] Such a notion underlies Russell Hardin's warning against too simple a belief in the good of collective action. See generally, Hardin (1995). Hardin shows us the evils of incomplete participation – ethnic cleansing occurs where only part of the relevant community is organized, participates, and, therefore, dominates. Phrased in terms of the analysis in this book, his warning is that traditional communities can often be quite different from ideal communities. I would add that this deviation is more likely as numbers and complexity increase.

[13] As we shall see in Chapter 7, William Simon's theory of republican property is constructed on participation.

frictionless transactions. In turn, other goals such as equality of opportunity and various notions of liberty are also directly based on the ability to
participate.

We can see the dynamics of majoritarian bias, its interaction with minoritarian bias, and the relationship of this interaction to participation
and to numbers and complexity by returning to the facts of the *Boomer*
case discussed in Part I of this book.[14] The location of the cement plant
and its neighbors is represented roughly in the following diagram:

A	B	C
D	E	F
G	H	I

Figure 1

Using the figures employed by the *Boomer* majority, the stakes of the cement company, located on plot E on our diagram, would be $45 million,
while the stakes of the neighbors (A, B, C, D, F, G, H, and I in the diagram)
would total $185,000 or $23,125 each.[15] We can see the implications of majoritarian bias by imagining that the nine boxes constitute a jurisdiction –
a small local government. Under the simplest rule of democratic government – one person, one vote – the more numerous neighbors would pass
an ordinance prohibiting the activities of the cement company. Since the
social costs of such a prohibition ($45 million) far exceed the social ben-
efits ($185,000), this would be an inefficient result. This result occurs be-
cause numbers of votes not impacts are counted. This is the simple civics
model of democracy gone awry.

We can trace the effects of increasing numbers by imagining that the
relevant population increases from 8 to 80 to 800 to 8,000 to 80,000 and
so forth. We can trace the effects of diminishing per capita stakes by associating these increases in population with proportionally smaller per
capita stakes: $23,125 to $2,312.50 to $231.25 to $23.12 to $2.31, and so
forth. Increased complexity can be reflected either by imagining more
complex land use conflicts or increasingly complex and larger legislatures

---

[14] Again, for simplicity, I am using the goal of resource allocation efficiency.
[15] I have taken the artistic liberty of including eight rather than seven plaintiffs in order to
make the diagram symmetrical. The changes in numbers and per capita impact are not
significant to the example.

and bureaucracies. At some point, the majority will become less active and the fear of majoritarian bias will diminish.

We also can envision those instances in which minority dominance is inefficient by turning to the issue of pollution in the Hudson River Valley raised by the dissent in *Boomer*. Suppose that the social impacts of the removal of the cement plant pitted the $45 million loss to the cement company against $90 million of benefits to the occupants of the Valley, who number, let us say, 9 million. Per capita impact now averages $10 per person. As we saw from the previous example, as the numbers rose and per capita impacts fell, the chance of effective majoritarian participation fell. Such a setting would likely be characterized by a more complex governmental structure (a state government, for example) with more legislators to watch and more complex records to police. Cost of participation would also likely increase as it becomes increasingly more difficult to trace the causal relationship between the activities of the Atlantic Cement Company and the loss to the populace.

All these factors make it more likely that the majority will be dormant and that, therefore, needed regulations would not be imposed. One can fiddle with these hypothetical fact patterns by, for example, altering the governmental process or introducing low-cost information in the form of a journalistic exposé on pollution. These variations underscore my point that a skewed distribution of impacts – concentrated on a few on one side and dispersed over many on the other side – can itself be consistent with a variety of outcomes and even with diametrically opposite outcomes. The outcome depends on those factors considered by the participation-centered approach.

For our purposes, a central issue is the correct characterization of the political process. Is it more likely that local zoning is characterized by an image of minoritarian bias in which developers are overrepresented and underzoning is likely or by an image of majoritarian bias in which developers are underrepresented relative to an active homeowner majority? Zoning is one of those areas where it is quite plausible to characterize the decision making in either of the two extreme models.

This possibility arises in part because of the large range of locales covered by the term "local zoning." New York City is a local government larger than many states (and nations). Its land use patterns and potential conflicts as well as its zoning and political processes are highly complex. At the other end of the spectrum are small sparsely populated jurisdictions with a relatively simple existing land use pattern – often largely undeveloped. As number and complexity vary so do the cases for majoritarian and minoritarian dominance.

The case for majoritarian bias in the zoning of relatively small and homogeneous suburbs seems strong. Homeowners have relatively high stakes. For most people, their homes are the single largest financial investment they will ever make. More important, home is where the heart is. Basic senses of security, indeed the most basic senses of self-definition are associated with one's home.[16] It is hardly surprising that homeowners are often active political participants.

Imposing restrictions via the public political process provides homeowner majorities with possibilities unavailable to homeowners as transactors. Where imperfect markets do not reflect the adverse external effects of development, the political process provides a vehicle to correct these effects. But in the name of correcting effects unrepresented in the market, the political process can create its own external and unrepresented costs. Homeowners as local voters may seek to impose restrictions on new development that make new housing less dense and more expensive than their own housing and impose losses on others that significantly exceed the amount that these homeowners would be willing to bear themselves. Regulation via the political process allows these homeowners to gain benefits, while shifting the costs to others. For resource allocation efficiency purposes, that is an obvious problem.[17] When in fact decision makers in any institution do not take into account important impacts, the resulting decisions are suspect. To the extent that homeowner majorities in various locales fail to consider the cost of restricting development, serious problems ensue.[18]

The dynamics of majoritarian bias for smaller locales can be dramatically seen in the facts of *City of Cleburne v. Cleburne Living Center, Inc.*[19] The City of Cleburne had a relatively common, if somewhat archaic, provision in its zoning laws which declared homes for the "feebleminded" as special uses in a district in which multifamily or multiperson housing would otherwise be allowed. Special uses require a special permit issued

---

[16] See the discussion of Margaret Radin's approach to property in Chapter 7.

[17] This shifting of costs raises problems for goals other than resource allocation efficiency. Because it treats similar housing in different ways, it can violate horizontal equity. Because, as we noted earlier, the resulting exclusion falls most heavily on lower income groups, it can violate vertical equity or equitable distribution.

[18] There are indirect ways in which these costs can come to roost including competition among jurisdictions. We will return to this issue in Chapters 5 and 6.

[19] 473 U.S. 432 (1985).

by the local zoning authority. Cleburne Living Center sought such a permit to allow it to use an existing structure as a home for the mentally retarded.[20] The City of Cleburne refused. The applicants sought judicial review and invalidation of the City's decision. They were successful. The facts of the case present a poignant picture of the dynamics of majoritarian bias.[21]

One need not be unsympathetic to the Cleburne homeowners in order to see the zoning decision as highly suspect. The stakes to the homeowner majority are strong enough to make them sensitive to any threats. Since, for most people, a house is the largest investment – both financially and emotionally – it is hardly surprising that people are sensitive to any risks or dangers to this central asset. In the *Cleburne* context, outside observers, including the Court, may see the risks or damages to neighbors as largely irrational. But even irrational fears translate into property values and become a self-fulfilling cost of the homeowner.

The issue in *Cleburne* is not the reality of the loss to the homeowner, but its scale and scope. More important, the issue is who will balance these impacts on homeowners against the sizeable losses of forbidding a home for the mentally retarded.[22] The problem lies in the inability (or unwillingness) of the local political process to balance the severity of the losses to the homeowners against the severity of the impact on "others" – those not considered by the homeowner majority – those considered to be different. The homeowner majority has little or no reason to weigh what may be relatively small losses (or, more exactly, small chances of loss) to them against what may be sizeable losses to those who are excluded.

Stereotypes about the mentally retarded are all too common, perversely providing the catalyst for majoritarian activity. Mental retardation provides a simple symbol to which these homeowners can react. The mentally retarded may also be safe targets for mistreatment. Because local homeowners are unlikely to be mentally retarded, they are unlikely to

---

[20] I recognize that the term "mentally retarded" is not the most contemporary or thoughtful. Since the term was used throughout the case, however, I use it here to avoid confusion.

[21] I discuss *Cleburne* and its difficult institutional choices at length in Komesar (2000). Here it is only the political malfunction that concerns us.

[22] "Group homes currently are the principal community living alternatives for persons who are mentally retarded. The availability of such a home in communities is an essential ingredient of normal living patterns for persons who are mentally retarded. . . ." *Cleburne,* 473 U.S. at 438, n. 6.

need this specific facility and, therefore, they can react with little need to count the cost to those they exclude.

Whether and to what extent majoritarian bias characterizes local zoning depends on familiar variables such as the size of the jurisdiction, the complexity of its land use, the per capita stakes of the relevant parties, and the distribution of the stakes. In turn, each of these will vary depending on the zoning jurisdiction and the zoning issue. What is true for the simpler setting of local zoning where homogeneous populations of homeowners may feel direct (if exaggerated) threats to their property values, is not necessarily or even likely to be true for large-scale (state or national) regulatory programs dealing with complex, indirect impacts on property owners. What may be true for housing in Cleburne, Texas or Petaluma, Califorma may not be true for particle pollution in the Hudson River Valley, which so worried the dissent in *Boomer*.

These issues can easily be extrapolated beyond zoning and beyond the United States. The form of political malfunction can vary across jurisdictions within any nation and across national and international borders. Determining the form of political malfunction will require asking the same questions whatever the setting. The same sort of issues will be at play when we compare political malfunction for the European Union (EU) versus any of its member states or the character of the World Trade Organization (WTO) versus its member states. The answers to these questions will vary with context. What may be true for corruption in Indonesia may not be true for ethnic relations in the former Yugoslavia. But understanding the form as well as the extent of any political malfunction is crucial everywhere.

III. JUDICIAL RESPONSES

In reacting to political malfunction of either variety, the courts have a range of responses analogous to the spectrum of responses we saw in *Boomer*. They can provide strong property rights by a sweeping denial of all power of the state to interfere with individual landowners – thereby leaving the decision on land use to the market. No court has ordered this – although, for a brief moment, one appeared to.[23] They can provide more qualified rights by substituting adjudicative balancing for regulatory bal-

---

[23] But legal commentators have maintained this position. See Siegen (1972); Kunstler (1996).

ancing and evaluating each ordinance and restriction case by case. Or they can provide no remedy or right at all by refusing any real judicial review, thereby leaving the decision to the political process. Here they may condition this judicial inaction on reforms of the political process ranging from more procedural due process to more direct democracy (referenda and initiative) to more regional rather than local zoning. These responses vary depending on perceptions of the degree and form of political malfunction and of the resources and competence of the courts. Once again law and rights depend on the characteristics and relative merits of the underlying decision-making institutions. There are tough choices and complicated tradeoffs here and we can see them in three cases – *Fasano, Petaluma,* and *Mt. Laurel.*

In *Fasano,* the Oregon Supreme Court expanded the role of the Oregon courts in reviewing local zoning. As we saw, the court's fear of minoritarian bias caused it to focus on rezoning decisions where it feared that concentrated minorities, in the form of developers, were undermining the general zoning plan. Our prior discussion cast some doubt on the court's perception that minoritarian bias is the prevalent political malfunction. But even if severe minoritarian bias is present and there is significant reason to distrust the political process, we only have a single-institutional case for judicial intervention. Courts must still face questions about their ability to replace even a highly defective political process.

In *Fasano,* the Oregon court controlled the scope of its review, in part, through the use of the administrative/legislative distinction. The court rationalized its expansion of judicial review for rezoning decision on the ground that these zoning decisions were "administrative" rather than "legislative." Although the zoning changes had been made by a legislative body, the *Fasano* court declared them to be administrative by pointing to the small scale of most rezoning decisions where usually only one parcel was rezoned. There was nothing in the court's precedent that required such a result and other courts faced with a similar decision have chosen to adhere to the simpler definition.[24] Although it is always tricky to read between the lines, the *Fasano* court's distrust for the political process articulated so clearly in the case indicated that the court saw a significant need for judicial oversight, and it seems likely that this perception produced the resulting definitions. As is so often the case, the legal formula

[24] See, e.g., *Arnel Development Co. v. City of Costa Mesa,* 28 Cal.3d 511, 620 P2d 565, 169 Cal. Rptr. 904 (1980)

articulated – if administrative, then greater judicial scrutiny – really works
in the opposite direction. The *Fasano* court perceived a need for greater
judicial scrutiny and chose the appropriate label. Whether a decision is
"legislative" or "administrative" is not being decided in the abstract but
by considerating the consequences of one label or the other. These consequences commonly are institutional.[25]

As we have seen, the *Fasano* court's focus on rezoning and small scale
land use conflicts concentrates judicial review on those zoning decisions
that, at least in the *Fasano* court's view, are most likely to be subject to minoritarian bias (although, as we shall see, there are good reasons to doubt
that even these are subject to that bias). But this focus also helps to control the strain of this added responsibility on both the competence and resources of the Oregon courts. Focusing on the subset of small-scale zoning decisions, rather than all zoning decisions, means fewer cases to review
and the simpler and more confined nature of these zoning decisions
makes judicial review substantively easier.

Even if review of these more confined zoning decisions is easier, however, it is not easy. Faced with this difficulty, the *Fasano* court sought help
in making these substantive determinations. Because its concern about
minoritarian bias was focused on rezoning which it feared would undermine the general zoning ordinance, it could put considerable trust in the
process that formed the general zoning plan. There are two possible reasons for the *Fasano* court's greater faith in the original plan. First, as I have
shown elsewhere, there is more reason to fear minoritarian bias at the less
observed, more complex administrative level than at the more exposed
(publicized) legislative level[26] and, therefore, there is a realistic basis for
the Oregon court to be more worried about minoritarian bias in the less
observed, more particularized rezoning process. Second, even if the court
were suspicious of the general plan, they might think twice before taking
on so large and difficult a set of decisions.

Immunizing the general zoning plans, whatever the reason, provides
the Oregon courts with help in reviewing the rezoning decisions. The
courts can use the overall plan as a rough guide on rezoning. This sort of
"plan jurisprudence" has been attacked as unrealistic on several

---

[25] We saw the same analytical point in Chapter 2 in connection with the use of the construct,
"physical invasion," to define the border between trespass and nuisance. I will examine
the issue in general in Chapter 9.

[26] See the discussion of the growth of the bureaucracy in Komesar (1994), 90–7.

grounds – some of which we will discuss subsequently. But it allowed the *Fasano* court to reduce the complexity and difficulty of judicial review. Attachment to a well-defined plan produced by another institution provided a more restricted, more clearly defined judicial role.

As we have already seen, however, the world of institutional choice and, therefore, the world of law and rights seldom run so smoothly. There are at least two problems with the *Fasano* strategy. First, the subset of cases that would receive *Fasano*-type judicial review may be neither small in number nor substantively simple. Second, these decisions may be characterized by majoritarian not minoritarian bias and, therefore, the *Fasano* strategy may at best waste judicial resources and, at worst, aggravate political malfunction.

In good part, the problems with *Fasano*-type judicial review lie in the character of the so-called comprehensive zoning plans and the role that rezoning plays in the implementation of local land use plans. In reality, comprehensive plans appear to be haphazard and vague and, therefore, likely to frustrate the hopes of the *Fasano* Court. A number of authors have been critical of judicial attachment to comprehensive plans because of the serious impediment to flexibility produced by restricting exceptions and rezoning. Some believe that project-by-project variation in zoning is a superior method of evolving a comprehensive plan.[27] In the view of these authors, these rezoning decisions are the core of sensible local land use planning.

An even more troubling feature of the *Fasano* court's decision, however, lies in its basic assumption that it is minoritarian bias that characterizes the local zoning process and creates the need for constitutional judicial review. Although the characterization of political malfunction for local zoning remains controversial and can vary with factors such as the size and homogeneity of the jurisdiction and the complexity of the particular local land use decision, the overrepresentation of concentrated special interests, the bias most often perceived in American politics in general, is not likely to dominate local zoning. The case for majoritarian bias in local zoning – at least in smaller and less developed locales – is strong.

The crucial ingredients of majoritarian bias are an active majority and a disproportionate impact on the minority. Local homeowner majorities

---

[27] See, e.g., Krasnowiecki (1980); Rose (1983); Rose (1984–85); Tarlock (1975). These articles criticize either *Fasano* itself or its intellectual antecedent in the famous work of Charles Haar (1955a and 1955b).

are smaller in number and larger in per capita impact than majorities in most other political settings. Organization is easier and the stakes are high enough to produce both an appreciation of the issue and a willingness to act. Local land use decision makers are more accessible both geographically and procedurally (simpler, less formal procedures) than most political bodies. It is relatively easy to monitor the actions of the zoning board members and sanction unpopular behavior. This active majority can impose serious burdens on the concentrated minority. The impact on the local minority – developers – and, through them, on housing consumers outside the jurisdiction, can be immense. In the context of local zoning, especially suburban local zoning of the sort in *Fasano,* majoritarian bias, overrepresentation of local homeowners, and problems of overregulation are likely to be the major threats.[28]

Direct judicial review of rezoning such as that proposed in *Fasano* or structural changes aimed at greater direct democracy such as increased use of referenda and initiative[29] can provide antidotes to minoritarian bias. But, by the same token, they can aggravate majoritarian bias. If the majority is already overrepresented in the local zoning process, providing additional majoritarian bites at the apple can eliminate even those instances in which the underrepresented group (the minority) is able to prevail. If the voices of the majority are sufficiently heard even at the level of rezoning, then the complex bargaining that goes on between zoning authorities and developers and the ensuing increases in density provides a decision-making process with little possibility of serious underzoning.

---

[28] Employing an early version of my two-force model, two prominent observers of the zoning scene have concluded that while minoritarian bias might characterize the decision of larger jurisdictions (such as big cities) the activity of smaller more homogeneous and to some extent more élite suburbs is likely characterized by majoritarian bias. Ellickson (1977), 404–10; Fischel (1995), 271, 277, 294, 297–8. This close to the margin, one might expect to find fluctuations or even cycles in the presence of minoritarian versus majoritarian bias. For an interesting examination of fluctuation between minoritarian and majoritarian bias, see Pierce (1989).

[29] Referenda operate to lessen minoritarian bias by lowering the cost of political activity for the majority. Rather than having to lobby, cajole, or contribute to legislators, the majority can make its will known directly at the ballot box. In addition, referenda focus on one issue rather than a legislator's multi-issue agenda. In this sense, referenda voting is more straightforward and easier than voting for representatives. Lowering the cost of participation raises the chances that the majority will be active.

For extensive discussion of the various shortcomings of initiatives and referenda, see Schacter (1997); DuBois and Feeney (1992); Magleby (1984); Fountaine (1988). For interesting examination of referenda in the land use context, consider R. Rosenberg (1983).

This is hardly to say that neighbors will never lose but it suggests that their losses may be justified. In a world in which majoritarian bias is the more likely evil, granting considerable discretion to local zoning authorities through such devices as contract zoning need not cause the courts much worry. Majoritarian reaction will hold the zoning boards in check.[30]

There are broader lessons here for the understanding of administrative agencies in general. The *Fasano* court quite correctly saw the local zoning process as similar to the action of administrative agencies in the sense that these small-scale zoning decisions involved application of general mandates to specific settings. But it then made the more questionable assumption that the political malfunction involved was minoritarian bias. That assumption would have been sensible for the prototypical administrative agencies – a regulatory agency at the federal or national level applying complex legislation. But one view of administrative agencies does not fit all.

The issue is not the label "administrative" or "administrative agencies." The issue is the level of systemic variables like per capita stakes of the various interests and the costs of participation and, in turn, variables like numbers and complexity. There can be significant variation in these factors between administrative agencies at different levels of government and even among administrative agencies at any given level. Even federal administrative agencies are not all subject to minoritarian bias. Once again it is wise to look to the parameters of institutional choice to better understand the intuitions that underlie conventional labels.[31]

My analysis of *Fasano* emphasizes the importance of dealing with majoritarian bias. But that is no easy task. In the world of serious majoritarian bias, there are two judicially intensive strategies for reform – expansion of the coverage of the takings clause and of just compensation (discussed in the next chapter) and expansion of direct judicial review of zoning restrictions themselves. In the face of majoritarian bias, this direct judicial review of the restrictions is an expensive and difficult strategy. It is even more daunting than the serious judicial response to minoritarian bias in cases like *Fasano*. The *Fasano* court could justifiably avoid serious

---

[30] As we shall see in the next two chapters, the ability of these zoning authorities to bargain may act to ameliorate the adverse effect of majoritarian bias.

[31] I will return to the subjects of legislative versus administrative and local verus national decision making in Chapter 5 in the discussion of William Fischel's proposal for just compensation and in Chapter 7 in the discussion of Carol Rose's affection for localism.

review of the overall zoning plan and focus on the limited subset of smaller scale rezoning decisions. To some degree, the overall plan served as a guide that reduced the substantive task confronting the courts. No such limits are plausibly available to courts asked to review the zoning decisions characterized by majoritarian bias. Now the issue is the overall plan itself or, more often, a wholesale change in the plan that substitutes a new and far more restrictive general zoning scheme. What was trustworthy in the context of minoritarian bias is now the focus of distrust in the context of majoritarian bias.

I will explore the monumental tasks confronting direct judicial response to majoritarian bias in two settings – the *Petaluma* case we have already discussed and the famous *Mt. Laurel* cases from New Jersey. In cases like *Petaluma* and *Mt. Laurel*, where courts have seriously shouldered the task of substantive review of local zoning, they have been confronted with intimidating tasks. In both cases, the substantive issues go beyond the individual jurisdiction and its plan for zoning. The District Court in *Petaluma* saw the evil of the Petaluma plan in the repetition of that plan by other similarly situated suburban or exurban jurisdictions. The San Francisco Metropolitan region was the focus of the *Petaluma* court. In turn, large regions within the state of New Jersey rather than individual locales were the concern of the judges in *Mt. Laurel*.

Even given the severe forms of political malfunction perceived by the *Petaluma* and *Mt. Laurel* judges, assessing so many local land use plans in so many contexts must give courts pause. Paradoxically and perversely, the severity of political malfunction that motivates the substitution of the courts makes the task for the courts more uncertain, expensive, and frustrating. Political jurisdictions subject to strong majoritarian bias can be aggressively uncooperative. They make obtaining compliance with court interventions difficult by every delaying and obfuscating tactic that they can employ.

The *Petaluma* and *Mt. Laurel* courts approached the challenging task of judicial review in different ways. The *Petaluma* court employed a sweeping solution. It denied the validity of an entire growth control strategy for public land use restriction. Places like the City of Petaluma would not be allowed to restrict growth below the amount of housing demanded in the market. The *Petaluma* court swept aside any attempts by local jurisdictions to mitigate the adverse effects of growth on existing homeowners. Faced with the kind of complexity involved in the Petaluma plan and the real possibility that variants of this plan would show up in most suburban and exurban jurisdictions in the San Francisco region, the court sought a simple solution. Serious, individualized judicial review of each restriction and each permit request when extrapolated over the San Francisco region was at least implausible if not impossible. The District Court's market-based remedy was strong, even dire, but it promised to be simple to implement. In terms of our prior analysis, the *Petaluma* court employed a strong property right that allocated responsibility for determining correct land use to the market. Like the simple trespass rule analyzed in Chapter 2, the court provided a strong remedy that left most of the substantive determinations to another institution.

The general problem with sweeping solutions is that they are likely to suppress valid exceptions – those instances in which the simple formula employed does not reach the correct solution. Whether such a result is tolerable depends in part on how frequent and how important these exceptional instances are. In the land use setting, the possibility that growth can have negative impacts that are not necessarily picked up in market solutions cannot be denied. There are benefits as well as costs in controlling growth. The most tangible negative impacts of growth involve the attempt to match population and natural resources such as water and sewage treatment capacity. The *Petaluma* court dismissed the City of Petaluma's attempt to make these environmental arguments by claiming that the City of Petaluma's demands could be met easily by existing regional capacity. But, like the impact on housing, the negative impact of growth across the region, not just in Petaluma itself, is the relevant issue. Here it is not so easy to dismiss the need to control or channel growth.

Massive residential development across the region might well strain Northern California's water supply and even sewage treatment potential. Like the impact of increased congestion on highways, the impacts of increased population density on basic environmental resources are not directly reflected in market transactions and market choices. These potential benefits for regulation or control in this setting are largely ignored by the *Petaluma* court. The *Petaluma* court may have treated the city's environmental arguments lightly because it believed, quite plausibly, that these were not the major reasons for the no growth ordinance. But another jurisdiction might be more concerned about these factors or might at least shrewdly appear more concerned. Then a court could not so easily avoid this difficult issue.

The benefits of controlling growth actually emphasized by the City of Petaluma raise confounding issues concerning goals and values. The City emphasized its desire to preserve the small town or community character of Petaluma. Such a desire to avoid change can stem from unattractive motives. Within the folds of the desire to preserve community character may be the desire for income, class, or racial segregation. But it is impossible to preclude the prospect that attractive values may also be present and that further confuses the land use balance and makes a sweeping rejection of zoning uncomfortable. The desire to preserve community has been applauded by commentators whose views would generally be considered sensitive to issues of race and class. These commentators have emphasized the central importance of home and community in personal definition and human fulfillment. As we have seen, there is a growing sense across the ideological spectrum that informal communities and relationships serve a wide variety of beneficial societal roles. I will examine this affection for communitarianism in Chapters 7 and 8. For present purposes, it's enough to note that the concerns of the City of Petaluma resonate with goals or values generally applauded or respected as well as those generally deplored.

Petaluma raises basic issues of institutional choice about the definition of community. The problems with Petaluma's plan, as seen by the district court, lie in the impacts of that plan on the region and even the nation. This larger community is not defined by the city limits of Petaluma – and that is the problem. The ideal community and the actual political community do not coincide. I have spoken often about "numbers" as a crucial factor in the performance of institutions. The correct "number" is synonymous with the relevant population impacted by a particular problem. Local zoning raises problems because, at least normatively, the correct community and, therefore, the correct number extends considerably beyond the border of the local zoning jurisdiction.

The realities of complex societal decision making as well as the realities of complex societal decision makers place a court like the *Petaluma* court in a quandary. A court fully appreciative of both the benefits and the costs of growth and the potential for both market and political process failures might still attach itself to the imperfect market. The *Petaluma* district court may well have felt inadequate to make the judgment case by case, restriction by restriction, but not wanting to leave the decision to a highly suspect political process opted for the market. By contrast, like the Ninth Circuit Court of Appeals in reversing the district court, such a court might attach itself to an admittedly highly imperfect political process rather than shift these tasks to the judiciary. Again, the choice among highly imperfect institutions is likely to be accompanied by highly imperfect strategies.

In the end, the district court in *Petaluma* was reversed. The opinion that accompanied the reversal harkens back to the *Boomer* discussion. Like the *Boomer* court, the circuit court in *Petaluma* avoided the broader land use issues. It did so by raising a procedural barrier in the form of standing to raise the interests of those excluded from Petaluma or the San Francisco area, even though the dynamics of litigation largely foreclosed those excluded from raising these issues themselves. The circuit court also limited its scope of inquiry by viewing the case solely in terms of the single jurisdiction. Through both these strategies, the circuit court, like the *Boomer* court, left larger and more complex land use issues to the political process.

Although the *Petaluma* district court's attempt to construct a strong rights strategy for judicial review of zoning was nipped in the bud, several state courts have seriously reviewed and invalidated local zoning ordinances.[32] By far, the most ambitious of these endeavors occurred in New Jersey. In a series of cases, most under the title *South Burlington County NAACP v. Mt. Laurel Township,* the New Jersey Supreme Court positioned itself to actively review and invalidate local zoning decisions in the state of New Jersey.

In the first of these cases, low and moderate income residents or former residents of the southern New Jersey township of Mt. Laurel along with various public interest groups brought action claiming that the township's zoning plan failed to consider adequately the housing needs of low- and moderate-income individuals. In particular, they alleged, and the courts believed, that the township severely restricted housing density with the effect, if not the intention, of excluding low- and moderate-income residents. Although the township offered half-hearted attempts to rationalize its zoning ordinance in terms of environmental impact, its primary purpose was to control the adverse fiscal impacts of further

---

[32] See, e.g., *Britton v. Town of Chester,* 143 N.H. 434, 439–41, 595 A.2d 492, 495–96 (1991); *Fernley v. Board of Supervisors of Schuylkill Twp.,* 509 Pa. 413, 502 A.2d 585 (1985); *Robinson Twp. v. Knoll,* 410 Mich. 293, 302 N.W.2d 146, 149 (1981); *Schwartz v. City of Flint,* 426 Mich. 295, 395 N.W.2d 678 (1986); *Suffolk Housing Services v. Town of Brookhaven,* 70 N.Y.2d 122, 517 N.Y.S. 2d 924, 511 N.E.2d 67 (1987); *Norwood Builders v. City of Des Plaines,* 128 Ill. App.3d 908, 471 N.E.2d 634 (1984); *Board of County Commissioners of Brevard County v. Snyder,* 627 So. 2d 469 (1993 Fla.); *Kaiser Hawaii Kai Development Co. v. City of Honolulu,* 70 Haw. 480, 777 P.2d 244 (1989).

development. The township attempted to minimize the demand for public services – in particular, public education.

This focus on fiscal impacts is endemic to local decision making. Because local services commonly are paid from local property taxes, development that increases the demand for local services can have significant financial impact on existing landowners. Existing landowners are motivated to mold new development in order to obtain the best balance between property taxes paid and public services demanded. The most significant local expenditure is usually public education. Existing homeowners can reduce demand for local services by assuring that new development is as childless as possible. It is hardly surprising then that a significant portion of the undeveloped land in Mt. Laurel Township was zoned for light industry only. Such a land use pays taxes but sends no children to school.

As in *Petaluma,* it is easy enough to debate the validity of these concerns by local landowners. To some degree, both on grounds of fairness and efficiency, fiscal concerns are valid. The amenities of a community include its fiscal position. It would be attractive to put housing in a community that had high property values relative to its school costs. New housing that was more dense, lower cost, and had more children would free-ride (or more cheaply ride) on the lower density more expensive property around it. The older, lower density housing would pay more than its share of local property services relative to the new housing. It seems appropriate to have new housing bear its share of these services.[33]

But, because local landowners control the process, there is no reason to believe that they will limit their fiscal desires simply to correcting the tendency of developers to free-ride on fiscal amenities.[34] They can and do

---

[33] Whether it is appropriate depends to some extent on one's conception of goals. From the standpoint of horizontal equity, it seems fair to have each development bear the allocated cost of its public services. As a general matter, from the vantage of resource allocation efficiency, better allocative decisions are made when such costs are taken into account by the relevant actor. On the other hand, from the standpoint of vertical equity, it is at least arguable that it is fairer for wealthier, larger landholders to bear a proportionately larger share of the cost of public services. Income distribution or vertical equity effects are especially difficult to establish since the final negative impact of the restrictions on housing can fall variously on the developers, housing consumers, or construction workers. It is likely that some if not most of these will have lower income or wealth than the local landowners who receive the benefits of the restrictions. See Inman and Rubinfeld (1979) for analysis of the horizontal equity considerations of these fiscal arrangements and Downs (1973) for a broader analysis of the implications of exclusionary zoning.

[34] These desires may be limited indirectly by competition among jurisdictions. I will return to this point in Chapter 6.

seek to reverse the situation and fiscally free-ride on the new development. Instead of developers free-riding by putting in lower cost, more child-dense housing, the existing homeowners seek to free-ride by requiring that new housing be even more expensive and child scarce than existing housing. Mt. Laurel Township sought this fiscal free-ride by requiring larger lot size than existed, by zoning for industry only, by zoning for senior citizens (without school-age children), and by assessing charges on developments based on the number of children. This fiscal zoning exacerbated the problems of low- and moderate-income families by making Mt. Laurel less accessible and by decreasing the supply of housing in the region.

The problem lies not in the abstract validity of the concern about fiscal impacts, but in a process that disproportionately weights these concerns relative to the benefits of expanded housing opportunities. Whatever the societal goal, this tendency to overrepresent the interests of local homeowners is disturbing. Yet, if local landowner majorities have total control over decision making, such "overuse" of the power is predictable because it maximizes their position. The societal impacts of this parochial maximization are similar to those in *Petaluma* – higher cost of housing, concentration of the poor in highly crowded central cities that, in turn, aggravates the negative impacts of overcrowding such as crime and pollution, as well as economic and racial segregation.

Although the effects in *Mt. Laurel* were similar to those in *Petaluma*, the remedy was quite different. The *Mt. Laurel* court, unlike the *Petaluma* court, did not attempt a sweeping solution via strong rights and the allocation of decision making to the market. Instead, it offered more qualified property rights and allocated the land use balance to the courts. As such, the New Jersey judiciary took on the prodigious task of case-by-case (or locale-by-locale) analysis.

The core of the *Mt. Laurel* remedial strategy was the determination of what the New Jersey Supreme Court referred to as "regional fair share." The regions were to be associated with various metropolitan areas such as the area around Camden or around Newark. The housing needs of each region would then be divided among the zoning jurisdictions in the region. Under this plan, the New Jersey courts must determine the needs for housing – and in particular low- and moderate-income housing – in each region of the state and the allocation of that housing among the various zoning jurisdictions.

The first *Mt. Laurel* decision placed great emphasis on removing those aspects of local zoning ordinances that impeded the development of higher density housing in locales like Mt. Laurel. Like *Petaluma,* the engines for development of housing would primarily be market forces. Unlike *Petaluma,* the extent and form of the optimal zoning restriction would be allowed to vary with the circumstances of each jurisdiction. As might have been expected, the strength of local homeowner majorities made local zoning authorities disinclined to abide by the precepts of this remedy. These communities found every excuse to avoid loosening the restraints on higher density housing. They read the long opinion in *Mt. Laurel I* carefully and made use of any possible escape. For example, the court had associated its remedy with "developing" communities so some locales argued they were not "developing." Others attempted to rationalize their zoning constraints on more attractive goals, in particular, environmental goals. The lower courts and even the New Jersey Supreme Court itself offered some indications that these sorts of claims would receive deferential treatment.[35]

Eight years later in 1983, the Supreme Court of New Jersey issued a second, even longer opinion in *Mt. Laurel* condemning the slack response of the townships to the problems set out in *Mt. Laurel I.* The court saw the need for a stronger judicial hand in determining what fair share allocation should be and in ordering not only the removal of restrictions but affirmative steps to accommodate low and moderate income housing. Every municipality, not just developing ones, was required to bear its share of housing. More important, the court constructed a streamlined and robust administrative apparatus with specialized courts and extensive roles for court-appointed masters along with a builders' remedy that offered developers additional incentives to bring actions against wayward municipalities.[36]

Mt. Laurel confronted the Supreme Court of New Jersey and, in turn, the entire judiciary of New Jersey with demanding institutional choices. First, the complexity and difficulty of local zoning with its significant variations across locales made the job of assessing the validity of the various land use restrictions in varying land use contexts demanding. Faced with these problems, the New Jersey Supreme Court did not opt for the sweeping solution employed in *Petaluma.* Instead, it set up an iterative process in which local zoning authorities would propose and trial courts would examine a variety of plans that presumably would allow for variation from locale to locale as relevant factors supported such variation. Second, the

---

[35] See Haar (1996), 30–5.   [36] See id. at 37–54.

Supreme Court of New Jersey faced one of the great paradoxes of institutional choice and constitutional judicial review – the worse the political malfunction, the more difficult the task for the courts. Thus, on one hand, courts should and do respond more aggressively when faced with greater reasons to distrust the political process but, on the other hand, the more severe the political malfunction the less likely it is that the courts will get cooperation from these political entities, making it more difficult for courts to respond. In turn, this ability to avoid and delay depends on the complexity of the substantive issues.

Court orders do not remove the political reality of determined local majorities and the resulting pressure on political representatives to respond to the desires of these majorities. Recalcitrant and unwilling political jurisdictions can use the complexity and difficulty of the situation to avoid or at least delay the increased housing density that their homeowner majorities disfavor. They can use loopholes, pretend compliance, or offer excuses more easily because the complexity of the issues makes it easier to offer false, but plausible excuses or otherwise cover their tracks. In the face of the recalcitrant response by local authorities, the Supreme Court of New Jersey had a difficult choice – either abandon the project or increase an already significant commitment to judicial review. One cannot help but admire the courage and commitment of the New Jersey Supreme Court in choosing the more difficult alternative in *Mt. Laurel II*.

Two recent books paint a picture of innovative and successful judicial implementation of *Mt. Laurel II*.[37] The courts aggressively tailored, imposed, and enforced housing requirements. This era of aggressive and innovative judicial review, however, lasted only three years. In 1985, the New Jersey state legislature enacted a response to the problems of exclusionary zoning – the Fair Housing Act. This complicated bill put an end to some of the more aggressive judicial interventions and offered a series of weaker administrative remedies and local zoning requirements. In 1986, the legislation was constitutionally tested and the New Jersey Supreme Court validated it.

The original *Mt. Laurel* cases were based on violations of the New Jersey Constitution and, therefore, the court was not required to accede to legislative direction. When it made its decision, the New Jersey Supreme Court knew that this political/administrative substitute for the courts was likely to remove the teeth from attempts to curb the excesses

---

[37] Haar (1996); Kirp, Dwyer, and Rosenthal (1995).

of local zoning. And, indeed, various reports indicate that the legislation has done little to correct the problems of exclusionary zoning.[38] The source of the Court's reluctant acquiescence can be found on the supply side. Courts face an enormous strain on both their competence and their resources when they attempt to replace a defective political process at high numbers and complexity. The history of *Mt. Laurel* through several voluminous appellate decisions and through various episodes in New Jersey politics is an uncomfortable reminder of the quixotic nature of judicial attempts to deal with serious political malfunction in general and with the quite serious problems and evils of suburban overzoning in particular.

Direct judicial review is a taxing response to serious political malfunction. It is hardly surprising that most courts offer little serious review of land use regulation. Most courts allocate decision making to the political process and, therefore, offer weak or no property rights. But this decision not to decide is an unstable equilibrium. There remains a serious distrust of local zoning that manifests in various ways. There will be hit-and-miss activism in which courts strike down particularly offensive pieces of legislation and then, recognizing the long-term costs of this activism, retreat back into dormancy. There will also be instances of serious and sustained judicial activism like *Mt. Laurel* and the nearly fifty-year effort at school desegregation in the federal courts.

This struggle between distrust of the political process and the difficulties of judicial review also manifests itself in judicial attempts to cure political malfunction through structural changes rather than direct judicial review. Here judicial passivity is conditioned on changes in the political process that remove or lessen majoritarian bias. At least at first blush, regional zoning – the allocation of the zoning decision to a larger jurisdiction – seems an effective means of decreasing local majoritarian bias. High-stakes developers underrepresented in local zoning decisions are now joined in a larger political jurisdiction by the consumers of the hous-

---

[38] See Dukeminier and Krier (1988), 1249 for citations to newspaper reports indicating the dubious nature of the New Jersey Fair Housing Act. The New Jersey Fair Housing Act of 1985, N.J. Stat. Ann. §§ 52-27D-301 to 52-27D-329 (1986) was held constitutional in Hills *Development Co. v. Bernards Township,* 103 N.J. 1, 510 A.2d 621 (1986). At least one of the recent books on *Mt. Laurel* is very critical of the actions of the Council on Affordable Housing (COAH); see Kirp, Dwyer, and Rosenthal (1995), 136–64. Even Charles Haar can offer only weak praise for COAH and only Haar sees much hope of serious judicial review. Haar (1996), 96–116, 117–26.

ing the developer might have produced. Augmented by these potential housing consumers, the antirestriction side appears to have the votes to adequately represent their position. In a world in which the only alternative antidote to majoritarian bias is extensive judicial review, beleaguered courts see regional zoning as an attractive alternative. Thus, in the *Mt. Laurel* cases, the New Jersey Supreme Court continuously exhorted the state legislature to substitute regional zoning for local zoning. To the New Jersey courts caught up in the arduous task of reviewing the decisions of so many local zoning jurisdictions, the prospect of regional zoning must have seemed like Nirvana.

As always, however, the ability of regional zoning to cure majoritarian bias depends on the true – not the idealized – character of the regional zoning process. If regional zoning ends up in the same hands or affected by the same distortions that characterize local zoning, we not only have a continuation of the same problem but its aggravation. Moving the decision to a larger level of government removes a possible source of amelioration of the problems of majoritarian bias at the local level – competition among jurisdictions. This competition would be suppressed if the local governments could agree not to compete – forming, in effect, a cartel. Cartels are likely to be undermined by the greed of members attempting to cheat. Cartels work better if they have enforcement mechanisms or cartel managers. Governments are excellent cartel managers. A regional zoning authority captured by the local zoning authorities (and the associated local homeowners) could operate as an effective cartel manager and, thereby, increase the problems of overzoning.

The threat of these adverse effects of regional zoning depends on the likelihood that regional zoning will be captured by the prorestriction forces that exist at the local level. That possibility is not remote. The new participants – the potential consumers of housing – are more likely to be passive or dormant than opposing pro-restriction homeowners. The per capita stakes of potential home owning associated with any adjustment in restrictions are low and diffuse and the uncertainty of both the location and timing of that ownership attenuates and complicates political participation by these potential owners. What we may see is a version of minoritarian bias at higher levels of government characterized by a larger dispersed majority of potential house buyers whose stakes are so small that they are largely passive. In this world, the largest active group is still the existing homeowners who have the advantage of an organizing mechanism in the form of existing local zoning jurisdictions. In such a world, regional zoning may be a dangerous reform.[39]

IV. CONCLUSION

I have spent considerable time on the political malfunctions of U.S. local zoning and the possible judicial responses to these political malfunctions. This attention could be justified simply by the importance of local zoning in the United States. Issues of vast importance such as environmental protection, affordable housing, racial and income segregation, and access to public education are at stake. But the themes of this chapter are relevant beyond land use and beyond the United States.

Political malfunction, involving both the fear of the few and the fear of the many, is everywhere. So is the strain on judicial resources and competence presented by difficult social issues with conflicting social goals. Especially where serious political malfunction emanates from high numbers and complexity, courts can expect dogged and creative litigation that will confront them with challenging and complicated decisions. This will be true whether the issue is protectionist legislation before the European Court of Justice or the WTO or human rights claims before any national or international tribunal. The same issues of political malfunction and judicial capacity raised here in the context of U.S. land use haunt the establishment, interpretation, and implementation of law and rights of all sorts in all places.

The lessons of U.S. land use law are both fascinating and disturbing. Governmental regulation of land use, and in particular local zoning, is ostensibly meant to protect private property by protecting one individual from another. But serious imperfections exist in these political responses. These imperfections provide the impetus for protection of individuals from governmental interference. The provision of this protection from government is complicated on two levels. First, there are two traditional and credible, but nevertheless conflicting forms of the political malfunction – overrepresentation of concentrated minorities and overrepresentation of dispersed majorities. Second, there is the question of how to provide protection from either of these political malfunctions. Many people look to the courts, usually under the aegis of constitutional judicial review

---

[39] We will return to the issue of regional zoning in the discussion of solutions to exclusionary zoning in Chapter 6.

and constitutional property rights. As we have seen, despite important societal stakes and serious political malfunction, constitutional property rights – legal protection of individuals from the government – are weak. At least as a matter of description, protection of property by direct judicial review of local zoning is limited.

All of the judicial reluctance is easily understandable. But is it correct? Social issues involving high numbers and complexity severely strain both the substantive competence and resources of the courts. Courts function better with more confined and simpler societal issues. This is the supply side of legal protections and rights. These supply side concerns explain judicial reluctance to review legal zoning aggressively.

But the simple and confined issues so comfortable for courts are also the context in which alternative institutions function well. Courts are most needed where these other institutions do not function well and that will be where numbers and complexity are high. This is the demand side for legal protection and rights. The opposite pulls of supply and demand create basic quandaries about land use, property protection, and property rights.

Yet, perhaps that suggestion is premature. We have not finished our examination of judicially based sources of property protection or property rights. We have to explore the issue of just compensation upon which U.S. courts and commentators currently place so much emphasis.

5

Just Compensation – The Problems of Judicial Pricing

Tucked neatly into the end of the Fifth Amendment is the Takings Clause: "Nor shall private property be taken for public use, without just compensation." In four prominent cases in the last decade, the United States Supreme Court's rendition of the Takings Clause in general and of the doctrine of regulatory takings in particular has delighted property rights advocates and alarmed land use authorities. These seemingly revolutionary decisions have been heralded as the foundation for a new era of property rights protection.[1] They can even be seen as a cure for the problems in the land use process discussed in the last chapter by forcing wayward zoning authorities to pay for and, therefore, to account for the adverse impacts of overzoning.

On the *Boomer* spectrum, these cases appear to provide at least the moderate to serious property rights inherent in close judicial review and perhaps even the strong, simple property rights inherent in allocation of decision making to the market. But such readings of these cases ignore central systemic realities that will limit their potential impact. In the end, these systemic realities confine the role of the courts and, therefore, the power of these property rights. Again, there are important lessons here not only about land use and takings in the United States, but about the dynamics of rights in general throughout the world.

The principal case is *Lucas v. South Carolina Coastal Commission.*[2] *Lucas* sets out the new approach to regulatory takings and it will be the

---

[1] See Kmiec (1995), 148, 156 (asserting that "the Court has awakened to its responsibility under the Takings Clause and that [t]here is no constitutional basis for confining [these cases to] complete value deprivation or property concession"); see also Huffman (1993); Washburn (1993); Krotoszynski (1997); Williams (1988); Callies (1999).

[2] 505 U.S. 1003 (1992).

primary focus of this chapter. Two other cases, *Nollan v. California Coastal Commission*[3] and *Dolan v. City of Tigard,*[4] address the indirect imposition of restrictions. They deal with exactions – situations in which land use authorities offer to loosen valid land use restrictions conditioned on the developer-landowner granting some land interest to the government. I will deal with these cases at the end of this chapter.[5]

After presenting the facts and basic holdings in *Lucas,* I examine its central question: How broadly will or should the *Lucas* doctrine be read? In that connection I consider two proposals for a broad regulatory takings doctrine. Richard Epstein offers the most expansive existing reading of the takings clause and regulatory takings. William Fischel's approach is more tailored but still ambitious. We can then consider what *Lucas, Nollan,* and *Dolan* can and should mean.

I. THE LIMITS OF *LUCAS*

In 1986, David Lucas, one of the developers of the Isle of Palms, located near Charleston, South Carolina, purchased two seaside lots for $975,000. In 1988, the State of South Carolina passed the Beachfront Management Act which had the effect of barring construction on Lucas's two parcels. It was not Lucas's position that the purpose of the Beach Management Act was invalid or that the state's desire to stop construction on his two lots was necessarily improper. He conceded the validity of the underlying governmental project – the restriction of development along the seashore in order to control the erosion or loss of shoreline. But, he argued, the government should not carry out this project without paying people like him compensation. To Lucas, the issue was not the validity of the overall project, but the validity of the mode of funding it. The resulting distribution of the benefits and burdens of the project was unconstitutional. He pointed to the fact that the restriction stopped him from developing the property in any commercially viable way and convinced the trial court that in effect the restricted property had no value. The trial court

---

[3] 483 U.S. 825 (1987).   [4] 512 U.S. 344 (1994).

[5] The fourth case is *First English Evangelical Lutheran Church of Glendale v. County of Los Angeles,* 482 U.S. 304 (1987). I do not spend much time on *1st Church* because its scope and importance are determined by the scope and importance of *Lucas. 1st Church* provides for the powerful remedy of temporary takings if a jurisdiction regulates when it should have used eminent domain. *Lucas* defines these instances.

invalidated the regulation and ordered that the government pay Lucas $1,232,387.50 if it wished to reimpose the restriction.

The government appealed to the South Carolina Supreme Court arguing that even if the restriction constituted a dire prohibition on development, the state's purpose in imposing the restriction was to prevent serious harm caused by Lucas's development. The government contended that, since Lucas never contested the validity of the state's purposes which involved the prevention of serious harm, Lucas had conceded that his prohibited use constituted a "noxious use" and, therefore, did not require compensation under the Takings Clause. The South Carolina Supreme Court reversed the trial court. But the Supreme Court of the United States ruled for Lucas reversing the state supreme court's decision.

The constitutional doctrine in issue is regulatory takings – whether and when government can restrict the use of land without paying compensation or, more exactly, when government must (rather than may) pay compensation before it restricts land use. The Court in *Lucas* sought to clarify and strengthen the regulatory takings doctrine in two ways. First, no doubt trying to avoid the weak, complex, and watered-down balancing that characterized earlier cases, the Court sought a categorical ground for compensation in the form of the total takings doctrine. Land use regulation that "denies all economically beneficial or productive use of land" requires compensation without regard to the validity or character of the regulatory scheme.[6] If there was a "total takings" – a total deprivation of value – then the government could impose a restriction only if it paid just compensation. Second, the Court recognized the serious loophole created by the existing noxious use doctrine. If the definition of noxious use is broad and, more important, if it is left to the political process to define noxious use, the political process can eviscerate any regulatory takings doctrine by identifying (or inventing) some negative impact associated with the unrestricted use. *Lucas* attempts to close this loophole by narrowing the noxious use doctrine to common law nuisance and offering serious judicial examination of political process use of this rationale.

Lucas makes property rights advocates optimistic and land use authorities nervous. But, the extent and degree of judicial activity and, therefore, the strength of the legal rights in question remain to be seen. The language of the opinions in *Lucas* and the concepts used in the case lend themselves to a broad range of interpretations. Some legal scholars join

---

[6] 505 U.S. at 1015.

the dissenting and some of the concurring justices in interpreting *Lucas* narrowly. To them, *Lucas* is severely narrowed by the concept of "total takings" that they view as requiring reduction in the value of the premises to virtually zero.[7] Seldom if ever will even severely encumbered land be worth nothing. Even if total takings means that the land in question cannot be developed in any standard way, the number of land use restrictions that trigger the new doctrine will be small. Most land use restrictions – even those that severely limit development and severely reduce value – will be beyond the scope of *Lucas*.

But the language of the majority opinion and the concepts used allow for much broader definitions. In his much-discussed footnote 7, Justice Scalia, writing for the Court, provides the basis for a broad-based definition of total takings:

Regrettably, the rhetorical force of our "deprivation of all economically feasible use" rule is greater than its precision, since the rule does not make clear the "property interest" against which the loss of value is to be measured ... unsurprisingly this uncertainty regarding the composition of the denominator in our "deprivation" fraction has produced inconsistent pronouncements by the court.... The answer to this difficult question may lie in how the owner's reasonable expectations have been shaped by the state's law of property – i.e., whether and to what degree the state's law has accorded legal recognition and protection to the particular interest in land with respect to which the takings claimant alleges a diminution in (or elimination of) value....[8]

In theory, this footnote and the "denominator issue" it raises could be the source of a virtually infinite expansion in regulatory takings. In the extreme, every regulation could be considered a total takings since, by imposing restrictions, all regulations "take" negative easements, a well-recognized property interest. Those who wish to see the *Lucas* precedent expanded and strengthened look to this footnote.[9]

There is much to be said for an expansive vision of the Takings Clause, in general, and of regulatory takings, in particular. It presents a picture of takings and property that is conceptually less arbitrary. The existing narrower definition of the Takings Clause is characterized by strained distinctions and arbitrary cutoffs. Acquisitions of title, physical invasions, and zero value restrictions are far more likely to be defined as takings even though the actual loss caused a property owner by these governmental

---

[7] See, e.g., Freilich, Garvin, and Martin (1996) and Mandelker (1996).
[8] 505 U.S. at 1016–7, n.7.   [9] See, e.g., Berger (1996).

actions may be far less than the loss caused by governmental actions that do not fall into these categories. Arbitrary differences, such as accidents of location, seem to determine whether a claim of takings will be seriously considered.[10]

Conceptual consistency is not, however, the most compelling reason to expand the coverage of the regulatory takings doctrine. Such an expansion could provide a powerful antidote to malfunction in the political process. As we saw in the previous chapter, land use regulation is riven with political malfunction. Excessive regulation can be both unfair and broadly inefficient. These impacts go significantly beyond the initial landowners and affect all those in the housing chain. Although protection against governmental excesses under the Takings Clause is usually seen as a "conservative" position, this perception, like many ideological generalizations, misses much. As we have seen, the excesses of local zoning have serious adverse ramifications on the supply of housing, the equitable distribution of public education and economic and racial integration. These adverse impacts are likely to be quite regressive – disproportionately falling on lower income families. It is myopic to envision protection against these excesses solely in terms of the interests of "private property."

The real problems with the expansion of the regulatory takings doctrine are not ideological. They are systemic or institutional. There are clearly benefits to protection against the excesses of land use regulation and they can be felt across the ideological spectrum. But there are also costs and these costs and benefits can only be understood by examining the institutional choices – by examining both the problems associated with governmental regulation and the problems associated with protection against the problems of governmental regulation.

It is easiest to see these points by looking at two proposals for expansion of the takings doctrine. These proposals are clearer about scope and meaning than *Lucas* and carefully examining them will help to better understand the potential scope and meaning of *Lucas* and, more broadly, the scope and meaning of rights in general.[11]

---

[10] Compare *U.S. v. Willow River Power Co.*, 324 U.S. 499 (1945) to *U.S. v. Cress*, 24 U.S. 316 (1917) (on the river and up the creek); compare *U.S. v. Causby*, 328 U.S. 256 (1947) to *Batten v. U.S.*, 306 F.2d 580 (10th Cir. 1962) (fly over and fly by).

[11] The classic analysis of the takings balance in general remains Michelman (1967). Michelman does not, however, directly address the underlying issue of who will strike this balance – the basic issue of institutional choice addressed here.

II. THE PROPOSALS

Writing ten years apart, Richard Epstein and William Fischel advocate radically enlarging the coverage of the Takings Clause in general and of the regulatory takings doctrine in particular. Epstein offers the most sweeping of proposals.[12] At base, he argues that any government action that interferes with any aspect of the use of private property protected at common law constitutes a takings whether or not the government acquires title, reduces the value to zero, directly invades the premises, or fulfills any of the seemingly arbitrary criteria that characterize existing takings jurisprudence. This conception of private property straightforwardly reflects an economic reality. In terms of economic impact, it makes little difference whether the government acquires title to ten of fifty acres or restricts use of all fifty acres in such a way as to reduce their value by one-fifth. A loss is a loss is a loss.

Given that Epstein's definition of property includes all possible economic resources including land, materials, labor, and even good will and trade name, virtually all forms of regulation and taxation would become presumptive takings. Each regulation would be subject to careful examination by the courts to check government claims that the regulation is protecting the rights of other private property holders against the restricted party or that the regulatory program offered implicit compensating benefit to the restricted party. If these claims failed, the regulation would be invalidated. Much of the activity of national, state, and local government would be subject to serious judicial review.

It hardly seems a surprise that a libertarian like Epstein should be delighted with the prospect of government action carefully scrutinized. Legal scholars from across the ideological spectrum must be and are severely critical of the workings of the political process. Especially for legal scholars interested in property law, it seems natural to turn to the courts and the Takings Clause to solve these problems. But neither life nor law is that simple. Serious problems involving the structures of law and rights and, therefore, institutional choice undermine Epstein's proposal.

First, Epstein believes that just compensation will "control rent-seeking and political faction." Such a correction of political malfunction would be a significant gain. Unfortunately, Epstein has not sufficiently thought through the connection between just compensation and the form or forms

---

[12] Epstein (1985).

of political malfunction he addresses. In fact, the chances are significant that just compensation will aggravate rather than correct the forms of political malfunction that seem to concern Epstein most. Second, Epstein sets a task for the adjudicative process that far outstrips the resources and sorely strains the competence of the adjudicative process.

William Fischel presents a more carefully tailored approach to regulatory takings.[13] He limits his proposal not only to land use regulation, but also to land use regulation emanating primarily from local as opposed to state and federal governments. This more focused plan for expansion of the Takings Clause has the potential of avoiding the perverse effects of using just compensation on the wrong form of political malfunction as well as limiting the amount of judicial activity. Unfortunately, like Epstein, Fischel largely ignores the systemic characteristics and limits of the adjudicative process.

A closer examination of the Epstein and Fischel proposals will allow us to better understand the role of just compensation and the regulatory takings doctrine and, more generally, the role and limits of courts and, therefore, the role and limits of law and rights. Such an examination provides an opportunity to observe the dynamics of the supply and demand of law and rights in general.

III. THE DEMAND SIDE: JUST COMPENSATION AND POLITICAL MALFUNCTION

Epstein asserts that "the takings clause is designed to control rent-seeking and political faction."[14] Epstein, like others who have employed the interest group theory of politics, sees government malfunction largely in terms of minoritarian bias.[15] Epstein is correct when he asserts that the compensation mechanism can serve to correct political malfunction by forcing the political process to internalize losses. As any economist will tell you, a societal decision is less trustworthy if the decision maker does

---

[13] Fischel (1995). In addition to his proposal, Fischel's book is filled with valuable insights about land use regulation.

[14] Epstein (1985) at 281.

[15] Although Epstein is somewhat vague in his views on political malfunction, his references to political malfunction in most parts of this book seem to support this interpretation, and it is also the interpretation given his views by other readers. See Elhauge (1991).

not take into account all the important impacts – all the costs and benefits. But internalization through compensation corrects only one form of political malfunction, and it is not the form of political malfunction that Epstein identifies when he speaks of rent-seeking. Compensation corrects majoritarian bias, not minoritarian bias.

We can see the point in the following hypothetical example based on the nine-box diagram from the *Boomer* setting. Suppose that we are dealing with a nine-voter jurisdiction and that there are two regulations each of which will prohibit the concentrated minority, depicted by E, from doing something that would harm the majority.

A	B	C
D	E	F
G	H	I

Figure 2

For regulation X, the impact of the regulation on E will be –$4,000 and the impact on each member of the majority will be +$1,000. For regulation Y, the impact of the regulation on E will be –$8,000 and the impact on each member of the majority will be +$500. We are now concerned with whether a given regulation will be passed by one of three political processes – an efficient process, a majoritarian-bias process, and a minoritarian-bias process.

The first process, the perfect process from the perspective of resource allocation efficiency, weights the aggregate costs and benefits and decides in favor of the largest net benefit. Such a process would decide in favor of regulation X ($8,000 benefit, $4,000 cost) and against regulation Y ($4,000 benefit, $8,000 cost). The majoritarian-biased process would count only the *number* of voters benefitted versus the *number* of voters harmed. Such a process would pass both regulations – eight voters are benefitted and one is harmed by both. The minoritarian-biased process gives undue weight to the concentration of interests and, therefore, can be seen as rejecting both regulations because both are opposed by the concentrated minority, E. The results can be summarized in the following figure (where R stands for "regulation"):

	X	Y
Efficiency	R	No R
Majoritarian-biased	R	R
Minoritarian-biased	no R	no R

Figure 3

In such a regulatory setting, compensation corrects majoritarian bias, not minoritarian bias. Compensation is paid out of the general tax funds. If the majority controls the political process, as majoritarian bias supposes, then the compensation requirement, by making the majority pay the minority for any losses inflicted by the majority, would internalize the minority's loss to the controlling majority. One can see this point by referring to the nine-box hypothetical setting.

The concentrated minority ("E" in Figure 2) would lose $8,000 from the government action while each of the eight members of the majority would gain $500 for a total gain of $4,000. Here we have negative-sum legislation: a net social loss of $4,000. Under a simple majority model, the legislation would pass – eight votes to one. But, if compensation of E is required, the vote changes. All nine of the citizens of the jurisdiction will now be forced to bear the cost of compensation, presumably through taxation. That means an average tax bill to each of the nine citizens of approximately $889 ($8,000 divided by 9). Each member of the majority will now be faced with a net loss from the government action. Each member of the majority would have to pay $889 to receive a benefit of $500, leaving a net loss of $389. Even E would be a net loser, since E would receive a net payment of $7,111 in compensation for a loss of $8,000 leaving a net loss of $889. Now the vote would be 9 to 0 against the program.

But if concentrated minorities control the political process, the requirement of compensation will not correct the political malfunction and ensure the absence of negative-sum regulation. One can again see this outcome in the nine-box hypothetical setting. For program X, the concentrated minority E received a benefit of $4,000 from the government action and each of the members of the majority lost $1,000. Because of the overrepresentation of concentrated interests associated with minoritarian bias, the concentrated minority prevails and again we get negative-sum legislation ($4,000 benefit minus $8,000 loss).

Compensation, however, will not correct this bias. Each of the nine members of the community would be taxed $889 to cover the $8,000 needed to compensate the losers. Minoritarian bias means that the minority controls. If this taxation is to correct minoritarian bias, it must change the incentives of the concentrated minority – E in our example. E would now have his or her tax bill raised by $889 – only a fraction of the true cost of $8000 and a fraction that begins to disappear as the population of the polity increases (9 to 90 to 900 to 9000). E would still push for the negative-sum legislation.[16]

In fact, in the presence of serious minoritarian bias, the availability of compensation may itself create negative-sum, rent-seeking government action. Like other government functions, a massive compensation program would have a complex administrative apparatus and generate the distinct possibility of minoritarian bias. In a setting where, as even Epstein's analysis shows, essential concepts like the presence or absence of nuisance and the extent of in-kind compensation are difficult to define and measure, mistakes and manipulations in the compensation program can be expected. Given the existence of minoritarian bias, these mistakes and manipulations will not be random. Overcompensation will be paid to concentrated interests who will employ the various avenues of influence (bribery, replacement of officials, lobbying, or propaganda) to gain these favorable determinations.[17] Rather than decrease the attractiveness of rent seeking as Epstein believes, the prospect of compensation can increase its attractiveness by providing additional rent-seeking

---

[16] It might be argued that the payment of compensation would more dramatically bring home the costs of the project to the majority and, therefore, increase the possibility of majority reaction and remove the possibility of minoritarian bias. In the simple hypothetical, a special tax of $889 might bring the eight-person majority to their senses and cause them to realize what E is up to. However, the realities of taxation and compensation negate this possibility. First, compensation is only a small part of the total tax burden for most taxpayers in most jurisdictions. More important, figuring out what part of total taxes are associated with compensation for a given program is likely to be as difficult and, therefore, as defeating of majoritarian activity as understanding the impacts of the program itself. Second, even if we assume that taxpayers get the message, what message will they get? As members of the dormant majority faced with a piece of minoritarian-bias legislation, each member of the majority will be both payer and payee. In the simple hypothetical, the majority (A, B, C, D, F, G, H, and I) are both the losers and the payers. If they are awakened, it will be to puzzlement not outrage.

[17] For a study of eminent domain showing that higher value (higher stakes) parcelholders are likely to receive more than fair market value and lower value (lower stakes) parcelholders to receive less than fair market value, see Danzon (1976).

opportunities.[18] Given Epstein's massive compensation program, the possibility that just compensation will aggravate minoritarian bias seems significant. For someone so distrustful of government programs in general, it is surprising that Epstein is so sanguine about the performance of the huge bureaucracy his plan establishes.

From the perspective of the one-force model of politics Epstein employs, a judicial requirement of compensation at best offers no possibility of correction of the political process and even threatens to increase malfunction. From the perspective of the two-force model proposed in this book, the requirement of compensation can have corrective effects. These corrective effects, however, are limited to legislation where majoritarian bias is present. Across the vast range of settings for just compensation proposed by Epstein, however, the prevalent form of political malfunction will be minoritarian bias, not majoritarian bias.

Fischel offers a far better focused program than Epstein. He limits his proposal not only to land use regulation but also to land use regulation emanating primarily from local as opposed to state and federal governments and, therefore, more likely to be subject to majoritarian bias.[19] This more focused plan for expansion of the Takings Clause has the potential

---

[18] In a somewhat more complex version of the two-force model, just compensation can serve to aggravate minoritarian bias in another way. There may be a series of interests graded from most concentrated to least concentrated with minoritarian bias translated into a decreasing tendency to be represented in the political process. For example, suppose there are three groups in the relevant population – a very concentrated group that would profit from a given regulatory program, a somewhat less concentrated group that might be harmed by the program, and the mass of the rest of the population who would also be harmed by the regulation but in much smaller per capita amounts. Employing the two-force model from Chapter 4, one could imagine a situation in which the first two groups were active but the general majority was not. Imagine, in addition, that the program benefitted only the most concentrated group. If the legislation in question was inefficient, the most concentrated group may be unable as a matter of private action to pay off the moderately concentrated group. If, however, its power from concentration allows it to control the compensation mechanism, then the moderately concentrated group can be bought off at the expense of the general population. Once the opposition of the moderately compensated group has been removed (at the expense of the dormant majority), the inefficient governmental program, which would have been blocked by an uncompensated moderately concentrated group, will now go through. So long as the combination of the small per capita indirect effects of the program and small per capita compensation burden are not enough to wake the dormant majority – and and they may often not be enough – compensation would aggravate the situation. For an excellent treatment of these perverse effects of just compensation on minoritarian bias, see Farber (1992).

[19] Several other prominent approaches to just compensation focus dominantly on underrepresented minorities. See, e.g., Farber (1992) and Levmore (1990).

of avoiding the perverse effects of using just compensation on minoritarian bias and perhaps of limiting both the amount and the difficulty of judicial activity.[20] But correctly understanding the form and extent of political malfunction and its interaction with just compensation are not the only or even the most severe problems facing serious expansion of the Takings Clause. For those, we need to turn to the supply side.

IV. THE SUPPLY SIDE: THE COURTS
AND JUST COMPENSATION

We can begin with Epstein's grand plan. The amount and scope of judicial activity Epstein proposes violates even the simplest senses of scale. Without regard to the competence of the courts or the chance that they would make worse decisions than even a rent-seeking, liberty-usurping political process, the range and complexity of the issues that the courts must now consider would break the judicial bank several times over. Whatever the evils of government regulation or the goodness of judicial decision making, reallocating such a mass of social decisions from the political to the adjudicative process is impossible without a change in the size of the judiciary so massive that it would alter the basic character of the judiciary.

Epstein's only consideration of this issue is a one-paragraph assertion that the problem will go away because government, confronted with new

---

[20] Fischel and I differ on the reasons for focusing the Takings Clause on local governments. Fischel finds larger jurisdictions like states and the federal government more trustworthy because, by their nature, they include more of the relevant parties associated with any land use conflict and, therefore, decrease the possibility of spillover or external effects. I am less sanguine about the move to larger jurisdictions. The two-force model indicates that such a move tends to trade one form of political malfunction for another. Moving to the larger, more complex, more diverse political landscape of the larger jurisdictions may decrease the chance of majoritarian bias, but often at the expense of increasing the chance of minoritarian bias. I agree with Fischel's focus on local majoritarian bias not because it is necessarily the greater evil but because it is the evil that matches with just compensation.

As a general matter, our differences are more than academic. The choice of level of governmental decision making is one of the most important and difficult institutional choices. We saw it in Chapter 4 in the discussion of the difference between administrative agencies at the local and national levels. Fischel's comfort with higher levels of government papers over too much. In that connection, Fischel's focus on localism as the greater evil can be contrasted with the great affection for localism of another able observer of local land use, Carol Rose. Both visions suppose too much for their favorites. I discuss Rose's view in Chapter 7.

signals from the courts will become minimal and will therefore stop creating faulty legislation to be reviewed.[21] Epstein is proposing a complex
set of tests to apply to a vast and varied range of government action. To
expect that the dynamics of litigation on such a massive scale and faced
with such uncertain outcomes would produce such a smooth convergence
requires heroic assumptions. As we shall soon see, this is not a world in
which litigation will go away easily.

Fischel offers a version of the Takings Clause that is more confined and,
therefore, puts less strain on the courts. Like Epstein, however, Fischel
spends little thought on the systemic characteristics of the courts. For Epstein and Fischel, the issue is whether and to what extent it is legitimate
for courts to take such a significant role in societal decision making. To
Fischel, Epstein's proposal seems an illegitimate and ill-advised imposition of court dominated decision making. In turn, Epstein chides Fischel
for his timidity.[22]

Given the diminutive scale of the adjudicative process as well as the
limits on its competence, this debate between Fischel and Epstein over legitimacy seems largely beside the point. The real problem for both Epstein and Fischel is not whether courts should be allowed to take over this
area but whether the courts in any realistic sense could shoulder the tasks
inherent in their proposals or even a small fraction of these tasks.

Legitimacy is largely a red herring. As constitutional scholars know,
there are no clear textual guidelines on the extent of judicial review – or
even on its existence. The extent of judicial review is a product of a series
of judicial decisions about the role of the courts versus the political
process. Legitimacy does not determine these institutional choices. It is
determined by them.[23]

The size and difficulty of the task that Fischel proposes for the adjudicative process is paradoxically inherent in his arguments about political
malfunction. Fischel continuously, and I think correctly, points out that local homeowner majorities are strong and doggedly determined to exploit
their zoning advantages. He is also correct that, *if* these local majorities

---

[21] Epstein (1985), 29.

[22] See Epstein (1996).

[23] Fischel sidesteps this institutional exploration by substituting John Ely's famous
process/substance dichotomy and arguing that just compensation is just a process issue.
As is true for Ely, however, this single-institutional analysis simply hides the basic underlying questions about the ability of the courts. I discuss Ely's single institutionalism
and the inadequacy of his process/substance distinction in Komesar (1994), 198–215.

were forced to pay just compensation, they would no longer be able to obtain the benefits of restrictions without their costs and would, therefore, internalize the interest of the otherwise unrepresented minorities. In other words, *if* the local majorities would cooperatively pay the correct compensation, the problem of majoritarian bias and overregulation would disappear. Once they pay, all the impacts are internalized and the local land use decision is optimal. But past experience and the realities of the compensation process militate against so docile a majoritarian response.

Consider the example of local zoning in New Jersey. *If* the local authorities and the local majorities had conscientiously cooperated with the task of meeting regional needs ordered in *Mt. Laurel,* the problems of local zoning would have been solved in New Jersey. These local authorities, however, did just the opposite. They dragged their feet and clogged the courts, using every possible excuse and loophole and exploiting every complication.

Local homeowner majorities have the stakes and organization to participate actively in whatever decision-making processes confront them whether political or adjudicative. They will push their representatives to defend local zoning ordinances and resist any attempts by the courts to "correct" the bias that gives them their political advantage. The courts can expect that any plausible substantive defense will be pushed strongly and that any plausible issue will be litigated. It took herculean efforts by the New Jersey courts to obtain any results. Why should these local authorities now go gently into correction by compensation? They will do so only if there are no loopholes to exploit, no complications or tough issues that can be used to resist the payment of cooperation. Unfortunately, that is far from the reality.

The issues of just compensation – who should be paid and how much – are inevitably complex and difficult, involving a number of factors that vary from context to context. For example, Fischel focuses attention on the question of whether the activity restricted is "subnormal" as opposed to normal or supernormal – an inquiry analogous to the so-called nuisance exception employed both by Epstein and the Supreme Court in *Lucas.* Under Fischel's proposal, restrictions of subnormal activities do not require compensation. Fischel recognizes a number of sensible factual criteria useful in discerning normality. In doing so, however, he opens the door to more complexity and, therefore, more room for manipulation by local townships.

Existing development in otherwise undeveloped suburbs or exurbs is usually located in one specific area or quadrant of the locale. This is where the local homeowner majority dwells. Quite commonly, these first homeowners zone the rest of the jurisdiction much more restrictively. Inevitably, different location means at least putative differences in context. Greater restrictions can, therefore, always be rationalized by variations in topography, ecological impact, historical preservation, access to highways, or any number of safety, health, moral, or other considerations. Aggressive local governments defending their zoning ordinances can seize these arguably valid considerations and manipulate, exaggerate, or even fabricate their existence in justifying the "normality" of the restrictions for which the developer seeks just compensation.

Similarly and inevitably, there are also relevant variations in the timing of restrictions. A township may argue that existing high-density uses are irrelevant to a determination of the normality of restricting the density of new development because these existing uses have a long history or long duration. Grandfathering in existing uses is common in zoning settings and accepted by Fischel. The issue of timing is further complicated by the issue of technological change. Existing patterns of land use that may have seemed normal or unharmful at one time may now be seen as threatening or harmful. Consider the *Lucas* case. The regulations invalidated in *Lucas* were intended to deal with the difficult but important problem of soil and beach erosion. The value of David Lucas's land was heavily dependent on the stability and existence of the beach on the Isle of Palms. Property owners like Lucas must and do depend on government for protection against serious threats like beach erosion.

Issues of beach and soil erosion has been with us forever. But increased shoreline development increases both concern about the problem and its severity. The perceived connection between construction and beach erosion changes over time. Developments in science and technology reveal the depth and intransigence of the problem. Various techniques have been tried and discarded.[24] In such a world, activity once considered innocent can now be considered harmful. Local zoning authorities can cloak their arguments against compensation in the credibility of science and technology. The complexity inherent in these arguments makes it increasingly difficult for courts to separate true from false claims. Contrary to the impression in the *Lucas* case, common law rights

---

[24] See Zalkin (1991), 211–16; Hwang (1991), 1–4; Houck (1988), 360; Permut and Snead (1998); Amend (1991).

are not well defined and these ambiguities can be exploited by local homeowner majorities doggedly determined to preserve their power.

My point is not that these land use authorities are always or even nearly always justified in their claims that the land use restricted is subnormal or harmful and, therefore, not due compensation. My point is that they can offer this justification with some reason to believe that it may work. Land use and its interactions are complex. This complexity means that there are a variety of relevant considerations and, at the same time, a variety of ways to cloak excessive regulation. These considerations operate spatially and temporally. A range of relevant objectives or concerns – ecological, safety, commercial, health, and aesthetic – provide room for manipulation. Jurisdictions can argue about the safety of children, the impact on drainage, and the impact on historical, cultural, and aesthetic features, to name a few. At base, a determination of what is normal will often require a determination of what is reasonable – a balancing of the costs and benefits of the proposed use. In the end, courts will face the very land use decisions that caused so much difficulty in *Mt. Laurel* and so frightened the *Boomer* majority.

Unfortunately, the task facing the courts under Fischel's proposal is not limited to this determination of normality. Courts must also determine the extent of any loss associated with restrictions on normal or supernormal activity. Even where the courts determine that the regulation restricts normal or supernormal activity, they must also decide whether the regulation imposes a loss and assess the extent of that loss. Lurking here is the confounding issue of reciprocity of advantage inherent also in Epstein's proposal and the *Lucas* decision.

The success of large privately planned communities shows both the glory and difficulty of reciprocity of advantage. In an effort to maximize the value of their land for sale, private developers impose restrictions on all or most of their parcels. They do so because they believe that purchasers will find the restriction of their parcel more than justified by the protections provided by restrictions on the other parcels in the planned community. Each purchaser receives reciprocal benefits that justify the restrictions on their parcel.

What appears manifestly true for private land use arrangements provides the justification for public land use arrangements. Public land use authorities, in theory, are providing the same benefits as the private land use arrangements on a grander scale. By now, we know that public land use authorities may not always or even usually achieve these results. But that hardly means that it will be easy to determine where, when, and to what extent the individual landowner is really a net loser – where, when, and to what extent the reciprocal benefits do not justify the claim.

Lucas presents an easy case because David Lucas would be unable to use the beach protected by the series of restrictions. It is unlikely that he would gain any reciprocal benefits.[25] However, had he been allowed to build even with severe restrictions, the question would have become much more difficult. It is this interchange or interaction of restrictions that makes determining the losers and gainers from these programs so vexing. The difficulty of assessing reciprocity provides local zoning authorities with room to argue that no compensation is due. The difficulty of the assessment and the resulting frequency with which the argument will be used impose an arduous task on the courts. Given the conditions that Fischel assumes – intractable local governments and complex land use settings – the possibility of protracted litigation and challenges to both the resources and competence of the judiciary is high.

Fischel's plan has virtues simply absent from Epstein's. Fischel focuses just compensation on those instances in which it will correct rather than aggravate political malfunction. However, although his program is more focused, more sensible, and more thoughtful than Epstein's, it still leaves the courts with an immense and difficult job. The problem is not one of legitimacy and it cannot be solved by the distinction between substance and process. It will not go away so easily. The problem lies in basic questions about the functioning of the adjudicative process. The U.S. adjudicative process is tiny compared to the mass of local political processes whose determinations would have to be reviewed. Local governments generate a monumental amount of land use regulation. The issues are complex and difficult and end up requiring courts to reassess reasonableness and validity restriction by restriction and area by area. The inherent difficulties that plagued the *Mt. Laurel* court do not disappear when we change the focus from exclusionary zoning to just compensation.

Lucas avoids or at least puts off most of these problems. A narrow definition of "total takings" directly eliminates or at least limits the de-

---

[25] Even this assertion needs qualification. The value of beachfront property is heavily dependent on beach preservation and flood control. Lucas was a developer of beachfront property on the Isle of Palms. By the time of the case, Lucas had already enjoyed considerable benefits from the preservation of the beach: he had developed much of the area, and presumably would have received far less profit from those developments if buyers had been unable to rely on the fact that government regulation would protect the area from serious erosion in the future.

manding issue of implicit compensation or reciprocal benefits. In the *Lucas* case itself, the total prohibition on development made the case easier. If a beachfront property owner cannot develop, he or she cannot gain any reciprocal benefits from beach erosion control. Control of beach erosion may be crucially important to beachfront property owners, but not if they cannot use their beachfront lots at all. A narrow "total takings" doctrine provides a way for courts to eliminate the most obvious unfairness without shouldering the worst of the tasks inherent in issues like reciprocity.

All of this works out very nicely so long as *Lucas* remains narrowly confined. Such an interpretation of *Lucas,* however, would hardly make it the foundation of a significant revolution in property rights. This narrow definition of total takings – zero value or no use – provides little solace to most landowners seeking to develop their land. Governments can still prohibit most of the use so long as they do not prohibit all. Quite severe restrictions and quite serious losses would go uncompensated and unexamined by the courts.

In order to offer more than a symbolic gesture or a bluff to temporarily impede overzealous land use authorities, the courts would need to expand property rights protection against the excesses of government beyond the rare instance of a complete refusal of development. But it is precisely this expansion that will trigger all the difficulties for the courts. Cases involving complicated, interactive land use restrictions produce costly and confusing litigation. Landowners, especially developers, are often large-scale players capable of generating litigation. Each expansion of the ambit of takings can generate a great many cases and it is likely that these new cases would be increasingly more difficult to deal with substantively as they involve increasingly more complex issues of reciprocal benefits and land use balance. Thus, if *Lucas* were expanded, both the number of cases and the costs of resolving each case would increase.

As a matter of description, *Lucas* appears to be narrow and weak. It looks as though the construct of "total takings" is being used to restrict the number of land use cases the courts see and that the threat to expand the total takings construct implied in Justice Scalia's footnote 7 is largely a bluff.[26] Even if the Supreme Court really intends such an expansion, the

---

[26] Most courts have declined Justice Scalia's invitation to expand the doctrine of regulatory takings to situations where not all viable economic use of the particular parcel of land is lost. See, e.g., the following state cases: *Reahard v. Lee County,* 68 F.2d 1131, 1134 n.5, 1136 (11th Cir. 1992); *District Intown Properties Ltd. Partnership v. District of Columbia,* 198

resulting deluge of difficult cases will induce a rapid retreat. If the federal courts expand the total takings construct to bring in partial takings, as several commentators hope, they will buy a task easily as daunting as that shouldered by the New Jersey court in *Mt. Laurel* and on a nationwide basis.

On a normative basis, this weak version of *Lucas* may be the best solution – although best is not very good. Society would benefit greatly if a device existed that would eliminate excessive land use regulation. These benefits can only grow as population pressures and complicated land use interactions increase both the likelihood and the adverse effects of these excesses. These benefits would resonate with concerns found everywhere on the political spectrum. But there is a familiar problem. The same increases in numbers and complexity that produce these excesses make it increasingly difficult to establish such a device. Both common law actions like nuisance and market transactions become less attractive as numbers and complexity increase. Both are likely to be impotent to deal with the pervasive land use interactions involved in phenomena like beach erosion.

Even if the regulatory process is highly flawed (and it is), the severe problems in the market and the adjudicative process may mean that the corrupt, excessive, and repressive regulatory process is the best of bad alternatives. In a quintessential example of the ironies of comparative institutional analysis, it may even be the best friend the Lucases of the world have. We are not finished, however, with the Supreme Court's attempts to control the appetites of land use regulators or with the examination of potential solutions in general.

V. THE STRANGE WORLD OF *NOLLAN* AND *DOLAN*

This chapter has focused on only one of the Supreme Court's recent just compensation cases. Even if I am correct that *Lucas* is likely to be nar-

---

F.3d 874 (D.C. Cir. 1999); *Del Oro Hills v. City of Oceanside,* 37 Cal.Rptr.2d 677, 690–91 & n.14 (Cal. App. 4 Dist. 1995); *Hansen Brothers Enterprises, Inc. v. Board of Supervisors of Nevada County,* 907 P.2d 1324, 1335 (Cal. 1996); *State Department of Health v. The Mill,* 887 P.2d 993, 998–1002 (Colo. 1994); *Hunziker v. State,* 519 N.W.2d 367, 370 (Iowa 1994). See also Meltz, et al. (1999), 132. Although there have been at least two lower federal courts that have played with the notion of a constraint on less than all use of the parcel as a total takings, *Florida Rock Industries, Inc., v. United States,* 18 F.3d 1560 (Fed. Cir. 1994) and *Loveladies Harbor, Inc. v. United States,* 28 F.3d 1171, 1181–2 (Fed. Cir. 1994), even these cases involve discernible and relatively easily evaluated property rights. See Meltz at 149.

rowly read, two other cases could provide the basis for a powerful judicially based strategy for property protection against the government. These cases deserve attention, not least of all because in the end they reveal another significant paradox about property protection and property rights.

In *Nollan* and *Dolan,* the issue is exaction. In both cases, the ability to develop in the manner desired required special permission from the government. In each case, the land use authority conditioned the granting of permission to develop on the deeding of an interest in land to the government. In *Nollan,* the landowners sought to replace a small outmoded cabin along California's Pacific coast with a larger home. The California Coastal Commission was willing to permit development if the landowners granted an affirmative easement (right of way) across their beachfront to the public. In *Dolan,* the landowner owned and operated a plumbing and electrical supply store in the central business district of the city of Tigard, a suburb of Portland, Oregon. She sought to expand her business by increasing the size of her store and her parking lot. The land use authority granted permission so long as the owner was willing to deed to the city the fee simple absolute interest in two relatively small areas of the parcel – a narrow band to be used as a bike path and a triangular area for flood and drainage purposes. In both cases, the landowners refused to provide the conveyances in question and sought protection from the courts. In both cases, the landowners succeeded.

On one level, *Nollan* and *Dolan* are simpler cases than *Lucas.* They involve the most traditional manifestation of taking – government acquisition of title. The California Coastal Commission and the City of Tigard wanted express grants of property interests from the landowners. Acquiring title, unlike restricting use, is the epitome of governmental taking of property. Indeed, for the majority of the Justices, this granting of title made the takings argument automatically stronger.

In each case, however, the government had a cogent response backed by precedent. It was the government's position that the exaction of the easement was itself a form of just compensation running from the landowner to the government. The compensation was due because of the burdens imposed on the public by the proposed new land use. Exactions in one form or another are quite common. Much of the law involving governmental approval of subdivisions – and, therefore, much modern land use law – involves landowners, usually large-scale developers, giving various land interests to the government. Most common is the granting of land within the subdivision for public streets and sewers. Such an exchange is a simple quid pro quo. The developer provides land for roads and sewers that will primarily serve the residents of the development.

The substantive issue in both cases is whether and to what extent the exaction in question is an appropriate response to the alleged negative impacts of the development in question. As always, however, the real constitutional question in both cases is *who decides* whether impact and exaction are in balance. *Nollan* and *Dolan* shift more of this responsibility away from the political process to the federal courts. The political process no longer unilaterally decides these issues. In *Nollan,* the Court asked the government to justify the connection between the loss to the general public associated with the Nollans' new construction and the easement along the beach requested by the government. The courts would evaluate rather than rubber-stamp the government's justification.

California claimed that development by the Nollans negatively impacted the public by blocking public view of the ocean and the beach. The Court conceded this impact, but found the government's exaction failed to match the government's concerns. How, asked the Court, is the blocking of the public's view from the road corrected by a right of way along the beach? Here was an issue of kind not degree. In the view of the majority, the State of California had not made out even the simple case that a right of way was an appropriate response to the adverse impacts of the developments.

After *Nollan,* however, important issues remained unanswered. First, was this new judicial scrutiny limited to issues of kind rather than degree? In other words, would the federal courts examine not just the general match but also the extent to which the exaction and the degree of negative impact matched? Second, how closely would the courts scrutinize this match?

Dolan allowed the court to respond to these issues. In particular, the exaction for the bicycle path in *Dolan* raised issues of both the degree of the exaction and the extent of judicial scrutiny. Unlike the beachfront right-of-way in *Nollan,* the Court had little doubt that, as a matter of kind, a bike path and its expansion was a valid response to the traffic increases associated with the expansion of Ms. Dolan's business. But, said the Court, the City of Tigard had failed to make out a strong enough case that the amount of land sought by the City for the bicycle path was commensurate with the amount of traffic increase generated by the new development. The government had to show more than a general match between the kind of negative impact and the kind of exaction.

The *Dolan* Court also responded to the issue of the extent of judicial review. The Court reviewed the varied responses of state supreme courts to exaction and adopted a Goldilocks approach. The Court noted that some state courts require a "very exacting correspondence described as the 'specific and uniquely attributable' test,"[27] but concluded that this test was too demanding. Some state courts required only "very generalized statements as to the necessary connection between the required dedication and the proposed development," but the Court felt this was too lax. Luckily, there are state courts that take "an intermediate position requiring the municipality to show a 'reasonable relationship' between the required dedication and the impact of the proposed development"[28] and that test was just right. The Court labeled the intermediate test the "rough proportionality" test.

A shift in institutional choice and, therefore, in law and rights occurred in *Nollan* and *Dolan*. Before these cases, the connection between exaction and impact was an issue left to the political process.[29] There were few rights against the government. Now the federal courts would take a more active role and, thereby, create more rights against the government. Put in traditional constitutional jargon, the Court was increasing the level and extent of judicial scrutiny. Where in the past government claims about the connection between exactions and impact would receive little or no serious judicial examination, these claims are now subject to a closer look.

Like *Lucas, Nollan* and *Dolan* can be interpreted very broadly. In the extreme, the base of cases for review can be expanded to include all land use restrictions by viewing these restrictions as exactions of negative easements. The degree of scrutiny can also be raised by forcing governments to show that the exaction was an exact quid pro quo – that the value of the exaction precisely equals the loss imposed by the development.

As with a tough version of *Lucas*, a tough exaction standard is attractive given the likelihood of political malfunction. If local homeowner majorities control zoning decisions, the zoning authorities have the incentive to exact not just the costs the development imposes on the community, but the full benefit of the development. They have the incentive to squeeze the developers for every concession they can obtain. Excessive

---

[27] 512 U.S. at 389.
[28] Id. at 390.
[29] At the very least, the *federal* courts had avoided this issue. As *Dolan* indicates, however, a few state courts have seriously reviewed exactions.

exactions would be unfair and would impose unwarranted costs on residential development with the adverse societal effects discussed in connection with *Petaluma* and *Mt. Laurel*.

As with *Lucas,* however, the scope of *Nollan* and *Dolan* cannot be decided by looking at only the demand side. The issue is not just the degree and kind of political malfunctions, but also the ability of the replacement decision maker – the adjudicative process. An expansive view of *Nollan* and *Dolan* underscores the problems in *Lucas* and adds another. A wholesale expansion of *Nollan/Dolan* would again require judicial examination of an uncountable number of complex land use contexts and conflicts. The negative easements that these restrictions exact are not commonly sold or traded separately. The courts would have to determine the value of these property rights without even the aid of comparable market sales. The task of comparing these values to the alleged negative impacts of development is like determining reciprocity under *Lucas.* Taken seriously, it would again exceed even the task undertaken by the New Jersey court in *Mt. Laurel.*[30]

There is, however, a short cut – a sweeping solution – that would save the courts from such case-by-case examinations. Recognizing that the exaction process has been severely abused and that they have neither the competence nor the capacity to examine each instance, the courts could simply prohibit exactions altogether, forcing governments to pay for these interests in land. Here we would have an example of strong property rights where vigorous judicial activism is accompanied by a sweeping solution that minimizes judicial activity. Such a sweeping solution would, of course, prohibit valid and fair uses of exactions along with the abuses. But there are inevitably trade-offs in the choice between imperfect decision makers.

Unfortunately, however, outright prohibition creates a more severe problem. Paradoxically, even if all exactions are unfair, developers sub-

[30] This task could be narrowed by making *Nollan* and *Dolan* applicable only to exactions where the passage of title is required. This subset is still quite large. Every subdivision approval involves a significant number of exactions for roads and sewers. These traditional exactions have been expanded to include parks and even schools. If the *Nollan* and *Dolan* level of judicial scrutiny is significant, it would again involve courts in case-by-case, exaction-by-exaction examination of the match between the alleged impact of the development and the level or amount of the exaction. In addition, it would involve examination of past practices to see the extent to which similar exactions were made for earlier developments and, if they were not, examining the rationales for the change or shift in policy. The task would still be immense and difficult.

ject to these exactions are likely to be worse off – not better off – if courts invalidated all exactions. If courts do not also seriously review land use regulations and prohibitions (the *Lucas* issue), land use jurisdictions suffering from majoritarian bias may well respond to the ban on exactions by simply prohibiting the use.[31] This shift would be worse for the developers and those in need of housing than is the regime of exactions. The bargaining process associated with exactions ameliorates somewhat the excesses of restrictions and prohibitions.

As a general matter, greater scrutiny of exactions relative to prohibitions and restrictions can have perverse effects on the protection of landowners, the fairness of the distribution and the efficient use of resources. This is the *Nollan/Dolan* paradox. It is, therefore, disturbing that the lower federal courts may be expanding judicial scrutiny via *Nollan* and *Dolan* rather than *Lucas*.[32] The perverse effects of expanding judicial scrutiny of exactions as opposed to regulation fall upon the very property owners the federal courts are seeking to protect.

This analysis again shows that, in a world of high numbers and complexity, the interaction between institutions can create unexpected and even perverse results. Strong rights can harm those whom they are meant to help. Defining the role of law and rights demands respect for the institutions of law and rights. Understanding whether and to what extent any legal response will further any societal goal tests our ability to understand the functioning of these underlying institutional decision makers, their interactions, and the choice among them.

VI. CONCLUSION

In this chapter, I have examined the cases that stand at the core of the recent revolution in U.S. property rights. From what we have seen, it is bound to be a limited revolution. These limits are not the product of lack of will or abstract notions of legitimacy. Nor are they the product of the absence of a strong case against the political process or the lack of a conceptual basis. As Epstein has shown us, the definition of the taking of property could easily support a regime of rights that provides protection against virtually every act of government. The limits of this legal revolution can be found in the structure of our legal institutions – in particular,

---

[31] Fischel presents evidence of this effect. Fischel (1995), 345–7.
[32] See Callies (1996), 3, 5, 12–25; cf. Hetzel and Gough (1996).

the adjudicative process. Concepts like "takings" and "property" are not defined in the abstract. They are defined in context and that context is dominated by institutional choice.

There are valuable lessons here for the meaning and impacts of law and rights in general. Any court-based response to political malfunction must consider the form as well as the extent of the political malfunction in question. Just compensation may serve to correct majoritarian bias but it is largely useless against and may even aggravate minoritarian bias. This issue is general. As I have shown elsewhere, many traditional constitutional responses such as protection of speech and press and procedural due process decrease minoritarian bias but not majoritarian bias. They may even aggravate it.[33] Because constitutionalism and the Rule of Law often rely on these sorts of protections, their validity depends on the correct identification of political malfunction.

Similarly, the costs and strains on the courts created by the vociferous political majorities that caused so much problem for Fischel's proposed use of regulatory takings and the *Mt Laurel* response to exclusionary zoning will haunt any judicial response to serious political malfunction especially in the context of high numbers and complexity. The most serious forms of political malfunction create the greatest need for judicial intervention. But they also provide the most difficulty for judicial intervention. The combination of an active interest group on one side with complicated and important issues often means that courts will have to struggle with complex and extensive litigation. This disturbing tendency is likely to be present across all rights and all nations. Any realistic attempt to import constitutionalism or the Rule of Law must confront these issues.

There is much wrong in the politics of land use and these evils cover the full ideological spectrum. Law and rights – and, hence, the courts – have a place in dealing with these excesses. But it is a role that cannot be defined by rhetoric, ideology, or even sophisticated single institutional analysis. Defining this role is the central task of the legal community, and it requires comparative institutional analysis. It is not an easy task. But, at least as an example of the analysis I propose, I will now try my hand at it.

---

[33] See Komesar (1994), 217–28.

6

High Stakes Players and Hidden Markets

When I was in graduate school, the students in another department told an apocryphal story at the expense of a not-much-beloved professor. When just a small boy, the professor-to-be was called to his mother's side. "How far is it from Baltimore to New York?" asked the mother. "I don't know," said the son. The mother turned to her son, eyed him sternly, and said, "Never say that again." And he never did.

Despite the obvious criticism leveled by the story, this mother's message has been taken to heart by many legal commentators. Most law review articles or books on law include strong, sweeping solutions to problems in law and public policy. These solutions are accompanied by confident rhetoric, making them seem obvious and attractive. Land use and property rights are often treated in this fashion.

I share the desire for answers. These land use issues have far-reaching social ramifications. A strong, sweeping solution would be welcome. For reasons now made clear, however, any real solution is unlikely to be either obvious or overwhelmingly attractive. As we have seen, all real world solutions involve important institutional choices. Because institutions tend to move together, these institutional choices are often close and, in that sense, difficult. As we have also seen, as numbers and complexity increase, all the institutional alternatives tend to deteriorate. Thus, at high numbers and complexity, institutional choices are not only close and difficult but quite likely unattractive.

But comparative institutional analysis points us in the direction of real answers. It provides an analytical framework that exposes the essential issues and the essential factors necessary to address societal issues. Analysts of land use issues and property rights – whether scholars, advocates, or judges – know they must focus on the relative abilities of the relevant institutions, that this institutional ability is a function of the pattern of participation in the institution, and that participation is a function of variables like per capita stakes, numbers, and complexity. In this chapter, I will explore the lessons this framework suggests for the treatment of local zoning and, by implication, the lessons it suggests for the analysis of legal issues in general.

I. FOCUSING ON MAJORITARIAN BIAS AND ENDING THE VILLAIN HUNT

The analysis in the last two chapters suggests that it is majoritarian and not minoritarian bias that characterizes local zoning decisions. By definition, the problems of both majoritarian and minoritarian bias stem from a "skewed distribution" in which a high-stakes minority faces off against a lower stakes majority. The central issue determining which bias prevails is whether the majority will be active – the extent to which they will participate. On the benefit side of political participation, the issue is how low the stakes of the majority are. The higher the per capita stakes of the majority, the more likely it is that the majority will be active rather than dormant. On the cost side of the political participation, the issue is complexity. The less complex the social issue and the less complex the political process, the more likely it is that the majority will be active rather than dormant.

Although there will be some variation, these factors indicate that the political malfunction most prevalent for *local* zoning is majoritarian bias. Homeowners have significant per capita stakes. A family's most valued asset is normally its home and, therefore, families are sensitive to government actions that affect their homes. Small local governments have relatively simple agenda that allow easier monitoring by local majorities. It is not difficult for homeowners to follow what their representatives are doing and to sanction unwanted actions at the ballot box.

If majoritarian bias is prevalent, then judicial intervention on behalf of local majorities against developers is perverse. In effect, the courts are aggravating the existing bias by providing an overrepresented group with a second bite at the apple. Cases like *Fasano* should be overruled and antideveloper courts like those in California should back off.

There is a considerable literature that views the primary problem with zoning as the overrepresentation of developers.[1] As in *Fasano,* the focus

---

[1] See, e.g., Anderson (1962); Bryden (1967); Dukeminer and Stapleton (1962); Reps (1955).

is primarily on small changes in the zoning laws such as variances or special permits. Although this fear of minoritarian bias seems justified if one focuses solely on these small changes, in the larger context of the locale's zoning as a whole, these changes should be seen as corrections of a larger majoritarian bias operating in the other direction. In other words, given the prevalence of majoritarian bias and overregulation, the deregulating changes associated with small-scale rezoning or the granting of variances are ameliorative and should not be made more difficult by additional barriers of judicial review imposed in cases like *Fasano*. There will be errors and even corrupt results, but, in the absence of systemic political malfunction, judicial intervention is likely to cause more problems than it will alleviate.

I cannot pretend precision for the two-force model. Given our present state of knowledge, it can identify tendencies and likely characterizations, but not exactly which jurisdictions are prone to majoritarian rather than minoritarian bias. In particular, it cannot define the point at which a jurisdiction becomes large enough to shift the likelihood from majoritarian bias to minoritarian bias. In the land use context, the difficult call will be for larger local jurisdictions, in particular, developed cities. But, at least for the exurban local zoning we see in *Fasano, Petaluma,* and *Mt. Laurel,* the political malfunction most to fear is majoritarian bias.[2]

Accepting this analysis also requires the difficult step of separating motive and systemic effect. Many developers, for all their rhetoric about low- and moderate-income housing, are interested in making a buck and many may even be insensitive to the damage they may do to the environment or to community serenity. That these developers may serve important interests in supplying housing is a product not of their intent, but of the totality of their activities within the larger housing market. Similarly, most local homeowners, for all their rhetoric about the environment, may be primarily interested in protecting the value of their property and even in excluding minority races and low- and moderate-income people. Yet their actions may still preserve open space and reduce the burden on ecologically sensitive resources.

There are villains lurking everywhere (with some saints among them). But the issue is not the existence of villains (or of saints). The issue is whether one side or the other is overrepresented in the local zoning process. It is the operation of large complex institutions like the market

---

[2] See also the sources cited in note 28 of Chapter 4.

and the political process, not the motives of individual actors, which makes the difference.[3]

II. DEALING WITH MAJORITARIAN BIAS

Assuming that we are likely dealing with majoritarian bias rids us of some perverse strategies. But it does not tell us what to do in response to the problems created by majoritarian bias. As we have seen, there are several potential responses. Reflecting the *Boomer* spectrum, they fall into three basic categories. First, the courts could establish strong, simple property rights and allocate the balancing of uses to the market by a sweeping invalidation of all local zoning.[4] This would be considered the ultimate in judicial activism, but it would involve limited judicial activity. The basic substantive decisions, such as the balancing of uses, would be made by the market. It would be analogous to the strong property rights associated with trespass or the strong constitutional rights associated with old-fashioned strict (always fatal) scrutiny in equal protection.

Second, the courts could assume the responsibility for balancing uses by aggressively overseeing the local zoning process. They could do so directly in a *Mt. Laurel* approach or indirectly by establishing "prices" for the political process under the Takings Clause as Fischel suggests. This would involve less judicial activism, but it would require more judicial activity. It is analogous to the judicial balancing found in private law nuisance discussed in Chapter 2 and in most forms of serious constitutional judicial review.

Third, the courts could allocate all responsibility to the political process by refusing judicial review of local zoning. Here both judicial activity and judicial activism would be minimized. This approach would be analogous to the decision of the *Boomer* majority to leave questions about pollution in the Hudson River Valley to the political process or, on the constitutional level, to the minimal (zero) scrutiny accorded most political process activity.

We are in the world of high numbers and complexity. All these strategies are far from ideal. We are left to choose the best of the bads. Indeed, as we shall see in the next chapter, these are the conditions that produce

---

[3] I discuss the limited relevance of motives in the functioning of institutions in general and the political process in particular in Komesar (1994), 58–65.

[4] See Siegen (1972), Kunstler (1996) and the District Court decision in *Petaluma* discussed in Chapter 4.

cycling between alternative approaches. That is what we have seen and will continue to see in the local zoning context. My own thinking on the subject has changed and, I suspect, will change again.[5] But, for a number of reasons, I would now choose the third alternative – a significant reduction in both judicial activism and judicial activity. I believe this is the best available way of achieving resource allocation efficiency, protection of property, and protection of the interests of low- and moderate-income families.

In a rough sense, this approach is closest to the status quo. The federal courts and most state courts already give most local zoning decisions virtually no scrutiny. Even federal takings jurisprudence is far more limited than its proponents hope. But adoption of this approach would require eliminating or at least severely reducing the judicial review of exactions set out in federal cases like *Nollan* and *Dolan* and in state cases that employ more than minimal scrutiny. It is in the unfettered negotiations over these exactions or, more broadly, in the market for exactions that the advantages of this approach lie.

As we saw in the discussion of the *Nollan/Dolan* paradox in the last chapter, local jurisdictions have an incentive to exact as much as they can. They will seek exactions that exceed the negative impact done by the particular development. As we also saw, if courts try to control this greed by carefully examining these exactions, it may make matters worse by inadvertently pushing zoning authorities to substitute less judicially scrutinized prohibitions and regulations for exactions. More important, if left alone, competition among local zoning jurisdictions for these exactions should control both excessive exaction and excessive regulation. There are many local land use authorities. Each would like to capture the gains of exactions that exceed the true cost imposed upon the jurisdiction by development. These are the conditions for competition; competition in turn will drive the exaction price toward true cost.[6] That is the tendency of competition in markets in general. This market for exactions – for permission to develop – provides a viable alternative to court supervision.

---

[5] See Komesar (1978) (favoring judicial intervention).

[6] For a powerful presentation of the evidence of competition in the exaction market, see Been (1991), 511–28. Been cites and summarizes a number of studies that show active competition among communities for both businesses and residents and adjustment of exaction fees in reaction to this competition. Been also points to several studies that show that "exactions allow growth that might otherwise be stalled by growth control measures." Id. at 483.

This solution has a number of advantages. Perhaps, most important, it confronts two institutional realities: the force of homeowner majorities as participants in the political process and as aggressive litigants in the courts and the great complexity of land use decisions. It blunts the force of homeowner majorities by conceding to them in both the political process and the courts. As the New Jersey experience shows, it is very difficult to stand against this strong and unremitting force in either context. But the market for exactions will prove a less manageable institution for these homeowner majorities. Here the strengths of these local majorities can be turned against them. They are high-stakes players and this makes them aware and protective of their self-interest. That will make them active players in the exaction market and, therefore, active competitors. In the land use setting, they are confronted with high-stakes players in the form of developers who are also aware and protective of their self-interest. We have a market made up of buyers and sellers who are both numerous and active.

At first blush, the deregulation solution – the first alternative discussed earlier – looks like the mirror image of this market for exactions. Under deregulation, the market is for restrictions; the developers have the right to develop without restriction and the municipalities must purchase the right to restrict. Given the extensive misuse of the zoning process, eliminating zoning completely is not a preposterous alternative. There are, however, at least two major problems. First, this "market" solution paradoxically turns out to be less dependent on the competitive mechanism than the more hidden market for exactions. The problem here is the availability of a nonmarket pricing device: eminent domain. Eminent domain provides a nonmarket mechanism for the municipalities to acquire restrictions if zoning is denied them. Here prices would not be set in the market but by adjudication. This would resurrect many of the problems associated with the Fischel and Epstein solutions and judicial pricing explored in the last chapter. Paradoxically, a stronger market is produced by initially allocating rights to the government.

Second, the deregulation solution would also run afoul of the power of homeowner majorities in the political process. As the New Jersey experience shows, the political backlash, especially to such sweeping deregulation, would be difficult for courts to resist. Both the reality and the illusion of environmental problems would haunt any sweeping judicial deregulation. It would be difficult to police the border between the local zoning invalidated by this plan and valid regulation of the environment.

As we saw in Chapter 2, there are strong arguments for some form of government intervention in contexts like the Hudson River Valley. These legitimate contexts will often be difficult to differentiate from feigned or exaggerated environmental claims.

This analysis, and especially the contrast with the deregulation solutions, suggests a familiar irony associated with protecting private property. Under quite plausible assumptions about institutional choice, private property owners are better protected with *reduced* rather than *increased* property rights. The result may be the most efficient and most equitable for society as a whole and may produce the largest supply of housing. Protection from governmental excesses can be provided by competition among the local governments rather than by rights or courts.

There are, of course, problems with this strategy. Like all real-world markets, the market for exactions will be imperfect. This competitive solution to the exactions problem will leave some landowners and developers unprotected, because they lack mobility or are in a monopolistic jurisdiction.[7] Relying on this market also will not completely eliminate all need for judicial oversight. Courts will have to remain active in order to defeat attempts by the municipalities to collude in pricing development rights. They will have to carefully review any regional or statewide zoning plan that constrained local governments from allowing additional development via exactions and strike down any attempt to control the exaction process at any but the local level. This reverses the preference of the *Mt. Laurel* judges and Fischel for regional zoning over local zoning.

This solution also offers little direct help for integration of the suburbs – a dominant theme in *Mt. Laurel* and, I believe, an important goal. Although the approach I suggest is a less expensive and intrusive judicial remedy than *Mt. Laurel,* I would think twice about giving up the *Mt. Laurel* solution if that solution showed any real promise of producing racial and income integration. Sadly, even the most optimistic perceptions of *Mt. Laurel* raise doubts about this possibility:

Putting an end to the exclusion of racial minorities from suburbia through the revision of local exclusionary regulatory power is the implicit theme of Mt. Laurel

---

[7] Been traces the standard list of market imperfections through the exactions context, id. at 529–33. She notes that developers are not totally mobile and that complex regulations mean that information on alternatives will be expensive and, therefore, imperfect. But these imperfections are likely to be present to at least the same degree in most real world markets. These imperfections are most likely to be overcome in markets, like the exaction market, where there are large numbers of high-stakes players on both sides.

I and II. Yet by and large the homes built so far have not gone to the inter-city poor; with their weak credit ratings and meager incomes, they can rarely qualify as purchasers or even as tenants. Instead, many of the new homes built to satisfy long-debated fair share obligations, bargain priced at between $40,000 to $70,000, are snapped up by people who qualify as low-and moderate-income buyers only because they happened to be at a low point in their lifetime earning potential – professional families just starting out ("junior yuppies"), divorced persons, graduate students, and the retired.[8]

My preference for the exactions market stems from the confluence of several systemic factors. First, the existence on both sides of high-stakes players – developers and municipalities representing local homeowner majorities – makes a market alternative credible. Both sides will actively participate and, because there are large numbers of both developers and municipalities, competitive forces have a real chance to operate. There may be evil lurking in the desires of the various actors, but at least these actors will have to pay for what they get. In particular, local homeowner majorities desirous of segregation will have to forego significant exactions payments to achieve these unattractive desires. In turn, given the availability of a system that will operate based on prices set by competitive forces, it seems imprudent to settle for solutions dependent on prices set by adjudication, such as the Fischel and Siegen solutions. Second, the aggressive and unremitting participation of local homeowner majorities severely burdens the realistic possibility of either a political or judicial solution to majoritarian bias in local zoning. Even in *Mt. Laurel,* the uniquely strong, creative, and courageous judicial remedy lasted only three years from *Mt. Laurel* II in 1983 to *Mt. Laurel* III in 1986. *Mt. Laurel* III, where the New Jersey Supreme Court surrendered to the legislative alternative despite its obvious limitations, showed that even a determined court can be worn down by the strain of resisting the homeowner forces. Third, even at its most successful, the judicial remedy in *Mt. Laurel* did not produce any real racial or income integration. Fourth, we are dealing with a world of high numbers and complexity in which simple, easy substantive solutions are unavailable. There are many interactions between land uses and many values of varying attractiveness on all sides. This market solution is a flexible device capable of recognizing and weighing (via pricing) these impacts.

These factors operate together. The first condition – numerous, high-stakes market participants on both sides of the issue – is particularly im-

---

[8] Haar (1996), 114–15.

portant. If this condition was not present, a *Mt. Laurel* or even a Fischel solution would seem the preferable alternative. These judicially based solutions would suffer from severe imperfections and yield results far from the ideal, but that is the character of all the realistic alternatives at high numbers and complexity.

The solution I suggest will satisfy few. To some, it is an anathema because it relies so heavily on the distrusted market mechanism. To others, it is an anathema because it allocates power to the political process and, as such, provides the weakest of property rights. The world of institutional choice under high numbers and complexity – the real world – yields incomplete and paradoxical results. Simplistic associations of good and evil with particular institutions and ideologies as well as demands for perfection no longer fit.

III. CONCLUSION

I must admit that I am less concerned with specific solutions than with the analytical approach employed to understand land use, property rights, and, more broadly, law and rights in general. I have offered an approach to analyzing U.S. land use issues that I believe clarifies these issues by showing the compelling role of systemic factors in understanding land use and property rights. The programmatic picture is complex, but the analysis is simple. It yields a vision of the essential issues, the essential factors, and the way in which these factors relate to the issues. Any advocate or judge dealing with land use issues and property rights now knows that they must focus on the relative abilities of the relevant institutions. For the public land use issues discussed in this part of the book, that means focusing on both the type and severity of political malfunction and the ability of courts to respond to these malfunctions. Is it more or less likely that the political decision maker is subject to majoritarian versus minoritarian bias? Although that is not an easy determination, the analysis I have presented provides a list of factors that determines the likelihood of one or the other bias, sets out the various responses to each of these biases and shows the adverse consequences of mismatching bias and response. The analysis also identifies those factors that cause variation in the ability of the judiciary to respond to the various political malfunctions.

I have tried my hand at solving the problems of U.S. land use law to show these factors in action. The results show the power of systemic factors and the inability to make simple associations between solutions and goals and ideologies. In the U.S. land use context, property interests may well be best protected by the weakest property rights and the strongest market may be one in which the competition is among governments. These results are highly sensitive to variation in the systemic factors that produced them. Other contexts will justify different outcomes – different allocations of decision making, different roles for courts, and, therefore, different patterns of law and rights. Many may differ with my solution. But to do so they must seriously address systemic factors and issues of institutional choice. Ideology, goals, and single institutionalism will not do.

What may be said about U.S. property law and constitutional judicial review of zoning and takings may be said with even greater force about more global uses of the courts to control the power of rulers and the excesses of government. When we look globally, we can see the same ingredients – the two forces of political malfunction and the severe strains on the competence and capacity of the courts – perhaps magnified by the problems of controlling the monopoly of force held by the government and retaining some semblance of judicial independence. Within the folds of comparative institutional analysis are moments for a strong judicial role, but finding and understanding these moments as well as dealing with less amenable possibilities requires us to accept and understand these powerful systemic forces. We can now explore these forces in the broader contexts of general theories of property rights and of law and rights in general.

PART III

LAW'S LAWS

CLAIMS/LAWS

7

Theories of Property –
From Coase to Communitarianism

I have drawn many lessons from U.S. property law: that understanding the demand for law and rights requires understanding institutions like the political process, communities, and the market; that political malfunction comes in at least two principal and conflicting forms and understanding them requires an appreciation for the dynamics of the two-force model; that understanding the supply side requires an appreciation for the dynamics of litigation and the limited scale of the adjudicative process as well as the competence of judges and juries and that understanding institutional behavior in general requires understanding the determinants of participation and the implications of increasing numbers and complexity. We can now apply these lessons to larger contexts. In this chapter, I examine general theories of property and property rights beginning with the economic theory of property rights and then considering several versions of the often counterposed communitarian view. In the next chapter, I address the Rule of Law and the role of law and rights in general.

There has been a recent outpouring of creative work on the role of property rights and about the choice between broad systems of property – primarily between private (individual) property and public (communal) property. This choice is often associated with broad themes and allegiances – right versus left; liberal versus communitarian; efficiency versus equality. But stalking this grand debate about various theories of property are basic questions about the institutions of property – those mechanisms that protect or oversee any of these systems of property. These are the institutions of law that we discussed in Parts I and II. When their role is examined here, the various theories of property and ideological allegiances take on different meaning. Simple definitions and associations break down and more basic questions and issues surface.

I explore these implications by examining a subset of the grand debate about property. I begin with the economic theory of property rights proposed by Harold Demsetz and Robert Ellickson. These authors have evolved a powerful resource allocation efficiency justification of private property rights. I will then turn to a critique of this theory by Carol Rose. Rose combines a concern for resource allocation efficiency with an affection for common property and a communitarian perspective. I will use this high-quality debate to once again show the importance of institutional choice and the influence of changes in numbers and complexity on institutional behavior, choice, and comparison. As these authors debate the merits of private property, they lose track of essential choices among the institutions of property. These neglected choices haunt the choice between common and private property and raise basic questions about the definition of private and common property.

Although the exchange between Rose and the economic theorists of property focuses primarily on the goal of resource allocation efficiency, the insights about institutional behavior, choice, and comparison are as applicable to other goals. I will show this applicability by examining the nonefficiency theories of property of William Simon and Margaret Radin. As a general matter, there is no fixed association between any goal or definition of the good and any institutional form. Especially at high numbers and complexity, we get unexpected results: The achievement of goals like resource allocation efficiency or liberty must depend heavily on the political process and the achievement of goals like equality and personhood must depend heavily on the market. Such a world tests existing definitions of property and existing worldviews and ideologies.

I. THE EVOLUTION AND FUNCTION OF PROPERTY: THE ECONOMIC THEORY OF PROPERTY RIGHTS

Imagine a small community (twenty-five families) that possesses a 2,500-acre parcel of land. The families meet and discuss their future. The community needs to know how to manage its resources so as to secure the highest yield. They do not want resources dissipated – all the game hunted out, all the trees cut down, or all the pasture devoured. They want a system of self-sustaining, renewable resources. They want a sensible balance between present and future yields. The basic issue is how they will organize the ownership and use of the land. Should they hold the land in one piece and allow everyone access to and use of all 2,500 acres or should they divide the land into twenty-five parcels of one hundred acres each and allocate one parcel to each of the twenty-five families?

According to work first done by Harold Demsetz[1] and expanded by Robert Ellickson,[2] this small group would and should decide to divide the land into parcels and create a system of private or individual property. Both Demsetz and Ellickson believe that choosing a private property system (parceling out) will, in general, produce the most productive use of the community's resources. In their view, private property best internalizes costs and benefits and, thereby, best stops the excessive use (grabbing) and severe underinvestment (shirking) that characterizes the "tragedy of the commons."[3] If I gain the benefits and bear the costs of what I do, then I will take into account the costs and benefits of my acts. I will invest in improving the land because I reap the rewards. I will not overuse the land because I bear the costs of overuse (and gain the benefits of conservation).

To some, this efficiency story of private property seems well established and comfortable. Others will be startled to find property considered primarily in terms of productivity rather than fairness and distribution. That I am spending so much time on theories focused on productivity or resource allocation efficiency might be justified by the importance of the size of the pie. In a world of scarce resources, concern for productivity seems essential.

But my focus on resource allocation efficiency stems from a simpler source. The theories of Demsetz and Ellickson and the critique of Carol Rose which focus on this goal are highly regarded and justifiably so. Careful examination of these influential analyses begins the process of showing that, whatever the goal, systemic concerns remain central in constructing a general theory of property or any general social theory. Examining theories of property based on resource allocation efficiency allows me to make these points in the context of a relevant – albeit not

---

[1] Demsetz (1967).   [2] Ellickson (1993).

[3] The mechanics of this tragedy lie in the same combination of free riding and failure of collective action we have seen throughout this book. (See, for example, the discussion of the logic of minoritarian bias in Chapter 4.) As a user of the commons, I may be aware that increasing my herd will inevitably cause serious adverse impacts on the common pasture through overgrazing. But if I cut back and, thereby, seek to preserve the pasture for later years, I will not capture all or even most of the benefits of my conservation efforts and indeed these efforts may be completely thwarted as others expand to fill the space I have left. Unless I can control others or trust their good behavior, it makes little sense for me to consider the long-term effects of overuse. Faced with this reality, I (and all others) will act to the detriment of the long-term best use of the land and of the group. The problems of collective action produce an ineluctable and systematic downward spiral – hence, the tragedy. The classic consideration of the tragedy of the commons is G. Hardin (1968).

the only relevant – goal and in the context of analytically powerful and creative work.

Demsetz and Ellickson find advantages for private property or parcelization in a simple and even prosaic source – the mechanics of monitoring. Monitoring is essential to assure that society's scarce resources are used wisely and productively. If the land is parceled out, each owner will have better incentives to monitor and apprehend those who attempt to grab. If the grabbing is localized to the hundred-acre parcel, then both the costs and benefits of monitoring are localized to the individual. For Demsetz and Ellickson, it is in these localized events that it is most clear that the costs of monitoring decrease as we move from common to individual property.

Clear borders reduce the costs of monitoring. Where everyone is allowed to use and enjoy the proceeds from all the land (the character of common property), grabbing cannot be discerned simply by establishing that someone is present or is using a particular parcel of land. For common property, the issue is whether someone is *excessively* or *wrongly* using it – a violation more complicated and difficult to define and apprehend. With private property, the act of crossing the boundary, let alone the consumption of any product of the land, would constitute a violation. Private property makes it easier to know when rights have been violated and provides greater incentives to monitor and sanction such behavior.

Even where adverse effects extend beyond a single hundred-acre parcel to others – say involving four or five such parcels – the apprehension of bad behavior and correcting it by sanctions or by transaction is easier because there are fewer people involved and each has higher stakes. If the activity on one parcel harms another parcel, the owner of the second hundred-acre parcel has the incentive to trigger whatever devices are available to stop the bad behavior. If the property is held in common, then relevant activities like monitoring, sanctioning, and bargaining involve greater numbers of people and more complex arrangements. Problems of collective action are likely to increase. There are, of course, many complicated permutations and combinations to follow. We will get to them subsequently.

But first, notice that the story that Demsetz and Ellickson are telling is quite familiar. Their story of property rights is about *participation* – parcelization operates to maximize productivity by increasing participation by the relevant parties in the administration of the economic system. This participation is discussed in much the same terms as we saw in Parts I and II – in terms of the variables of the "participation-centered" model.

In the Demsetz/Ellickson approach, monitoring is dependent on the stakes and costs involved. As Demsetz and Ellickson tell it, the stakes are higher and the costs are lower under parcelization than they are when the property is held in common. Demsetz and Ellickson are not extolling private property in philosophical or visionary terms. They are speaking in basic institutional terms.[4]

The variables and even the vernacular employed by Demsetz and Ellickson in their discussion of monitoring make it easy to bring in our experiences from Parts I and II. As we saw, the real-world systems for dealing with land use conflicts depend directly on the degree and quality of participation by the impacted parties. As a general matter, these systems work better the greater the participation of these parties. This is the story that Ellickson and Demsetz are also telling.

But the lessons of Parts I and II also warn us that this story of private property may not work out so neatly. When we examine the impact of changes in numbers and complexity on the underlying structures of private property, a more complicated story appears. This story does not necessarily refute the case for private property. It may strengthen it. But that judgment will be more difficult to make and the ensuing analysis will raise important questions about the functioning and even the meaning of private property.

Ellickson and Demsetz focus their story of private property on a familiar setting – a society with a small population, basic needs, and simple technology. This is the world of small numbers and low complexity.[5] Here, private property and its advantages are easy to describe and envision. Land can be divided neatly and any productive activities – hunting, grazing, and farming – are localized and simple. They can be carried out by a single family. Monitoring is easy because we know who should be there and who should not.

It is even easy to imagine the mechanism that sanctions any illicit activities. Since this is a small community, once the norm of private property is established, the community will provide informal incentives such as

[4] Those who do not find efficiency-based analyses of property law compelling may be especially dubious about analyses focused on the seemingly mundane subject of monitoring. But concerns about issues like monitoring transcend any particular goal or any particular system of property. All goals require implementation. In a world of large numbers and complexity, this implementation will be both central and demanding. Unless one envisions a society of angels, any system of property depends on monitoring.

[5] Indeed, for Ellickson, this world of small, closely knit communities is necessary for the most efficient choice of property system. Ellickson (1993), 1320–1.

shunning or gossip or guilt to keep people in line. This is a world of simple and strong norms with relatively straightforward mechanics for monitoring, apprehension, and sanctioning. Both the institution of private property and the institutions of private property are simple and admirable.

However, although private property may have advantages in such a setting, these advantages are not dramatic. The common property system may not do as well, but it is not bad. The chance of a true "tragedy" of the commons is small so long as numbers and complexity are relatively low. In a small community, norms against grabbing or shirking can operate by themselves to control these activities even in the context of common property. Although it may be somewhat more difficult to observe and sanction excessive use in the common property context, one could easily imagine that it would be done. In such a setting, even if parcelization or private property were precluded, we can easily imagine that the worst tragedies of the commons would still be averted. In fact, we have considerable empirical evidence to that effect.

In her important book on common property resources, Elinor Ostrom presents a number of instances of successful communal or cooperative governance of the commons.[6] In these settings, parcelization is precluded or made difficult by the type of resource involved. Ostrom deals with classic instances of resources that are difficult to divide – such as fisheries or irrigation systems. Yet even here, so long as numbers are low and technology simple and relatively homogeneous, tragedies of the commons are averted and common property systems seem to operate effectively.

We should not be surprised, however, that the case for private property over other systems is not overwhelming where numbers and complexity are low. Anyone familiar with the Coase Theorem will understand why. At zero transaction costs, systems of formal governance or law are largely irrelevant. Everything can be worked out instantly, frictionlessly, and costlessly. Any system of property will work. Although, in a world of low numbers and low complexity, we are not at zero transaction costs (an unachievable world), we are in the world of low transaction costs. If, at zero transaction costs, law and systems of property are irrelevant, then at low transaction costs they are not very important.

The real problems for communal or centralized arrangements occur as we increase numbers and complexity, and, thereby, increase transaction and other governance costs. As Ostrom's work shows, greater numbers or

[6] Ostrom (1990).

greater complexity (usually in the form of heterogeneous interests associated with different production technologies) cause serious problems in
connection with common property resource governance and communal
effort. Here we see the downward spiral of resource use associated with
the tragedy of the commons. Resources are grabbed. Renewable resources
are dissipated. Conservation is shirked. External sanctioning mechanisms
are problematic. The possibility of sanctioning by gossip and shunning or
of operating through close bonds of trust, kinship, or long-term relationships diminishes as numbers and complexity grow.

This world of large numbers and high complexity seems to be the place
to make the argument for private property. It is here that the alternative
systems of common or collective property seriously disintegrate and true
tragedies of the commons show up. It is also this world of large numbers
and complexity in which we most often function. Here the comparative
advantages of private property should be greatest or most meaningful.

Unfortunately, however, the case for private property, although prob-
ably quite valid, is increasingly more difficult to make as numbers and
complexity increase because the simple virtues of parcelization and participation through monitoring are more difficult to establish and describe.
We have, in fact, told this story already. In Parts I and II of this book, we
saw real difficulties for the institution of private property at high numbers
and complexity. These difficulties reflected problems in the institutions of
property – markets, communities, political processes, and courts – at high
numbers and complexity.

At high numbers and complexity, the modes of organizing production
in private property systems, such as corporations, partnerships, and complex contractual arrangements, must often employ coordinating, cooper-
ating, and ordering strategies that bring "common ownership" attributes
into the system. "Borders" are no longer so clear and problems of grabbing and shirking invade private ownership. It becomes increasingly difficult to determine who is supposed to do what or to get what. Principal-
agent issues abound. The technology of monitoring is much more
complex – grabbing and shirking get more difficult to define, monitor, apprehend, and sanction.

My point here is not that private property and common property have
no differences. Nor am I arguing that the case for private property decreases as numbers and complexity increase. I strongly suspect that it increases. My point is that it is not so easy to make or assess that argument
and doing so requires an appreciation for parallel impacts on the alternative systems. A familiar phenomenon has set in. The private property

system taken in isolation works less well as numbers and complexity increase, in good part, because the mechanisms available to define and protect private property deteriorate as numbers and complexity increase. That is a lesson of Parts I and II. The system of private property may well do better in a relative sense (better than the other systems), but it will do worse in an absolute sense.

This analysis requires a closer examination of the systemic elements implicit in analyses like those of Demsetz and Ellickson. We can begin with the central subject of monitoring. How does monitoring operate to improve the use of property? How does monitoring operate to control or sanction grabbing and shirking? That parcelization increases the possibility of monitoring either by increasing the stakes or decreasing the costs of monitoring only suggests that the transgressions can be spotted and revealed. Can the mere revelation of transgression curtail transgression?

The answer is yes – in the world of small numbers and low complexity. In this world of strong simple norms against transgression, guilt and shame can easily convert the revelation of transgression into sanctions – revelation and enforcement are virtually synonymous and simultaneous. It is a short distance to more external, but still informal sanctions like gossip and shunning. Damage to reputation is an informal sanction that surfaces even in quite sophisticated business settings.

But, when the social setting becomes more complex as the number of parties grows and as communities and relationships become less stable and less easily defined, informal mechanisms become less effective. We may then have to turn to more formal mechanisms – common law courts and the regulatory state. This potential shift in the institutions of property was the core of the Part I discussion of *Boomer* and central throughout Part II.

In the more complex world in which formal institutions of enforcement come into play, control of grabbing and shirking requires more than monitoring. At the least, the transgressions will have to be reported to an official – a police officer, bureaucrat, or prosecutor. If common law courts are to be used, the monitoring will need to be joined with litigating and, as we saw in Part I, where impacts are dispersed, it must be joined with some mechanism for working out collective action problems such as class actions. If the regulatory apparatus is to be used, it is likely to require lobbying, demonstrating, or reacting at the ballot box as well as reporting the transgression.

As numbers and complexity increase and formal mechanisms come into play, the case for private property made by Demsetz and Ellickson seems less forceful and less compelling. In this more realistic version of the modern world, the case for private property seems to be fading. For reasons we have seen throughout this book, however, that judgment is premature. The efficacy of private property may decrease in an absolute sense as we move from a simple to a complex world. The choice between private and common property, however, is not determined by the *absolute* performance of private property. It is determined by the performance of private property *relative* to other systems of property.

There are reasons to believe that the relative advantage of private property may increase as numbers and complexity increase. As we saw in Parts I and II of this book, the participation-centered view of institutions treats activities like negotiating, organizing, litigation, lobbying, and voting in the same manner that Demsetz and Ellickson treat monitoring. If, as Demsetz and Ellickson argue, private property increases the stakes and decreases the cost of monitoring, there is good reason to believe that it operates similarly for all the other activities necessary for protection of property. The determinants for all these activities are stakes and costs. Although this brief treatment only indicates the *possibility* not the *actuality* of the superiority of private property, there is at least a plausible case for the better relative performance of private property here. The important insight here, however, is that the case for private versus common property lies in the relative merits of these two forms of property and, therefore, in the impact of systemic variables such as stakes, numbers, and complexity on the patterns of participation in the institutions of property (markets, communities, courts, and political processes).[7]

The operation of these systemic variables also raises provocative issues about the definition of private property. As we have seen throughout this book, increasing numbers and complexity can mean a shift in the relevant institutions of property. We saw such a shift in *Boomer*. As numbers and complexity increase, we saw a shift from informal to formal mechanisms of enforcement and a shift within formal mechanisms from common law courts to political process regulation. Are these simply shifts between different means of enforcing or implementing private property or are they shifts between different systems of property – from private to common property?

---

[7] These considerations are as relevant to common property and to nonefficiency goals such as equality and redistribution. William Simon's attempt to design a system of communitarian or republican property reflects these same concerns for participation in the design and promotion of nonprivate property. Simon (1991). We will consider this work in greater detail later in this chapter.

For some advocates of private property, the movement toward political process regulation seems intrinsically at odds with the essence of private property. This is a shift toward common property and a cause for consternation. To use an old phrase, this shift is "creeping socialism." As we shall see, others less devoted to individual property also see the shift to regulation and even shifts in forms of judicial enforcement from rules to standards as a shift toward common property, although these commentators are not alarmed by this shift.

It is not clear, however, that we are seeing a shift in systems of property. As we saw in Part II, even the most ardent devotee of private property may have to turn to the political process for monitoring and enforcement as numbers and complexity increase. This increasing reliance on the political process may well accompany decreases in absolute levels of such goals of private property as resource allocation efficiency. But again the relevant measure is the relative not the absolute levels of these goals and, as numbers and complexity increase, these levels may be higher with protection via the regulatory state than with protection via courts under either common law or constitutional rights. As Part II showed, whether and to what extent use of the courts versus use of the political process promotes resource allocation efficiency or liberty or any other goal is a difficult issue of institutional choice.

To the extent that this institutional choice favors the allocation of responsibility to the political process, it is not clear why this allocation is a shift from private to common property as opposed to a shift in the mechanisms for enforcement of private property. Even Richard Epstein is comfortable with nuisance as a core form of private property law. Yet, as we saw in Chapter 2, the move from trespass to nuisance is a move from valuation by transaction to valuation by courts. As we also saw in that discussion, the same considerations that justify that move can also justify valuation by the political process. Have we now crossed into common property or some hybrid? I am not pushing one definition or another. My point is that the shifts in institutional choice that accompany increases in numbers and complexity will inevitably create tensions between the denotation and connotation of terms like private, common, and mixed property.[8] Associating given institutions with given goals or philosophies of property is dangerous, especially at high numbers and complexity.

---

[8] There is another consequence of increased numbers and complexity that may more easily be seen as a shift to common property and this time it involves the *absolute* not the *relative* performance of the private property systems. As numbers and complexity increase,

If, in the unkempt world of high numbers and complexity, private property is superior to the other property systems, it is not because private property improves in its performance as numbers and complexity increase. The case for private property must lie in the fact that, as numbers and complexity increase, its ability to function – its ability to establish the correct incentives and produce the correct level of participation – disintegrates more slowly than the ability of alternative systems of property. Once again, the central questions of law require consideration of the character of its institutions and the choice among them. These same themes, issues, and problems apply as well to more consciously communal systems in property.

II. THE SEARCH FOR COMMUNITIES

There are many who reject private property and promote more communal visions of the organization of societal resources. The gap between these two views of property is usually so great that it is difficult to address them in the same analysis. Differences in goals as well as in styles of analysis make comparison and close examination awkward. But a recent work makes analysis of these positions easier. In a thought-provoking book,[9] Carol Rose seeks to bridge the significant gap between what she refers to as "the two currently dominant traditions": "neoconservative utilitarianism," which covers the advocates of strong private property rights including the proponents of the economic theory of property and "liberal communitarianism," which covers the resurgent civic republican movement. Like the proponents of the economic theory of property, Rose emphasizes the importance of resource productivity in assessing the role of property law and property rights. In her view, however, the economic theory of property fails to appreciate the central importance of cooperation and informal collective endeavor and, therefore, places too much emphasis on the role of the individual and individual property. Thus, even with her

---

all the mechanisms for enforcement – all the institutions – of private property deteriorate and, as such, the ability to sanction or enforce decreases. Costs of enforcement go up, effectiveness of enforcement goes down and more nonenforcement occurs. The supposed owners of the private property will now find it uneconomic to protect and capture some of the benefits of this property and these uncaptured benefits will become generally available. In effect, they become common property and this form of common property increases as numbers and complexity increase. Property rights economists like Yoram Barzel have chronicled and analyzed these situations. Barzel (1989). Harold Demsetz is a founder of this field. See also North (1990), 33.

[9] Rose (1994).

abiding interest and sympathy for the resource-productivity purposes of property law, she sees a central role for common as opposed to individual property.[10] In this vein, Rose criticizes two prevailing visions of law – the economic theory of property rights and the Federalist image of the Constitution. She faults both for a failure to envision a greater role for informal communities.

Rose's analysis reminds us that the the list of institutions is drastically incomplete without an appreciation for informal communities and norms. But her analysis, like the analyses she critiques, neglects basic issues of institutional choice that have surfaced throughout this book. Exploring her work allows us to examine critically the basic systemic characteristics of those communities and norms that have captured the imagination of so many legal scholars. This exploration returns us to themes and questions raised in the discussion of the economic theory of property rights and in the earlier discussion of land use and provides a way to further understand the role of the courts and the limits of law in general. I begin this exploration with Rose's critique of the economic theory of property rights and then turn to broader communitarian visions in the next section.

When Rose examines U.S. property law, she sees a considerable role for common property even in the achievement of resource allocation efficiency. Her most expansive claims involve the important issue of rules versus standards. Here she most directly confronts what she sees as the analytical deficiencies of the economic theory of property. In particular, she focuses on Harold Demsetz's vision of the evolution of property rights, which she refers to as the "scarcity story." She finds tension between property law and property rights and the scarcity story told by Demsetz:

[E]conomic thinkers for several centuries have been telling us that the more important a given kind of thing becomes for us, the more likely we are to work toward hard-edge rules to manage it. We draw ever sharper lines around our entitlements so that we can identify the relevant players and so that we can trade instead of getting into confusions and disputes – confusions and disputes that would otherwise only escalate as the goods in question became scarcer and more

---

[10] This emphasis on cooperation and community leads her to fault traditional communitarians for too quickly moving from the proposition that communities count to reliance on the formal regulatory state rather than on informal communities. She is also concerned that communitarians too easily dismiss issues of wealth promotion and resource productivity in their pervasive programs of wealth distribution via rearrangement of property rights. Id. at 4.

highly valued.... The trouble with this analysis (which I will here call the "scarcity story") is that things don't seem to work this way, or at least not all the time.[11]

Rose sees the failure of the "scarcity story" and the absence of hard-edged rules not only in conventionally recognized instances of communal or common property, but in the broader world of seemingly individual or private property:

> Even with respect to these divisible and exclusive properties, we sometimes seem to start out with perfectly clear, open-and-shut demarcations of entitlements – and then shift to fuzzy, ambiguous rules of decision. I call this the substitution of "mud" rules for "crystal" ones.... These odd permutations on the scarcity story must give us pause. Why, in ordering our bargaining for scarce resources, should our legal patterns shift back and forth between crystal and mud, instead of relying on crystal? Is there some advantage in the mud rules that the courts are paying attention to? And if so, why do we not opt for mud rules instead?[12]

Consistent with the "scarcity story," Rose finds that property law possesses hard-edged, simple rules: fail to make mortgage payments and you lose your house; fail to pay your rent and you lose your apartment. Rose's examples all concern contractual aspects of property law. But we saw the same choices in the discussion of common law responses to land use in Chapter 2. We saw a clear example of a hard-edged rule in trespass law: physically invade someone's land and you will be enjoined. Property law in all its aspects contains crystal.

As she shows, however, property law is not just a world of crystal. There are many instances in which courts, eschewing clearly stated, simple rules, will delve more deeply and impose their vision of what is reasonable and fair. We saw this in the judicial balancing approach to nuisance law chosen by the *Boomer* court.[13] Thus, Rose shows that the world of property law is made up of both crystal and mud. More important, she shows that crystal evolves into mud as well as mud evolving into crystal. Contrary to the scarcity story, the evolution operates in both directions. In fact, there seems to be cycling between crystal and mud.

---

[11] Id. at 199.   [12] Id. at 199–202.

[13] Even the hard-edged world of trespass has been invaded by the mud of balancing as some courts and legal authorities have allowed the "balancing of hardships" to condition the issuance of injunctions, even given a clear physical trespass. See *Urban Site Venture v. Levering Associates,* 340 Md. 223, 665 A.2d 1062 (1995); Restatement (Second) of Torts, section 941.

Rose's argument is straightforward and compelling. The scarcity story emanating from the economic theory of property rights envisions a steady evolution toward hard-edged, well-defined property rights. Yet we as often observe evolution from crystal to mud as we do from mud to crystal – much more a cycle between the two than an evolution from one to the other. At least as a matter of description, Rose seems correct. Property law – indeed all law – is filled with mud as well as crystal and change is cyclical. We have seen shifts between hard-edged rules and more flexible standards throughout this book beginning with the discussion of *Boomer*. As we will see in the next chapter, this cycling is important in understanding the limits of the Rule of Law.

However, issues concerning institutional choice lurking in Rose's observations raise basic questions about the character and role of communities and even about the definition of private property and create problems for both Rose's theories and those that she criticizes. According to the standard economic analysis, simple rules (crystal) promote transactions by reducing transaction costs. Transaction costs are reduced because parties can understand more easily the consequences of their behavior and the behavior of their bargaining party. The proposition is about simplicity and is straightforward: Simple, hard-edged rules make for lower cost knowledge of legal consequences and, therefore, lower cost transactions. Unlike "maybe it is, maybe it isn't" mud rules, one knows and can rely upon the straightforward association between a simple occurrence and a legal consequence such as that a failure to make mortgage payments means forfeiture. The clearer the consequences, the lower the transaction costs and the lower the transaction costs the more likely we are to have value-enhancing transactions.

But, suggests Rose, the same concerns about complexity, knowledge, and transaction costs also justify mud. Crystal rules can not reduce ignorance and uncertainty to zero. Part of this ignorance and uncertainty is irreducible. Even the most knowledgeable participants do not know what the future will bring. There will also be instances in which one party may have cheaper or better access to information than another. This "asymmetric information" is more likely where the disadvantaged contracting party has lower per capita stakes and less transactional sophistication.

Unattractive results can occur where there is irreducible ignorance, residual uncertainty, and the possibility of asymmetric information. First, unfair and inefficient bargains may be formed. Second, and perhaps more damaging, many parties, fearing the implications of their ignorance, will not take part in transactions that otherwise might be value enhancing for them, the other party, and society. Here the promise of protection in the form of court review of contracts might enhance both transacting and resource allocation efficiency.

Rose attempts to connect this case for mud or standards to the informal communities and relationships for which she has so much affection. As she points out, contracting parties often deal with inherent ignorance or fear of asymmetric information by informal, long-term, commercial relationships. Parties who know each other and deal with each other over the long run will have the incentive to work out any unforeseen difficulty as it occurs. Rather than enforce a contract by its letter, the parties adjust when and if an unforeseen event occurs. This adjustment occurs without coming near a court. Parties may even avoid the cost of serious *ex ante* contracting altogether and depend upon their relationship to work out the relevant terms as they go along. This is the world of contracting described by my colleague, Stewart Macaulay.[14] The ability to trust the contracting process decreases transaction costs, increases the willingness to transact and, thereby, increases resource productivity.

But this analysis takes on a different look when we raise familiar systemic issues. Consider Rose's basic assumption that the choice of mud or standards indicates greater affinity for informal communities and relationships. As we have seen throughout the book, a move from crystal or rules to mud or standards usually means that courts will now make judgments about use and valuation formerly made elsewhere. For example, the move from trespass to nuisance, discussed in Chapter 2, meant that courts now weigh and balance the value of the competing uses – a decision made elsewhere under trespass. In Chapter 2, "elsewhere" was envisioned at least initially as "the market," but, as we have seen and as Rose herself notes, in many settings, market decision making means decision making by informal relationships.

Thus, even if mud were the most efficient or fairest approach, a move toward mud would be a move *away* from informal relationships and communities to courts. The *real* community – to the extent it exists – is part of the "elsewhere" and is, therefore, more associated with crystal than mud. It may be that courts are better approximators of the outcome of the *ideal* informal community than is the *real* informal community. But the institutional choice implied in a shift to mud is that courts will make substantive

---

[14] Macaulay (1963).

decisions that they formerly allocated to informal communities and voluntary arrangements under a regime of rules or crystal. This choice decreases rather than increases the role of community decision making.

The use of the courts as approximators of the ideal "elsewhere" is, paradoxically, also central in conventional law and economics. Richard Posner's standard treatise on law and economics is filled with instances in which the substitution of common law courts for *real* markets is viewed as efficiency enhancing because these courts are allegedly superior to the imperfect markets at replicating *ideal* market outcomes.[15] Even if substituting the courts enhances resource allocation efficiency, it is a move *away* from, not *toward* markets. That law and economics scholars so often count standards and, therefore, courts substituting for markets as efficiency enhancing is inconsistent with the notion that hard-edged rules (crystal) and market decision making are equated with an economic approach to law in general and with an economic approach to property in particular.

Whether and to what extent imperfect courts approximate the outcome of perfect or ideal markets and communities better than imperfect markets and communities is a tough institutional choice, and, once again, it is a choice dependent on numbers and complexity. At low numbers and complexity, everything works just fine. Courts can formulate rules with ease. They can also formulate standards and apply them with ease. But, in this world of low numbers and complexity, highly effective continuing relationships and small communities make both rules and standards largely superfluous. Parties work things out informally. At low numbers and complexity, the choices may be relatively close, but they are attractive.

As numbers and complexity increase, however, the comforting world of continuing relationships and small communities based on trust deteriorates. Complications, uncertainty, and opportunistic behavior increase. Now law can make a difference. It is here that Rose would like courts to replicate trustworthy continuing relationships and simple communal interactions. But the same increases in numbers and complexity that diminish the abilities of continuing relationships also make court replication of continuing relationships more difficult. We have substituted formal decision makers, the courts, for informal decision makers, just when the ability of these formal decision makers is also deteriorating. At high numbers and complexity the choices are again close, but not as attractive.

We can now understand the cycling between crystal and mud that Rose observes in terms of increasing numbers and complexity. As we have seen

---

[15] R. Posner (1998).

throughout this book, institutional choices can be quite close and, there-fore, difficult. As numbers and complexity increase, however, these close choices are among increasingly less attractive alternatives. As the existing institution becomes increasingly unattractive, it is natural, if not necessar-ily correct, to move to another institutional alternative, thereby escaping the present institution and its unattractive consequences. The thought is that anything would be better than this.

Sadly, since all alternatives are growing increasingly unattractive, we soon find ourselves disenchanted with the new choice and in search of yet another alternative. Yesterday's panacea becomes today's disaster and vice versa. This analysis suggests that cycling will increase as numbers and complexity increase. It also suggests an increasing need to better under-stand these difficult institutional choices so that we can avoid unnecessary cycling and, where possible, make real improvements. Cycling creates se-rious costs in the form of increased uncertainty and the information costs of constantly adjusting to a new system. In a world of high numbers and complexity, these costs can be very high and likely will be distributed in a regressive or skewed manner.

Careful consideration of institutional and systemic factors also throws doubt on the basic premise of the debate between Rose and the propo-nents of the scarcity story – that private property is somehow equated with hard-edged rules or crystal. As we have seen throughout this book, there is no simple correlation between any social goal and any institution. Similarly, there is no simple correlation between private property and ei-ther mud or crystal or, more broadly, between private property and any particular mode of or institution for protecting private property. As the first two parts of this book show, the protection of private property is con-sistent with a vast array of mechanisms and decision makers. Individual or private property can be protected via hard-edged rules propounded by courts leaving the resource allocation efficiency balance to markets and informal communities or via standards that leave the resource allocation efficiency balance to the courts. At very high numbers and complexity, the best of unattractive choices may leave the resource allocation efficiency balance to a highly defective political process unconstrained by judicial activity and legal rights.

Especially when numbers and complexity are high, identifying private property with a particular institution or enforcement mechanism is treacherous. Both Rose and the proponents of the scarcity story seem to exclude standards or mud from private property. Such a definition, how-ever, runs contrary to common usage as well as precluding quite viable

ways of protecting private property. In turn, Rose seems to equate cooperation, communities, and norms with common property. Although this
position is more consistent with common usage, it is inconsistent with the
significant role of informal institutions – like the market and communities – in the workings of private property. Communities and informal relationships are basic building blocks of market activity. Nor can serious
governmental intervention be viewed as synonymous with common as
opposed to private property. As we saw in Parts I and II, when numbers
and complexity increase, government regulation can be a valuable if
highly imperfect device for protecting individual or private property.

This association between communities and the market will likely be
jarring to some readers. Many people see communities as havens from the
atomistic market. This reaction reflects the ambiguous nature of the term
"community" and perhaps the term "market." As Rose uses these terms
in her discussion of mud and crystal, community and common property
are associated with the sort of small-number, ongoing business relationships described by Stewart Macaulay. Such market relationships are
clearly consistent with private property in its narrowest sense. As many
studies have shown, long-term and intricate ongoing relationships are
present and even necessary for the functioning of markets.[16]

Quite clearly, communities and ongoing relationships also facilitate
those collective efforts associated with common or communal property. I
have no desire to deny these more common associations with the term
community. My only point here, and it is basic, is that in defining the role
of communities as well as in defining either common or private property
the dynamics of institutional behavior, choice, and comparison can easily
produce startling connections and results. The operation of these forces
mean that there can be no simple correlation between any value, ideology, or philosophy of property and any particular institutional arrangement and, therefore, any particular legal or public policy outcome.

The problem of equating private property with hard-edged rules or
with any particular enforcement strategy can be seen if we retell the
scarcity story in terms of numbers and complexity. Increased scarcity occurs because increased numbers and complexity, operating through expanded and more sophisticated markets, increase demand for an asset
previously held in common. Since the input now has greater value, the

---

[16] See Bernstein (1995); Macaulay (1963); MacNeil (1985); Palay (1986); Scott (1990).

benefits of monitoring and the benefits of improved conservation and production increase. In other words, increased demand for the input increases demand for a system of property likely to maximize its conservation and production which translates into an increased demand for hard-edged private property rules. But the story is incomplete because it only looks at the demand side.

As we know by now, as numbers and complexity increase, all the mechanisms for monitoring and protecting private property (or any form of property) deteriorate. The ability to sharply define parcels and police their borders decreases and the costs of doing so increases. Thus, although increased demand for well-defined property can be associated with increased scarcity, decreased supply of well-defined property can also be associated with increased scarcity. Supply goes in one way and demand in the other. Rehearsing only those factors that increase the need or demand for the protections of private property does not tell us either the extent or the form of these protections.

Like simple associations of goals and institutions, simple associations between institutions and systems of private or common property suppress fundamental systemic issues. Even analysts as sophisticated as Carol Rose and the authors of the economic theory of property rights she critiques are adversely affected by the failure to break out of traditional associations between goals, systems of property, and institutions. As we saw in Parts I and II and are now seeing again, the protection of property has many paradoxes. Protection of private property may be achieved in vastly different ways – by rules or standards administered by common law courts, by government regulation, by constitutional judicial review, by some combination of these forms, or by no formal manifestation at all. It may be best protected by strong judicial protection of private property rights against the government (the conventional view) or, as we saw in Chapter 6, by weak judicial protection of private property rights against the government. It is the character of the institutions of property, their comparison, and their interaction with factors like numbers and complexity that will determine whether and to what extent any of these strategies match with any system of property or with any social goal.

We have now seen this lesson primarily in the context of private property. We can now turn to common property and its institutions and to non-efficiency goals by broadening our examination of communities and communitarianism. Here we can consider localism and civic republics along with a range of social goals beyond resource allocation efficiency. We can then return to the world of private property by a parallel consideration of the minimal state and the Rule of Law.

III. COMMUNITIES AND NORMS
MEET NUMBERS AND COMPLEXITY

Carol Rose is not the only legal scholar attracted to communities. Legal scholars representing a wide range of viewpoints see informal communities and community norms as a fruitful area for study and a potential source of social reform. Sociologists, associated with the law and society and law-in-action traditions, have long focused attention on communities, long-term relationships, and norms. Even those interested in law and economics and private property, such as Robert Ellickson and, more recently, the "new Chicago school," have focused significant attention on communities and norms.

This significant interest in communities and norms helps to inform institutional choice by exploring a vibrant range of institutional alternatives. But the interchange works both ways. The fervent outpouring of interest in communities and norms must confront the systemic realities inherent in institutional choice and comparative institutional analysis. Whether and to what extent informal communities and their norms are attractive institutions depends on the sort of factors we have discussed throughout this book – in particular, numbers and complexity.

Informal communities are not, however, the only popular institutional images vying for attention. While some exalt informal relationships, communities, and civic republics, others glorify a minimal state kept in place by a rule of law based on well-defined constitutional rights and common law doctrines. These two popular images, often representing quite different ideological positions, have captured the debate about property law and rights, in particular, and law and rights in general. In this section, I will focus primarily on communities and norms leaving most of the discussion of the Rule of Law to the next chapter. I begin with Carol Rose.

In an excursion into the U.S. Constitution and U.S. constitutionalism, Rose contrasts the formal U.S. Constitution and its Federalist underpinnings with the more amorphous "ancient constitution" and its connections with the Anti-Federalist position and civic republicanism. She sees the U.S. Constitution in conventional terms – formally defined institutions designed to check and balance one another through differing modes of election and differing powers and further controlled by a formally enunciated bill of rights. Rose refers to this arrangement as "the plain vanilla constitution." This is the Federalist constitution and its ratification and continued existence supports the common notion that only the Federalist's vision of governance survives. But, says Rose, that is too simple a perception. According to Rose, Anti-Federalism survives in the form of local government. In her view, unlike the conventional constitutional structure, localism operates and should operate largely without formal checks and balances in a more organic manner.

Consistent with her attraction to communities and informal relationships, Rose is drawn to the informal give-and-take of local government decision making. Local officials are more likely to be part of the traditions and customs of the community and they work through informal channels. For Rose, these communal relationships and customs supply an informal constitution akin to the ancient unwritten constitution of custom and tradition. Checks and balances and formal protection of rights are replaced by a significant increase in effective popular participation.

Rose makes her case for this informal constitution in terms familiar to readers of this book. Local officials are more easily accessible, more limited local agenda make their positions more easily known, and local citizens know and deal with each other more easily and directly. In other words, the cost of participation is much lower at local levels and, at least for some issues, the per capita stakes of a majority of citizens are high enough to give them the incentive to bear these costs. This more serious possibility of participation leads Rose to suggest that James Madison had it exactly wrong when he thought that factionalism would be controlled by moving away from localism. As Rose points out, the concentrated special interests that walk the pages of the public choice literature are far more likely to prevail in the more complex, dispersed world of larger government than they are in the more accessible, informal halls of local government.

Rose's view is consistent with the analysis of minoritarian bias presented in Part II of this book. As we saw there, however, the overrepresentation of concentrated interests to the detriment of dispersed and dormant majorities is not the only form of serious political malfunction. Complicating the picture is the opposite bias: The overrepresentation of active majorities to the serious detriment of concentrated minorities – majoritarian bias. As we saw in Part II, serious majoritarian bias at the local level produces overregulation and exclusionary zoning in the land use setting. Once the conflicting forces of majoritarian and minoritarian bias enter the picture, it is no longer easy to unconditionally love localism. Greater local participation is not an unabashed good. The problems and dynamics of majoritarian bias and the trade-off with minoritarian bias complicate political reform.[17]

Civic republicans believe that participation and interchange in small communities create consensus and altruism. This is an appealing and attractive image. However, a familiar problem lurks. As numbers and complexity increase, localism becomes increasingly problematic. If the locale is defined more broadly so as to include all those who are impacted, increased numbers and complexity decrease the attractive possibility of working things out by deliberation and consensus. By contrast, if we keep local governments small and maintain a cohesive informal community that produces active local majorities, we can seriously harm the larger society if the societal issues with which these small, cohesive communities deal affect a much larger population.

As we saw in *Petaluma* and *Mt. Laurel,* the "ideal community" may be much larger than the actual one. Many with quite legitimate interests are not part of the cohesive actual community. These interests cannot be ignored or wished away without significantly diminishing social welfare. As we saw in Part II, as the relevant world grows in size and complexity, active participation by local citizens can be an evil. This lesson extends far beyond U.S. land use issues. For all the attractiveness of simple local communities, we cannot go back to a time in which social conflicts and issues were simple and impacted few. We live in national and global communities and cannot deny the accompanying interactions and interconnections without risking serious, even catastrophic hardships.[18]

Voice and participation, however, are not the only mechanisms that control local government. As Rose reminds us, there is also exit. Among numerous local governments, people can find possibilities that fit their needs and tastes and, by voting with their feet, constrain the excesses of local government. As we saw in the last chapter, exit and competition among communities can internalize external effects to local communities and create the paradox that private property can be best protected by reducing rather than expanding constitutional protections of private property.

But these exit-based mechanisms also contain a paradox for many civic republicans and communitarians. Their core image of social decision

---

[17] These insights were not lost on the framers of the Constitution. James Madison was aware of both minoritarian and majoritarian bias and quite consciously chose to deal with majoritarian bias. It is not obvious that he got it wrong. See Komesar (1994), 217–21.

[18] For a sophisticated and harrowing picture of the sources of evil inherent in communal and collective action, see Hardin (1995).

making is human interaction and deliberation. Exit is not a mechanism that operates by deliberation, discussion, trust, and consensus. It does not operate by increasing cooperation and altruism. Quite the opposite, it depends significantly on atomistic action and the forces of competition. Indeed, as we saw in Chapter 6, cooperation and deliberation among local jurisdictions, leading to larger regional decision making and cooperation, can undermine the exit mechanism. It is competition not cooperation and mobility not stability that make the exit mechanism work.

Most communitarians and civic republicans stress both different mechanisms and different goals than Rose. They emphasize goals other than resource allocation. They stress equality, especially equality of opportunity facilitated by broad-based participation. In a thoughtful article, William Simon summarizes and advances this social-republican form of property.[19] His system is structured to maximize voice and minimize exit. Simon seeks to increase the stakes of a broad range of societal actors; workers and renters are primary examples. But, in order to maximize participation, he severely restricts mobility and exit by conditioning ownership on continuing residence in the community in question.

As Simon himself recognizes, however, a community constructed to be so close-knit and stable will have serious problems with inclusion and, therefore, can create serious inequalities. To his credit, these inequalities concern Simon and he struggles with their solution. His principle suggestion is a familiar one – judicial review. He refers to *Mt. Laurel.* As Part II showed, however, using the courts to solve the issue of inclusion – whether based on a concern for resource allocation efficiency, equality, or any other goal – is a perilous and, at best, very limited undertaking. Simon's reference to *Mt. Laurel* reminds us that all societal goals face quite similar issues of institutional choice. In this world of difficult institutional choices, exit and competition remain important and perhaps necessary antidotes to the excesses of localism.

The tension between mobility and stability in institutions creates problems for those, like Simon, who seek an alternative to liberal private property. The inherent trade-off between voice and exit is based at least in part on the trade-off between majoritarian and minoritarian bias. By increasing the stakes of all citizens, Simon seeks broader-based participation in society's institutions. Greater participation associated with higher stakes is a basic tenet of the participation-centered approach and, as I

---

[19] Simon (1991).

have shown, broader-based participation is an antidote to control by the few. But if the price of this participation is artificially defined and closed communities, we get local majoritarian bias and spillover effects in return.

The tension between mobility and stability in institutions reflects another dominant institutional theme common to many communitarians – a deep distrust of large, atomistic institutions and, in particular, of the market. In Simon's case, this distrust triggers an attempt to structure a more vibrant collective process by designing a meaningful version of communal or republican property. Like Rose, Simon is drawn to a form of property that is neither all state ownership nor all individual ownership. Unlike Rose, however, Simon's conception places almost exclusive emphasis on voice. He purposely cuts off exit and, therefore, the use of atomistic competition to discipline governmental excesses.

In a world of high numbers and complexity, it is always dangerous to assume that the desire for any goal either anoints or precludes an institutional alternative – most definitely including the atomistic market. However, Simon's analysis is hardly the most severe instance of aversion to the market. That title belongs to Margaret Radin's well-known theory of property law where distrust of the market is a central theme. To Radin, the market and its rhetoric are harmful to community and to an essential sense of self.

This essential sense of self and community is central to Radin's work. She has developed a theory of property based on "personhood" that distinguishes fungible from personal property. People have little personal attachment to fungible property. It is the sort of stuff that is bought and sold in the market regularly. The difference here is not in the type of physical asset but in the relationship of that asset to its owner.[20] Houses may be owned by absentee landlords or speculators. Such owners do not have strong personal attachments to these houses. In these instances, a house is not a home. To Radin, personhood and personal property deserve more moral recognition and legal protection than fungible property.

Like many of the legal theories constructed around values and goals, Radin's theory has impressive philosophical credentials. Radin's philosopher is Hegel. She contrasts Hegelian theory with the Lockean theory most prevalently used to support conventional private property approaches. Her theory contains plausible distinctions and valid observations about the market.

---

[20] Radin (1982), 959.

She is clearly correct that people may value the same physical object in quite different ways and that this difference is often dominated by subjective attachments to the object. She is also correct in the assertion that these subjective values are crucially important. Indeed, they are what life is about. Subjective values may sometimes be difficult to measure and, as such, raise discomforts and uncertainties. But subjective values are easily as important as objective values. On a personal level, they must dominate them.

Radin is also correct to worry about the effect of markets and the activities of transacting on these central subjective values. Like many, including Simon, she is concerned with the dehumanizing effects of commodification. She sees in the language or rhetoric of market exchange a degradation of the essence of living. Like Epstein's abiding distrust for the political process, Radin's deep distrust of the market resonates with common experience. Materialism, displacement, and a sense of disconnection are not difficult to see in the atomism of mass markets. These effects are serious. The market is highly imperfect whether measured by the goal of resource allocation efficiency, equality of opportunity, or personhood.

But, contrary to Radin's view, a recognition of the value of personhood and a deep distrust of the market tells us virtually nothing about law, rights, and public policy. It does not tell us whether we should have rights or no rights, regulations or no regulations, alienation or no alienation, or indeed any response at all. It does not tell us whether courts should substitute for the market on a case-by-case basis thereby shifting valuation decisions to the courts, allocate these decisions to the local community, substitute for the market on a wholesale basis through restrictions on alienation, or even allocate the decisions to the market altogether. These are the decisions that define law and public policy.

Consider the *Petaluma* case discussed in Chapter 4 in terms of Radin's approach. It is easy enough to identify the dispute as one between owners of personal or personhood property and owners of fungible property. Those who favored limiting growth were local homeowners and their opponents were developers. Unlike the local homeowners, there is little reason to believe that these developers had any significant subjective attachment to their property. But if one's home, neighborhood, and community are essential aspects of defining who one is, it is centrally important when someone is not allowed to establish a home or when one is not allowed access to a better neighborhood or community. In protection of their already existing homes and their subjective connections to them, the citizens of Petaluma have adversely affected the ability of others to establish such personal relationships.

There is a strong connection or relationship between the fungible property interests of the developers and the potential for personhood property for those excluded from Petaluma. It is quite possible, even quite likely, that the Northern California developers represented in *Petaluma* sought nothing more than pecuniary profit when they attempted to build in the City of Petaluma. In the complex market system, however, the effect of this profit maximization can be the delivery or enhancement of precisely those personhood values which Radin justifiably emphasizes. When Radin and others focus on the immediate form of ownership and discount those who hold, buy, and sell for pecuniary profit, they ignore a creditable process by which others gain access to those important property relationships associated with personhood. The market is a fundamental instrument, albeit a highly imperfect one, for the achievement of goals like equality of opportunity, community, and personhood as well as the goal of resource allocation efficiency. This assertion does not require the rejection of any of Radin's serious indictments of the market or of her affection for personhood.

Judicial determinations or political decisions by local communities may do better than the market. But that is the central issue to be addressed and it requires attention to systemic factors. At low numbers and complexity, Radin may comfortably assume that courts and local legislatures will ably resolve the issues of valuation she addresses. But, at low numbers and complexity, the problems of the market she describes largely disappear. At low numbers and complexity, markets and communities become one.

When Radin excoriates markets, she is speaking of atomistic, mass markets – the world of high numbers and complexity. But, in this world of high numbers and complexity with its vast and complex interrelationships, the sizeable imperfections of nonmarket institutions like courts and political processes will also have to be seriously considered. The same sort of difficult institutional choices that we saw confronting liberal private property throughout this book also confront Radin's quite different goals and her seemingly quite different conception of property. Whether and to what extent Radin's conception creates a better or even a different system of property law directly depends on these choices. It is not obvious that the resulting configuration of institutions would reject the market or be much different than the real world system of liberal private property she rejects. One cannot seriously manifest a concern for the deep importance of subjective or personhood values (or any other value) without addressing these central and difficult systemic issues. It defeats the achievement of any goal to dismiss a serious institutional alternative on an *a priori* basis.

When one carefully considers these difficult institutional choices, the singular focus on values and their importance shared by Radin and so many other legal scholars can have unexpected results. Paradoxically, the importance of a value or interest may cut against legal protection – at least to the extent that protection means judicially based protection. Again, this paradox can be seen in *Petaluma*. As we saw in Part II, the importance of home ownership with all its strong personhood values is the very reason that homeowner majorities are politically active and often dominate the political process in places like Petaluma. That these homeowners are already well represented in the political process makes additional legal protection less, not more, necessary. Indeed, that they may be overrepresented makes out a strong case for legal protection of their opponents who, in this case, are the owners of fungible property.

There are two important points here. First, when commentators, depending upon established philosophical positions, identify what is socially important, they are much further from law and policy than they believe. No serious philosopher of law can derive a meaningful program of law or public policy from the claim that an interest is important. It is not that Radin's values or goals are wrong-headed. Like Epstein's values derived from Locke, there is much that is attractive in Radin's Hegelian-derived value system. However, without far more serious consideration of systemic issues than either of these authors manifests, we have no idea whether the programs of property law and property rights they propose have any relationship to the values or goals they espouse. Goal choice, no matter how elegantly executed, is no substitute for institutional choice.[21]

Second, even seemingly stunning parades of horribles will not settle institutional choice. The problems with the market described by its opponents are in many instances real and serious. The adverse impacts on productivity, morality, and personal satisfaction associated with effects ranging from dislocation to commodification are significant – and they are likely to grow worse. Yet these defective markets may often be the best (albeit far from perfect) means to deliver not only larger GNP but also a more open, satisfying, and equalitarian world. It may well be that

---

[21] I have shown similar problems in the application of Rawlsian conceptions of the good. See Komesar (1994), 44–9.

the correct institution for Radin's purposes would be a republican system as described by Simon where restraints on alienation create stability and more intense communal participation. But there is a price to pay for increased stability and the greater workings of voice: decreased mobility and the lesser workings of exit. Whether this trade-off favors Simon's republic, Rose's localism, or Epstein's rights-protected market as the best means of carrying out Radin's goals (or theirs) can be decided only by serious systemic analysis that takes as a given that we are choosing among highly imperfect communal, political, adjudicative, and market processes. As numbers and complexity increase and institutions deteriorate, strongly felt aversion to the evils of an institution is an increasingly unreliable way to decide issues of law and public policy.

At high numbers and complexity, there is a vast gap between the idealized images of community and cooperation and their reality. When only part of the true or normative community cooperates, we can get a wide range of evils ranging from special interest legislation to oligopoly and cartels to exclusionary zoning to gangs to ethnic cleansing.[22] Anyone who extols the virtues of community and cooperation must be careful that they are not carrying over images from low number and complexity contexts to much larger populations and much more complex issues. The same large numbers and complexity that turn evenhanded and simple market transactions carried out in ongoing relationships into the alienating and deadening atomistic market so distrusted by Radin also turn attractive cooperation within a self-contained simple community into quite different and far less attractive forms of cooperative effort. Comparability is, as always, essential. Images taken from the wrong context distort analysis and create disastrous results.

Like the idealized small communities or civic republics of communitarians, the minimal state of libertarians or neoconservative utilitarians (to use Rose's terminology) also faces serious problems as numbers and complexity increase. Commentators from Frederic Hayek to Richard Epstein have extolled the virtues of a minimal state limited to aiding the market by enforcing contracts and protecting private property. But this seemingly simple and attractive ideal, like the idealized civic republic, is transformed as numbers and complexity increase. Even a minimal state run by angels would grow with numbers and complexity – there would be more possible property violations and contracts to respond to.

---

[22] See Hardin (1995).

Real problems set in, however, once we recognize that the minimal state is an imperfect political process and, therefore, have to face the issue of how to keep that state minimal. As numbers and complexity grow, so does the possibility of political malfunction. Greater numbers and complexity mean the enhanced possibility of minoritarian bias and the prospect of "rent seeking." They can also mean pockets of expanded governmental action through majoritarian bias. This is the story of Part II where both minoritarian and majoritarian bias haunted local zoning and grew worse as the overall land use conflicts impacted more people and grew more substantively complex. None of this is solved by simply calling for a state limited to generally defined tasks like protecting property and enforcing contracts. As we have seen in the context of local zoning, where numbers and complexity are high, these tasks become difficult to define and can be manipulated to justify a wide range of government regulation.

What we have learned thus far tells us that the minimal state, like the civic republic, is a tricky notion. At low numbers and complexity, the minimal state is very workable. In fact, at low numbers and complexity, the minimal state is the civic republic. It is Macaulay's continuing relationships and Ellickson's Shasta County. There will be little use for formal government and little fear that it will exceed the correct size especially in a world where its constituency is small and observant and it is easy to identify and react to excesses. Lions lie down with lambs and liberals lie down with communitarians. As numbers and complexity increase, however, minimal states like civic republics fall from perfection. We saw these implications for the minimal state in Part II and we are about to see them again in the analysis of the Rule of Law in the next chapter.

IV. CONCLUSION

Virtually nothing follows from the choice of a goal or of a general philosophy of property. You cannot hardwire goals and institutions and, therefore, no program of law and public policy follows from goal choice. The simple correlations between goals and institutions that characterize so many ideological positions simply do not hold. Institutional choice, at least institutional choice at high numbers and complexity, is filled with paradoxes and counterintuitive combinations of goals and institutions.

This chapter has examined the implications of choice among the institutions of property especially as numbers and complexity vary. We have seen that every system of property and every institution of property functions at its best where numbers and complexity are low. Informal cooperative communities flourish. Markets and governments comfortably merge in the face of the significant ability of people to work things out and to trust one another. All relevant interests participate and participation is easy and straightforward. Norms, customs, and practices are simple, accessible, and trustworthy. We are near Nirvana.

As numbers and complexity grow, however, the trustworthiness of norms, customs, informal relationships, and communities diminishes. In terms of the *Boomer* spectrum, there is now a stronger case for formal responses perhaps beginning with the courts employing simple hard-edged rules that return the issue to the informal setting and then evolving into more complex standards in which courts seek to replicate the outcomes of ideal markets and communities rather than leaving the decisions to real markets and communities. Finally, as numbers and complexity grow still further, the political process takes over the task of the adjudicative process substituting regulation and public ownership.

As we have seen, however, the comparative institutional picture of rights is even more interesting. Because institutions tend to move together, we are as likely to see cycling as simple evolutionary shifts. As Carol Rose observes, there is cycling between rules and standards (crystal and mud). As Part II showed, there is cycling between judicial and governmental decision making: Regulation replaces common law adjudication and, in turn, is sometimes replaced by constitutional judicial review.

Simple, romantic notions of institutions must be abandoned. Civic republicans and communitarians, like libertarians and other advocates of private property, will have to face the realities of institutional choice. Localism may be the answer. But if it is, it will be brigaded by forces unattractive to and unfamiliar to communitarians. Just as the realities of institutional choice revealed in Part II may force supporters of private property to accept the paradox that the world of private property must be increasingly dominated by the collective political process, so civic republicans may have to accept a world in which localism operates through remote, competition-driven, atomistic mechanisms.

Civic republics and minimal states are among those attractive images that form the basis for countless programs and reforms worldwide. But these images are accurate only in the largely irrelevant world of very low numbers and complexity. As number and complexity grow, civic republics and minimal states may remain viable alternatives but in increasingly less attractive forms. Paradoxically, however, one of these ugly alternatives often will be the superior choice even to carry out goals thought foreign to them. Real reform requires confronting real institutional choices and that means choices among *comparable* institutions – institutions envisioned and compared in the same context of numbers and complexity.

Legal commentators, however, always have a simple way out if civic republics, cooperative communities, or minimal states fail to meet their ideal. They turn to the courts. For libertarians or neoconservative utilitarians, the courts are the bulwark of rights. Civic republicans see in courts the deliberative, consensus builders they sought in local communities. As we have seen, however, as numbers and complexity increase, strains on the courts also increase. We must now turn attention to the role of the courts and the Rule of Law in the difficult, but relevant world of high numbers and complexity.

8

Numbers, Complexity, and the Rule of Law

Embodied in the slogan, "a government of laws, not men," the Rule of Law is one of those phrases that seems to withstand the ravages of time while maintaining a significant if vague veneration. As an ideal, the Rule of Law evokes an image of stability and lack of arbitrariness. With the promise of impartiality and restraint as its core, the Rule of Law seems to transcend partisan concerns. Modern proponents of globalizing the Rule of Law, such as the World Bank, see it as a bulwark for the market as well as a control on the excesses of government. Most visions of the Rule of Law place heavy emphasis on rules as clear articulations of expected behavior applicable to all and give a central place to courts in articulating and applying these rules. But if the Rule of Law is a law of rules and a law overseen by courts, it must then be subject to the forces of institutional choice we have seen throughout this book. Examined through this prism, the Rule of Law looks far different than the simple and powerful portrait so often painted.

As Parts I and II showed us, U.S. court-made law is neither stable nor clear but rather is characterized by shifts and cycles between strong rights that depend heavily on market decision making, moderate rights that depend heavily on courts, and no rights that leave decisions primarily to the political process. As Part I showed us, systemic factors such as numbers and complexity push courts to move from one strategy to another – results underlined by Carol Rose's observation of cycling between crystal and mud. Part II showed us that even the most suspect and malfunctioning political process may sometimes be the best protector of property rights and the best strategy for achieving resource allocation efficiency, equality, integration, or any other goal. Similarly, Chapters 6 and 7 showed us that private property, whatever its advantages, is not a system dominated by simple rules or by common-law courts. Instead, society must increasingly depend upon the political process to protect property owners from one another and even to protect property owners from the political process itself.

This chapter projects these themes more broadly. The first section explores the implications of legal and institutional shifts and cycles for such Rule of Law attributes as clarity, stability, and evenhandedness. It examines the effects of numbers and complexity on shifts and cycles between rules and standards and, in turn, on judicial activity and judicial activism. The second section uses these lessons to expose the unrealistic perception of courts underlying various versions of the Rule of Law. The third section explores communitarian and critical legal studies critiques of the Rule of Law and, in turn, compares and contrasts the role of the Rule of Law and courts versus the role of informal communities. In the end, although there is a role for both informal communities and formal rules in the world of high numbers and complexity, both the Rule of Law and communitarianism must assume forms far from their ideals.

I. SHIFTS AND CYCLES: THE DECREASING
LIKELIHOOD OF STABLE AND CERTAIN LAW

Stability, clarity, and certainty are the hallmarks of the Rule of Law. In fact, the belief in certain, reliable, and stable rules pervades law in general. As we saw in Chapter 7, the economic theory of private property is based on the ability of clear rules, rights, and boundaries to facilitate better management of assets. This view of law underlies the theories of philosophers, lawyers, and social scientists. What we have seen thus far, however, casts doubt on the premise of stable, clear, and certain law, especially in a world of high numbers and complexity.

As the analysis of *Boomer* in Chapter 2 revealed, changes in systemic variables like numbers and complexity change the character of law and, therefore, the character of the Rule of Law. At very low numbers and complexity, there is little need for formal decision making. The ideals of the Rule of Law, such as clarity, stability, evenhandedness, and control of government, are easily achieved through informal communities and transactions. In this setting, the Rule of Law with its formal rules and careful applications is largely unnecessary. We can have the Rule of Law virtues without either rules or law.

As numbers and complexity increase but are still low, some disputes escape these informal processes. As long as numbers and complexity remain low, however, courts can make simple judgments – employ simple rules – that send the tougher issues of balancing back to markets and communities. This is a world of strong and simple rights – the world of trespass we saw in Chapter 2. The Rule of Law is in full flower.

As numbers and complexity continue to grow, however, disputes reaching courts force greater judicial activity. As other institutions deteriorate, courts may better approximate the ideal market or the ideal community than existing real markets or real communities. Courts now strike the necessary substantive balances. Simple rules are replaced by flexible standards and judicial balancing. Judicial activity increases, but judicial protections and judicial activism may decrease.

In turn, at even higher numbers and complexity, courts, recognizing their own limitations, increasingly defer to the political process. This allocation to another institution, however, is commonly associated with judicial passivity not strong protection of rights. We see a simple rule of law – go to the legislature. But it is a rule of law defunct of any promise of legally produced (or at least judicially produced) clarity, stability, and evenhandedness. Both judicial activity and judicial activism disappear. Gone is judicial protection against the excesses of government. It is a rule of law but not the Rule of Law.

Thus, even the *Boomer* spectrum reveals significant fluctuation in and qualification of the Rule of Law. However, because this simple account is largely single institutional, it understates the amount of fluctuation. From the more relevant comparative institutional perspective, the patterns of law will not be so neat. There will be close calls, controversy, ambivalence, and cycling – results even more inconsistent with the clarity and stability associated with the Rule of Law. As Carol Rose's work shows, property law reflects significant cycling between rules and standards (crystal and mud) and, therefore, cycling between imperfect markets and imperfect courts.

We saw another important type of cycling in Part II. The simple *Boomer* assumption, that at large scale – large numbers and complexity – the political process prevails, is subject to at least some exceptions. The troubling nature of land use regulation with its severe political malfunctions has drawn some courts into reviewing these land use decisions even at high numbers and complexity. This serious judicial review is and, to a significant extent, must be limited. But judicial concerns about severe political malfunction continue to produce ambivalence and cycling in judicial review of zoning and just compensation.

We are seeing the classic choice between rules and standards in a different light. For reasons exposed in our examination of Rose's analysis of crystal and mud, increased numbers and complexity are likely to put pressure on both rules and standards that can lead to cycling between the two strategies by courts and even by individual judges. This cycling can occur without any variation in goals, ideology, or political philosophy. Buried in these various shifts and cycles are important issues about judicial activism, judicial activity, the future of the courts, and the realities of the Rule of Law.

At least at first blush, increased numbers and complexity create a strong case for standards. Where societal issues become more complex and correct answers less obvious, there is a tendency toward a more cautious judicial examination of these issues. Greater complexity means greater uncertainty and greater sensitivity to the possibility of unforeseen twists and turns. Because judges will want greater flexibility to deal with this possibility, they are likely to articulate complex balances in which significant numbers of factors are listed – often without much guidance as to why a factor is listed or which are the most important factors. This vagueness represents an unwillingness on the part of judges to prematurely limit the inquiry. They want to be educated by subsequent cases. As numbers and complexity increase, judges, whatever their ideological bent, will be increasingly uncomfortable with what they do not know and with what surprises may be around the adjudicative corner.

Moreover, as numbers and complexity increase, alternative decision makers become less trustworthy. Courts face both more demand for their services and less comfort allocating decision making to other institutions such as markets and political processes through the use of simple, hardedged rules. Strong rights, in the form of simple rules, mean sweeping allocations of responsibility to other decision makers. Increasing numbers and complexity, however, mean that these alternative decision makers will be less reliable. For all these reasons, a Rule of Law as a law of clear rules becomes increasingly problematic and less likely.

But although concerns about competence or substantive judgment drive courts toward standards as numbers and complexity increase, concerns about physical capacity or scale, as well as a different aspect of competence, drive them in the opposite direction – toward clear rules. As markets, communities, and informal relationships deteriorate, the courts can expect more requests for both their common law and public law decision making. On the common law side, this increased demand may take the form of increased contracts litigation caused by a deterioration in the informal mechanisms that would otherwise have adjusted to changing circumstances or of increased tort litigation occurring because conflicts and injuries are not so easily worked out by informal communities and norms. Courts will be called upon to deal with difficult substantive issues concerning changing circumstances, injuries, and conflicting uses that once were handled by informal arrangements.[1] Similarly, deterioration in the ability of the political process associated with increasing numbers and complexity increases the call for judicial protection against the political process through constitutional law, administrative law, and statutory interpretation.

As courts are confronted with more litigation and more demand on their resources, simple rules or crystal will look attractive. These simple rules reduce uncertainty about adjudicative outcomes, facilitate settlement, and allow courts to allocate decision making elsewhere, thereby sharing responsibility with other institutions. In *Boomer*, we saw this allocation to other institutions not only in the trespass rules that implicitly allocate to the market, but also in the allocation of widespread pollution issues to the political process. These sweeping decisions not to decide are the essence of constitutional constructs such as the political question doctrine and the "hands off" minimal scrutiny used in equal protection and substantive due process. Strains on judicial competence and resources make the decision not to decide attractive.

Increasing numbers and complexity place strains on both the demand for and supply of law, thereby creating conflict between rules and standards. Increasing complexity means that courts will want more flexible formulations that allow them to learn and adapt in the more complex setting and yet, at the same time, increasing numbers mean that courts will want simpler, clearer formulations that reduce the amount and cost of litigation and allocate decision making elsewhere. They will want to allocate to other institutions at the same time that they are increasingly distrustful of these alternatives. As numbers and complexity increase, courts want more help, but there is less help available. We can expect tougher institutional choices with more compromises and more uncomfortable partnerships with these other institutions. And none of these changes, compromises, or cycles is dependent on shifts in the ideological make-up of courts or judges.[2]

---

[1] Again, the classic work showing the avoidance of contract litigation at low numbers is Macaulay (1963) and the classic work showing the avoidance of tort litigation at low numbers is Ellickson (1991). We have seen the adverse impact of increasing numbers and complexity on these informal mechanisms in Chapters 2, 4, and 7.

[2] Work by Kathleen Sullivan on the use of rules and standards by the Justices of the U.S. Supreme Court disputes commonly asserted associations between the rules-standards

This cycling between rules and standards and between the courts and other institutions takes its most elaborate form in constitutional law where courts employ two forms of "rule," representing either the weakest or the strongest of rights. Strong rights in constitutional law – such as old-fashioned (and always fatal) strict scrutiny under equal protection law or the absolutist position on free speech – allocate significant responsibility away from political processes to informal processes. But sweeping allocations elsewhere also characterize the weakest rights. Although there is plenty of language in the U.S. Constitution that invites courts to review all government activity (Epstein's interpretation of takings provides an example), courts can seriously review only a tiny and decreasing percentage of government activity. Through narrow definitions of thresholds like "takings" or "private property" or various levels of scrutiny like those in equal protection law, courts exclude vast areas of governmental activity from serious judicial review. These broad and sweeping allocations to the government are the weakest of rights. They are rules of abdication. The difference between strong and weak constitutional rights is not the presence of sweeping allocations elsewhere. The difference is the subject of that allocation. With weak rights, the sweeping allocation is to the political process rather than to the informal process (markets, communities, and individuals).

This choice between rules and standards at the constitutional level has created confusion about the meaning of judicial restraint and activism and the distinction between judicial activism and judicial activity. Justice Scalia, for example, is critical of standards because he believes that they mean more judicial activity and necessitate greater judicial activism than rules.[3] There is little doubt that standards mean more judicial activity. Judges will be doing more of the balancing and more complicated judicial formulations mean more uncertainty, more litigation and, therefore, more work for judges. But this judicial activity does not necessarily correlate with greater judicial activism.

---

choice and given ideologies. Sullivan (1992). Sullivan's observations indicate that it is no more likely for those on the left than those on the right to be attracted to either rules or standards. Id. at 99. Sullivan did note a correlation, however, between polar ideology and rules and more moderate centrist positions and standards. Ibid. Ideologues, of whatever stripe, are apparently more attracted to rules, and moderates are more attracted to standards. In our terms, this is explicable by a correlation between ideology and certainty. Ideologues see the world as simpler than moderates. The simpler the world, the easier it seems to use rules.

[3] Scalia (1989), 1179–81. See also Nagel (1992).

The opposite is often true. In constitutional law, the strongest activism and the strongest rights are associated with rules. Consider, for example, old-fashioned strict scrutiny under equal protection. This form of strong judicial scrutiny was rulelike. Find a suspect classification, such as race, and the legislation was invalidated. Similarly, the absolutist position on First Amendment speech relies on rules and bright-lined categories. As with common law rules like trespass, these constitutional rules are associated with strong rights and strong judicial activism, but limited judicial activity.

Constitutional law raises the central issue of who decides who decides. The choices here are the government and the courts. Thus, in the land use cases in Part II, the courts had to determine who would decide whether the government or the market would decide the location and amount of housing. In both *Petaluma* and *Mt. Laurel,* activist courts decided that they would decide who decided. But when courts decide that they, and not the political process, will decide who balances the societal benefits and detriments, they still have another institutional choice. The courts can themselves balance these benefits and detriments on a case-by-case, regulation-by-regulation basis (as in *Mt. Laurel*) or they can leave the decision to markets, communities, and individuals by a sweeping invalidation of a whole category of regulation (as in *Petaluma*). The second, more rule-like response requires less judicial activity than the more standardlike response. But it would constitute an increase – not a decrease – in judicial activism.[4] As we have seen, both the strongest rights and most activist po-

---

[4] The same phenomenon can be seen even in the common law. Consider here the famous landlord-tenant, implied warranty of habitability case, *Javins v. First National Realty Corp,* 428 F.2d 1071 (D.C. Circuit 1970). The *Javins* court not only found an implied warranty of habitability, but it also made this warranty unwaivable. This decision on waiver is grounded, at least in part, on the same concerns about bargaining that underlie unconscionability. The *Javins* court, however, replaced a case-by-case adjudicative determination about unconscionability with a sweeping determination that all bargains concerning waiver were unenforceable. The *Javins* rule on waiver is an example of rule-based activism in the common law. It increased judicial activism but decreased judicial activity.

The *Javins* court made a rulelike institutional substitution on another level. It declared the existence of an implied warranty of habitability in residential leases, thereby providing significant protection for residential tenants. But the *Javins* court avoided the task of setting the level of expected quality by substituting the determination of the political process in the form of the District of Columbia Housing Code. Whatever the wisdom of this strategy – as always a complex issue of institutional choice among imperfect alternatives – it had the advantages of greater certainty and reduced strain on judicial resources and competence.

sitions and the weakest rights and most restrained positions involve rules and allocate decision making away from the courts.

As a general matter, as numbers and complexity increase, we can expect increased ambivalence – and, therefore, increased cycling – in the choice between rules and standards within areas of law, within given appellate courts, and even for given judges. As numbers and complexity increase, each alternative grows more unattractive in an absolute sense and, therefore, the institutional choices inherent in the choice between rules and standards become increasingly unattractive. Even the best choice will not work well. There is a natural tendency to move away from a solution that does not work well – even if it is the best choice. There will be an increasing tendency to drop the unattractive choice for what appears to be a better choice, but may often just be another unattractive alternative.

Although this cycling may be understandable, it is costly. It decreases stability and certainty, increases the expenditure of societal resources to adjust to these changes, and deters important transactions and productive activities. These costs will fall disproportionately on those least able to adjust – most likely those who are generally disadvantaged. Adjusting to change is subject to the same parameters of participation we have seen in operation throughout this book. Once again, higher stakes players or those with lower information and organization costs can be expected to adjust more quickly and easily to change. This costly cycling can be reduced only if judges and other societal decision makers gain greater sophistication about institutions and institutional choice.

As numbers and complexity increase, the strains of increasing demand and constrained supply may well produce a law of rules – but not the law of rules envisioned by the proponents of the Rule of Law. The resulting rules of law will be rules of judicial abdication produced by the inevitable effect of the demand for judicial resources outstripping the supply. The adjudicative process is both smaller than its institutional alternatives and less able to expand. As increasing numbers and complexity continue to increase demands on the courts, courts may do more in an absolute sense but still be forced to allocate a greater percentage of issues elsewhere. We can expect sweeping allocation of responsibility away from the courts to other institutions and, therefore, more rules of abdication. Under this law of rules, the stability, clarity, and protection against the excesses of government envisioned by the Rule of Law cannot come primarily from the courts.

Stable, reliable, and certain rules remain a pervasive vision of law. There is a connection between this view of the Rule of Law and the concept of the rules of the game that underlies many social science theories. Both institutional economists, like Douglass North, and neoclassical economists, like Harold Demsetz, envision law and rights as the rules of the game – as parameters of the market. In their view, the success of any economy is based largely on the existence of stable laws and rules and, in particular, the existence of stable laws and rules of private property.[5] Economic and other social science analyses often proceed on the assumption of fixed and stable rules of the game.

But, even in the most successful economies, these laws and rights – these rules of the game – are often not fixed and stable. They shift and cycle. Moreover, these shifts and cycles are often determined by the same factors that determine the behavior of the larger institutions that these rules of the game are supposed to control. Changes in numbers and complexity often similarly impact both the makers of the rules of the game and the institutions meant to be controlled by these rules. As we have seen throughout this book, the dynamics of both private and public law create serious problems for any analysis that assumes that there are fixed rules. However discomforting this picture, it is analytically valuable. Connecting the Rule of Law and the rules of the game with the increasing instability associated with increasing numbers and complexity provides a powerful link between legal analysis and social science analysis and should improve both.

There are basic lessons here for the establishment of the Rule of Law around the world. We are most likely to hear cries for a stable, clear, evenly applied Rule of Law in those situations where it will be most difficult to establish this sort of Rule of Law. Where numbers and complexity are high, the Rule of Law will be most demanded, but it will also be in the shortest supply. This does not mean that the adjudicative process cannot play a meaningful role in dealing with these tough conditions but the chances are that it can do so on a broad basis for only a short time and that any long-term role for serious judicial intervention will require narrowing the band of societal issues allocated to the courts.[6]

The choice of both this stop-gap period and the narrow focus for long-term rights will confront judges and constitution makers with those tough questions of political malfunction and judicial limitations we have considered throughout this book. They will have to be conscious of both the

---

[5] See North (1990) and Demsetz (1967).
[6] See Madaro (1998); Klug (2000); Shaffer (2001a, 2001b).

form and severity of the political malfunctions of their political processes, the dynamics of litigation, and the competence and resources of their courts. Nothing can be resolved by simplistic images of either the Rule of Law and the courts or of court substitutes. We can see the problematic nature of such thinking by examining the conceptions of institutions that underlie the views of both the proponents and opponents of the Rule of Law.

II. CONFRONTING THE SUPPLY SIDE: IMAGES AND REALITIES OF COURTS

U.S. property rights provide an intriguing, if disturbing, picture of the judicial role. Courts can and will only play strong roles on occasion and, in good part, on the margin. Part I of this book showed this pattern in traditional common law rights. The struggles of U.S. courts in reviewing land use regulation depicted in Part II underscored this message for constitutional law. Moreover, this judicial role can only diminish over time. As numbers and complexity increase, judicial activity will decrease relative to the activity of larger institutions such as the market and the political process. Any attempt to define a role for the courts faces a quandary of increasing proportions: The most serious need for judicial protection and legal rights will generally occur in those settings in which it is most difficult to deliver this protection.

Unfortunately, even otherwise sophisticated analysts overlook these fundamental insights. An important example is found in Joseph Raz's updating of F. A. Hayek's famous theory of the Rule of Law.[7] Hayek's Rule of Law focuses on fixed rules, certainty, and the ability of the citizenry to know and rely upon the actions of their government. It emphasizes what Raz refers to as the "popular conception of law" – general, open, and stable rules upon which people can rely:

The doctrine of Rule of Law does not deny that every legal system should consist of both general, open, and stable rules (the popular conception of law) and particular laws (legal orders), an essential tool in the hands of the executive and judiciary alike. As we shall see, what the doctrine requires is the subjection of particular laws to general, open, and stable ones. It is one of the important principles of the doctrine that *the making of particular laws should be guided by open and relatively stable general rules.*[8]

---

[7] Raz (1979), Chapter 11 commenting on Hayek (1944).
[8] Raz (1979), 213 (emphasis in the original).

Like many analysts of the Rule of Law, Raz sees the courts as central in securing these general rules. According to Raz, this task requires an independent judiciary with broad, but in Raz's view, limited powers of judicial review. Courts would review the full range of legislative and administrative actions, but only to assure that they are consistent with society's general rules. Raz alludes to two kinds of general rules: "[T]hose which confer the necessary powers for making valid orders and those which impose duties instructing the power-holders how to exercise their powers."[9] He also refers to such "principles of natural justice" as open and fair hearing and the absence of bias. Although this judicial review covers all governmental action, Raz believes it is "very limited review" because it merely ensures conformity to these general principles and rules.

Whatever Raz's hopes, however, the review he proposes cannot be both meaningful and limited. Even the most activist U.S. courts have been able to review only very limited categories of government actions. Moreover, as we have seen, the coverage of this review can only decline as numbers and complexity increase. Raz like many constitutional commentators believes that it will be relatively easy to determine whether and when there have been violations of basic principles. But, as Part II of this book made clear, if review is meant to be anything more than the enunciation of meaningless abstractions, the searching out and correction of violations of basic principles, even in narrow categories of governmental actions and even for a limited subset of principles, will be excruciatingly difficult.[10] One only needs to consider the discussion of the Takings Clause in Chapters 5 and 6. There we contemplated applying a single constitutional principle to the limited world of land use decisions and yet any serious judicial review promised to overwhelm judicial competence and capacity.

Raz's – and, more fundamentally, Hayek's – version of the Rule of Law again raises issues about rules and standards and, more basically, the distinction between judicial activism and judicial activity. They envision a Rule of Law built on strong, certain, and clear rules. They believe that clear rules are simple to expound and enforce. And they are – in a world of low numbers and complexity. But, as we have seen, this is the world in which the protections of law and the Rule of Law are least needed. Supply is easy, but demand is low.

---

[9] Id. at 216.
[10] Komesar (1994), especially Chapters 2, 3, 7, and 8, contains many other examples.

My problem with Hayek is not his deep affection for the organic market. I have no argument with the notion that markets have advantages in terms of organic and spontaneous adjustments, innovation, organization, and information generation. My problem with Hayek is that he assumes away the essential and difficult tasks of determining the extent of market and government roles and of determining who will make this judgment. The basic issue raised by Hayek's Rule of Law is who decides who decides.

Even if one were totally devoted to market determination, there remains the question of who will decide when and where government is valuable as a support or supplement to a functioning market. Hayek is not an anarchist. Like so many, he wants a minimal state. The role of the government in enforcing contracts and protecting property which forms the basis of this minimal state is neither self-enforcing nor self-evident in application and becomes less so as numbers and complexity grow. Who will determine the state's role? The framers of the constitution? The legislature? The courts? Informal community ties?

Where numbers and complexity are low, there is little reason to worry and little reason to need formal constraints on government. Where numbers and complexity are high, there is great need for such constraints but great difficulty in finding a means of defining and enforcing them. An abstract announcement of commitment to the market will not suffice. The issue here is not whether the market should make most of society's decisions. Even if we all agreed that it should, the issue is how to achieve such a result in a world of imperfect institutions at high numbers and complexity.

It is in the world of high numbers and complexity – the real world in which we live and to which these theories are meant to respond – where political processes malfunction, produce governmental excesses, and create a need for judicial action. But the same factors that increase demand for judicial action decrease its supply. For the reasons we discussed earlier in this chapter, these factors make it increasingly difficult to formulate and enforce simple rules. Once again it is invalid to respond to problems derived from a world of high numbers and complexity with solutions derived from a world of low numbers and complexity.

What is true for Hayek and for Raz's carefully constructed narrow version of the Rule of Law is even truer for Ronald Dworkin's broad-based version of the Rule of Law. Dworkin sees theories like Hayek's as "rule book" theories of the Rule of Law – theories that require only consistent adherence to a prescribed set of rules without asking about the justice of these rules.[11] Like Raz, Dworkin indicates that these narrow theories cannot promise justice. Dworkin further argues that in practice these approaches cannot be confined because inevitably the interpreter of these rules will be forced to extrapolate and, therefore, infuse the narrow sense of the Rule of Law with difficult judgments. In critiquing theories like Hayek's, Dworkin emphasizes the problems of judicial decision making under high numbers and complexity. But this realization does not carry over to his own theory. Here he finesses the problem with the seemingly simple distinction between principle and policy.

Dworkin's "rights" version of the Rule of Law is based on his fundamental position that legal decisions should be focused on rights or principles rather that on policy. In effect, judges should decide based on the impact on individuals rather than on notions of the general or collective welfare. Dworkin's version of the Rule of Law has been critiqued as largely empty of content[12] and I must admit that I find his basic position hard to follow in practice. It is difficult to imagine an adequate consideration of the general interest that does not focus on the impact on individuals or a just set of rights that fails to give attention to the implications of these individual rights for society. Dworkin's distinction between principles and policy can easily lend itself to tautological conclusions based on the existing list of rights.

These problems can be seen by applying Dworkin's theory of rights to the important issues of land use regulation discussed in Part II. How do we pick out the individuals to receive preferential rights treatment from the mass of people lumped together in the less protected general welfare? For the *Fasano* court, the individuals whose rights needed protection were the local homeowners harmed by the public decision to allow development. For the *Petaluma* and *Mt. Laurel* courts, the individuals in need of protection were the developers and those who would occupy the housing stymied by the public decision to constrain development. Dworkin's approach does not have any way to tell us who the right holders are or should be. He does not even have a device, like Radin's distinction between fungible and personal property (discussed in the last chapter), to aid us in deciding.

The real difference between rights and policy lies in the character of the decision maker, not in the character of the decision. The term "rights" signals those substantive decisions made by courts rather than by the po-

---

[11] Dworkin (1985), 11.   [12] See Shklar (1987), 12, 14–16.

litical process and, as such, it indicates an essential and demanding institutional choice. The normative issue raised by rights is when and what issues courts should decide. Society's response to that issue defines rights.

Dworkin faces the systemic aspects of his theory of rights only when forced to answer arguments of legitimacy. Confronted with the argument that important societal decisions should be made by elected officials, he defends a significant judicial role by pointing to failings in the political process.[13] As we have seen throughout this book, it is always accurate to describe the political process as defective. But it is also fundamentally insufficient. Nowhere does Dworkin consider the systemic characteristics of the adjudicative process to which he assigns so much responsibility. For Dworkin, that process is simply the judge – who Dworkin envisions as Herculean. Judges are embedded in an adjudicative process that relies on the dynamics of litigation to bring judges societal issues and on the adversarial process to inform them. This adjudicative process is constrained by its severely limited physical capacity as well as by the competence of its judges and juries. Moreover, as we have seen repeatedly, instances of severe political malfunction, like those Dworkin uses to justify a strong judicial role, are most likely to arise where problems with judicial decision making are most severe. Dworkin's version of the Rule of Law will remain empty until he addresses these institutional choices and the profound systemic issues that underlie them.

Constitutional scholarship is replete with images of judicial review that promise that courts can easily face and cure the most troubling forms of political malfunction. Whether it is establishing principles, reinforcing representation, securing fundamental rights, creating deliberative democracy or setting an agenda for discourse, the ease promised by these images is illusory. As we have seen repeatedly, the most severe and damaging forms of political malfunction arise in those occasions in which it is least likely that applying the rules, calling for deliberations, seeking consensus, or correcting process will be easy or even effective. The real-world problems that exhausted the resources and severely strained the competence of the dedicated and courageous court in *Mt. Laurel* cannot be overcome or even understood by devices like the distinction between principles and policy.

The problem is by now familiar. Notions of deliberation, consensus, and process fit neatly into the easy world of low numbers and complexity.

---

[13] Dworkin (1985), 23–8.

But this is not where courts, judicial review, and the Rule of Law are most needed. The structural forces triggered by increasing numbers and complexity mean that where courts are most needed they may also be most strained. The tension between the demand and supply sides means that understanding and projecting the role for courts requires eschewing attractive imagery and easy answers. These problems promise to haunt courts in both Western democracies and developing nations.

III. CONFRONTING THE DEMAND SIDE: COMMUNITARIANS VERSUS THE RULE OF LAW

Proponents of the Rule of Law see it producing equal treatment and protection against the excesses of government. Not surprisingly, critics see a different picture. Roberto Unger, one of the most prominent of these critics, argues that the Rule of Law serves the privileged by masking hierarchy and exploitation and by destroying precapitalist communities.[14] To some degree, this critique is similar to Carol Rose's more moderated criticism of Federalist formality and praise of localism discussed in the last chapter. Both these critiques of the Rule of Law favor a more communitarian vision of law. For Rose, the alternative is robust and informal localism and, for Unger, it is fraternal community. There are important lessons here concerning the importance of the two-force model as well as the fallacy of comparing noncomparable settings.

Modern proponents of the Rule of Law, such as the World Bank, see it as an antidote to severe political corruption like that recently observed in Russia and Indonesia where political officials line their own pockets (or Swiss bank accounts) and favor the well placed and privileged. On one level, turning to the Rule of Law as an antidote to this severe minoritarian bias seems straightforward and sensible. If public officials can be made to apply the same rules to all, including to the privileged few and to themselves, these problems of corruption would disappear. This is simply a version of the Golden Rule – the great internalizer. The problem here is that the Rule of Law – with its reliance on the courts – is poorly structured to deliver the equal treatment that would correct this political malfunction.

At first glance, courts seem well equipped to deliver equal treatment. Judicial procedures exclude or at least reduce informal contact, informal prior relationships with decision makers and previously obtained special knowledge. This insulation would seem to preclude special interests well

---

[14] Unger (1976).

placed in the political process from exercising undue influence on judicial decision makers. But, as we have seen, these formal structures increase the cost of participation in the adjudicative process and, therefore, interact with the dynamics of litigation to preclude the dispersed and dormant majorities who are the victims of political corruption.

Even with the most independent judiciary, the worst forms of minoritarian bias will go uncorrected because they will go unlitigated.[15] It is possible to imagine judiciaries allowed to operate without litigants turning upon an openly corrupt political process. (Consider the Italian experience.) But the substantive issues would have to be particularly flagrant and obvious to be dealt with by an adjudicative process structurally insulated from informal sources of information and now bereft of even the aid of the adversarial process. The point is simple: Because the dynamics of litigation disfavor small, dispersed claims, the adjudicative process itself suffers from a structural minoritarian bias that makes it difficult for courts to correct minoritarian bias in the form of severe political corruption.[16]

The dynamics of adjudication provide a source of bias toward the privileged that does not require insidious motives. It is analogous to the minoritarian bias in the political process that produces the rent seeking that attracts liberals and libertarians to the Rule of Law. The Rule of Law is the rule of courts and, therefore, the systemic realities of the adjudicative process are essential in understanding the role of the Rule of Law.

This point provides a basis – without need to imagine evil motives or villains – to understand why critics like Unger and Rose are dubious about formal legal strategies. It also explains their affection for informal, unstructured communities. In many ways, minoritarian bias may be best corrected within the political process itself. But the need to understand the structure of institutions applies equally to the communitarian position.

The communitarian viewpoint moves us away from large-scale, formal decision makers to more informal, small-scale decision makers. It shifts us from minoritarian bias where high-stakes players are privileged to a system that hopefully better represents the dispersed majority – a system with lower cost, easier participation. But, as the local zoning experience portrayed in cases such as *Mt. Laurel* shows us, this form of correcting minoritarian bias creates increased possibility of majoritarian bias within the community and adverse effects on those outside. The reign of small communities may see the less privileged poorly represented and badly

---

[15] Consider the dynamics of individual and class actions discussed in Chapter 3.
[16] This point is discussed in greater detail in Komesar (1994), 136–8.

treated. The *Mt. Laurel* experience and, on a broader level, the experiences described by Russell Hardin show us that communities can produce distorted, biased results, and even atrocities.[17]

Once again, we are confronted with the realities of institutional choice at high numbers and complexity. High numbers and complexity produce a world in which neither the simple image of a frictionless Rule of Law or of caring communities fits comfortably. As numbers and complexity increase, the masking of hierarchies and the exploitation of the weak that so concern Unger are likely to be present in even the best available decision making. As such, Unger's critique becomes both increasingly accurate and increasingly irrelevant. Unless there is care for the institutional context, such critiques are destined to be nothing more than extended parades of horribles applicable to any of the available alternatives including the organic communities preferred by Unger and Rose.

The lessons of the two-force model and, in particular, the reality of majoritarian bias decrease the ability to equate the good with informality or even greater access to participation. In the world of high numbers and complexity in which we function, whether we choose the formal structures associated with the Rule of Law or the informal structures favored by communitarians critical of the Rule of Law depends on an assessment of the form of the political malfunction with which we are dealing. We are likely to need different responses for the political corruption in Indonesia than for the ethnic cleansing in the Balkans.

Exporting the Rule of Law or any other constitutional strategy requires us to understand how that strategy really works in its original context and how it will adapt. That means making judgments about the form of political malfunction and putting in place the most realistic countermeasures. This will involve difficult choices and the acceptance of the increased risk of other forms of political malfunction. U.S. constitutionalism, in its best light, can be seen as a combination of democratic localism as an antidote to minoritarian bias in national decision making and judicial review as an antidote to the resulting risk of majoritarian bias. Part II of this book shows how imperfectly the system works in the U.S. context. As I have shown elsewhere, the framers of the U.S. Constitution understood this trade-off and its difficulties.[18] Adaptation of U.S. constitution-

---

[17] See Hardin (1995).
[18] See Komesar (1994), 217–21.

alism for use elsewhere requires a similar appreciation for the balance between these two risks in the adapting nation.

IV. CONCLUSION

The Rule of Law is a widely employed notion appearing frequently in the popular press, political rhetoric, and scholarly work. But like the other vague images that seem to fuel legal and public policy analysis, it disintegrates in the face of serious comparative institutional analysis especially when one focuses attention on variables like numbers and complexity. At low numbers and complexity, the Rule of Law is easily accomplished but unnecessary. At high numbers and complexity, it is most needed and most problematic. Historically the Rule of Law was offered as a cure to serious excesses of the Crown and it is still offered for those purposes. But, like other approaches to law, the Rule of Law must be built upon the institutions of law and its reality and validity are dependent upon the real workings of and choices among these institutions.

Nations around the world – developed and less developed – must face the reality of societal institutions operating at high numbers and complexity. The Rule of Law depends on the workings of the courts and these courts cannot be assumed to be frictionless black boxes big enough and able enough to deliver society's needs for clarity, stability, and protection against the excesses of government. When and whether the courts and, therefore, the Rule of Law are the best strategies for providing these goals or any others is the essential issue and it cannot be addressed by assuming it away or by substituting attractive images appropriate, if at all, to simpler times and places. It can be adequately addressed only by considering the degree and form of political malfunction with which a nation must deal and the abilities and resources of the real adjudicative process available to deal with the issue. Determining whether and to what extent the Rule of Law will work for any nation always requires confronting these tough institutional choices. Although the correct choice will depend on local factors, the same questions about who participates and is represented and how this participation is impacted by numbers and complexity will be fundamental everywhere.

9

Changes

Tough institutional choices determine what law is and what it can be. These choices are tied to systemic factors like numbers and complexity. These choices and factors are as primal to understanding law as forces like gravity are to understanding nature. They are law's laws. Any relevant analysis of law must concentrate on these choices and factors and that necessitates transforming the way law is analyzed and taught.

I. CHANGING LEGAL ANALYSIS

Legal analysts, in general, focus on goals and values. Many books and articles about law spend most of their pages setting out and defending a view of the good usually by exploring the writings of a well-known philosopher such as Locke, Hegel, Kant, or Rawls. These explorations normally end with a program of court action, ostensibly based on the chosen goals. Debates rage about whether the goals are correctly described (your philosopher did not say that) or correctly chosen (my philosopher is better than your philosopher). But there is little about the character of the relevant institutions – the paths to these goals.

Many of these goal-based analyses depend on the implicit premise that there is a simple correlation between goals and institutions. Often they are animated by a deep aversion to a particular institution and a deep conviction that the goal they have espoused will insulate them from this institution. We have seen these positions exemplified in Richard Epstein's aversion to the rent-seeking, welfare state (discussed in Chapter 5) and Margaret Radin's aversion to the callous, atomistic market (discussed in Chapter 7).

But, in fact, virtually nothing follows from the choice of a goal. You cannot hardwire goals and institutions and, therefore, no program of law and public policy follows from goal choice. The simple correlations between goals and institutions that characterize so many ideological positions simply do not hold. Name any serious goal, define it well, defend it to the hilt and you are still a long way from law and public policy. You cannot address definitive questions of law and public policy such as liability versus no liability, regulations versus no regulations, and rights versus no rights. Dealing with every important issue from rules versus standards to capitalism versus socialism requires that you seriously address institutional choice.

Seriously addressing institutional choice means abandoning simplistic associations of goals and institutions. Institutional choice, at least institutional choice at high numbers and complexity, is filled with paradoxes and counterintuitive combinations of goals and institutions. Resource allocation efficiency and the protection of private property may best be achieved by a political process unrestrained by rights, while equality and communitarianism must increasingly rely on atomistic markets. Paradoxically, the dynamics of institutional choice often require that the most important goals will not be (and should not be) the subjects of strong rights and legal protection.

There is another prevalent short cut to institutional choice – one more directly concerned with institutions. Open most law reviews and books and you will find programs for judicial action generated by the evils in some other institution. The literature is replete with descriptions of the malfunctions, biases, and evils of the market or the political process and, in response, calls for judicial intervention. These arguments often show up as unsophisticated make-weights attached to goal-based analyses. But some are substantial and quite sophisticated – frequently borrowing from fields like welfare economics and public choice theory. Numbered here are some of the most prominent works in law.[1] The picture they paint of serious institutional problems is generally accurate. This is the demand side approach to the analysis of law, rights, and the judicial role.

But there is also a supply side approach that stresses the failings and malfunctions of the courts and calls for decreased judicial activity and a greater role for markets and political processes.[2] The harsh picture of the adjudicative process painted by these supply side analyses is also generally

---

[1] Included here are the works of Richard Posner and John Ely. I discuss these at length in Komesar (1994), Chapters 1, 2, and 7.

[2] See, e.g., Horowitz (1970); Huber (1985); Rosenberg (1991); Sugarman (1989).

accurate. Although still a minority view among legal scholars, this pessimism about the judiciary seems to be growing.

Both those promoting and decrying a larger role for the courts offer powerful pictures of the imperfections of the institutions they wish to replace. Moreover, these parades of horribles can only grow longer and more severe as numbers and complexity increase. But they also can only grow increasingly less relevant.

Neither judicial activism nor judicial restraint can be supported by an examination of the attributes of only one institution – by single institutionalism. Because institutions move together and tend to deteriorate as numbers and complexity increase, revelations even of severe institutional malfunction are of limited and decreasing relevance to public policy and law. The very existence of these two opposing single institutional literatures with their emphasis on the failings of markets and governments, on the one hand, or on the failings of the courts, on the other, shows that the only real way to define the role of the courts is institutional comparison.

The path of institutional choice and institutional comparison is necessary, but challenging. Analyzing law, rights, and the role of the courts entails facing a basic quandary: *The most serious need for judicial protection and legal rights will often occur in those settings in which it is most difficult to deliver this protection.* For too long, legal analysts have sought to sidestep this quandary by relying on a virtually inexhaustible supply of panaceas including minimal states, close-knit communities, deliberative courts, and the Rule of Law. But this quandary is systemic and cannot be avoided by distinctions between principle and policy or by imagining courts as promoting deliberation, reenforcing democracy or replicating communities or by any of the other simple and attractive images presently employed to carry debate. These attractive images are derived in the largely irrelevant world of low numbers and complexity. They have little relevance in the world of high numbers and complexity in which we live.

If we do not face the issue of institutional choice and the quandaries it poses, we will simply continue to cycle through the same panaceas. Today's panacea will be discarded when we discover its severe and increasing imperfections. But the substitute will be yesterday's discarded panacea whose imperfections we momentarily ignore perhaps because it is dressed in new verbiage. This useless cycling is more than wasteful. It can impose serious hardships on those who must adjust to the changes with the worst hardships saved for those least able to make adjustments – often those generally disadvantaged. Meaningful change is important. Empty cycling is destructive.

II. CHANGING LEGAL EDUCATION AND DISCOURSE

Although it cannot offer easy answers (because there are none), a comparative institutional approach to law and the role of the courts provides a powerful analytical framework that increases the understanding of law at all levels. It is a key to more powerful legal analysis and more meaningful legal education. Institutional choice and comparative institutional analysis can integrate all categories of law and legal inquiry. The same analytical questions arise and the same factors are relevant whether we are dealing with torts, contracts, procedure, administrative law, or constitutional law. Unconscionability and unconstitutionality are analytically parallel. Comparative institutional analysis has been used in this book to examine issues ranging from the choice of remedies for violation of common-law property rights to the role of class action to the lofty choice between private and common property to the meaning of constitutional protections like just compensation and equal protection. Elsewhere I have used it to examine issues ranging from tort reform to the growth of the bureaucracy to fundamental rights.[3] Others have used it to examine a wide array of legal subjects including international law,[4] corporate law,[5] environmental law,[6] patient's rights,[7] affirmative action,[8] separation of powers,[9] labor law,[10] intellectual property,[11] family law,[12] sports law,[13] urban sprawl,[14] and professional responsibilities.[15]

Most law – at least, most U.S. law – can be seen as a request to the courts to do something or to refrain from doing something – to substitute themselves for other decision makers or to be substituted for. Constitutional law, contract law, corporate law, administrative law, environmental law, civil procedure, and federal jurisdiction, to name a few, all centrally concern choices between courts and other institutions. Constitutions design the institutions of government and constitutional law is defined by choices among these institutions and, at least in the case of the U.S. Constitution, by hard choices between courts and the various levels and

---

[3] Komesar (1994).
[4] See Dunoff and Trachtman (1999); Sharer (2000); Trachtman (1996–97).
[5] See Fisch (2000); McDonnell (2000).
[6] See Cole (2000); Wagner (2000); Wiener (1999).
[7] See Palmer (1999).   [8] See Doherty (1999); Schwartz (2000).
[9] See Nourse (2000); Rossi (1999).   [10] See Dau-Schmidt (1996).
[11] See Rai (1999).   [12] See Knauer (1998).
[13] See Carstensen and Olszowka (1995).   [14] See Buzbee (2000).
[15] See Schneyer (1996); Wilkins (1996).

branches of the political process. As we have seen, the forces of supply and demand – the need for and limits on court intervention – define constructs like takings and equal protection. By its very nature, constitutional judicial review is institutional choice.

Similarly, administrative law requires courts to decide who will decide among markets, various political entities, and the courts themselves. Judicial review of the output of the bureaucracy under statutory authority is analytically analogous to constitutional judicial review. The severity and form of political malfunction and the constraints on the competence and physical capacity of the courts shape administrative law, leaving courts with some important decisions but forcing them to leave most to the political process.

Corporate law and contract law require courts to decide whether they or various market or transactional mechanisms will assess important questions concerning the allocation of resources. Corporate law is filled with concerns about market failures especially those inherent in the separation of management and ownership. Yet, for all this concern about market imperfections, courts generally avoid intervention in corporate decision making because of legitimate concerns about the limitations of the adjudicative process. The conjunction of these forces is most obvious in doctrines like the business judgment rule, but lies not far below the surface throughout corporate law. Contract law is replete with institutional choice ranging from the choice of remedies to issues about the validity of the contract such as unconscionability and issues about the allocation of risk by implied terms. In general, every area of law contains tough institutional choices and most are dominated by them.

Comparative institutional analysis is applicable to all levels of legal inquiry. It allows law students and lawyers to better recognize the strengths and weaknesses of any case or position, while providing a powerful framework for policy analysis by judges and legislators. Strategies for advocacy can be effectively constructed in comparative institutional terms. If you are asking courts to expand their role, stress the demand side: Show how badly the alternative system is doing. Sophisticated advocates must, therefore, know and understand political malfunction and market malfunction. If you want courts to back off, stress the supply side: Focus on the dire implications of judicial intervention – floods of cases, the substantive difficulty of the decisions, and the dangers of adjudicative mistakes. Sophisticated advocates must, therefore, understand the implications of the dynamics of litigation and the scale of the adjudicative process as well as the competence of judges and juries. Anyone seeking judicial intervention must be prepared to show courts that there is a way to control the strain on judicial competence and resources. Because able advocates must understand and be able to address both the strengths and weaknesses in their cases, they must understand the pros and cons of the institutional alternatives in each relevant context. Whether they are to become advocates, administrators, legislators, or judges, law students should leave law school with a deep understanding of society's institutions, their interaction, and their relative merits.

The role of institutional choice in legal analysis is sometimes straightforward and direct, but, in many instances, understanding it means translating doctrines that do not speak directly in comparative institutional terms. This translation provides a potent way to understand these traditional doctrines. At first blush, these doctrines seem to avoid the hard work of institutional comparison. The role of courts appears to follow from well-established legal constructs. Unequal bargaining power triggers judicial scrutiny of private contracts under the unconscionability doctrine, representativeness determines the availability of class actions and, as we have seen, the presence or absence of physical invasion dictates whether courts will balance impacts under the nuisance doctrine. Suspect classifications and fundamental rights dictate the role of courts in U.S. equal protection law. The takings of private property triggers judicial review of just compensation. On the broadest level, the construct of legitimacy delimits the judicial role in constitutionalism in general. Similar constructs are found throughout the law – both in the United States and elsewhere. Every area of law has doctrinal requirements or constructs that appear to define the role of the courts without recourse to careful comparison of the relative merits of institutions.

As one more carefully examines these constructs, however, a curious pattern appears. They seldom correspond to a straightforward construction based on the common meaning of their terminology. "Fundamental rights" do not cover all or even most of what is fundamental. The "taking of private property" falls far short of the full conceptual meaning of that term.[16] The term "suspect classification" omits many suspicious classifications.[17] "Physical invasion" excludes many physical invasions.[18] All these terms seem distorted and artificially limited.

---

[16] See the discussion of Richard Epstein's program for takings in Chapter 5.
[17] See Komesar (1994) at 213–16, 222–30.
[18] See the discussion at the end of Chapter 2.

There is, however, a straightforward way to understand the use of these terms in law. Reverse the causality. Although, in theory, these constructs define institutional choices, in reality, they are defined by them. As one examines their application, these constructs seem roughly based on considerations of institutional characteristics and the relative merits of judicial versus market or governmental decision making. Thus, although, in theory, constructs like physical invasion, unequal bargaining power, and fundamental rights define institutional choice, in reality, they are defined by institutional choice. They do not avoid institutional choice and comparison. They require them. If a doctrinal term seems vague, sophisticated lawyers should look to institutional choice and institutional comparison for guidance.

Courts have roughly reflected these tough institutional choices in doctrines and results. In that way, the courts have exceeded the grasp of many legal commentators who still operate from noninstitutional or at best single institutional analyses. On a normative level, however, the rough approximation of comparative institutional results implicit in doctrines and cases is no longer adequate. Judges and legal scholars must bring comparative institutional issues to the surface and integrate them into the determination of what law should be. All analysts of law must learn to speak openly and sophisticatedly about the institutional choices that are the core of law. This change in the way we think and talk about law should begin with changes in the way we train lawyers. Before addressing what this analytical change means for the future of the law, however, I want to address its implications for the economic analysis of law and public policy and for law beyond the United States.

III. CHANGING ECONOMICS

My approach to understanding institutions and institutional choice is economic. I have emphasized the importance of participation and cast institutional malfunction primarily in terms of distortions in the pattern of participation. Participation stands at the core of resource allocation efficiency and the economic sense of institutions and is the essence of basic economic constructs like externalities and transaction costs. As we have seen, participation also stands at the core of many noneconomic conceptions ranging from equality of opportunity to communitarianism and the Rule of Law. It provides a robust and largely unexplored connection between economics and other approaches to law and public policy.

The model of institutional participation I use in this book is also economic. Institutional participation is determined by the interaction between the benefits and costs of that participation. The benefit side focuses on the characteristics of the distribution of benefits across the relevant populations. The cost side focuses on the costs of participating in the institutions – transaction costs, litigation costs, political participation costs – and, in turn, on the costs of organization and information. The origins of this view of institutions lie in the economics literature. Ronald Coase's transaction cost approach to the organization of production emphasized the cost of information and organization in understanding institutional activity in general and transacting in particular.[19] The emphasis on the distribution of stakes can be traced to Mancur Olson's work on collective action.[20] Some noneconomists may see this economic approach as too sparse,[21] but I believe it provides a powerful analytical framework with which to organize analysis of law and public policy. It asks essential first questions and supplies an organizing framework capable of integrating other considerations.

But my stress on comparative institutional analysis rather than single institutional analysis represents a fundamental difference with the conventional economic approach to law and public policy. Economic analysts of law and public policy rely on single institutional concepts like market failure derived from welfare economics and even define resource allocation efficiency in single institutional terms. Paradoxically, this conventional economic approach to law and public policy violates the most basic tenets of economics.

A single institutional approach to analyzing law and public policy is incompatible with the notion of rational choice that underlies economic analysis. Although there is much debate both within economics and between economists and others about the degree of rationality and knowledge assumed by economics, it is unassailable that rational people – no matter how bounded that rationality – do not generally make choices by considering only one alternative. Choice among alternatives is the foundation of fundamental economic concepts such as opportunity costs and the role of substitutes and complements.

As this book shows, a single institutional approach cannot even be justified as a low-cost first approximation of comparative institutional

---

[19] Coase (1937); Coase (1960).   [20] Olson (1965).   [21] See, e.g., Rubin (1995).

analysis. The tendency of all institutions to move together and to deteriorate as numbers and complexity increase obviates such a role. At high
numbers and complexity, severely imperfect and deteriorating institutions
will often be the best choices.

The issue of institutional choice is already an integral part of most economic analyses of law and public policy. It is too late to deny it a place. But
having opened the door to institutional choice, economists cannot legiti-
mately approach the subject via single institutional analysis. That single institutional analysis is easier than comparative institutional analysis may
explain the prevalence of the single institutional approach to economics
and the prevalence of single institutional approaches in general. But it
does not justify them. Cheap but useless is neither rational choice nor good
economics. To be true to economics as well as to be relevant, the economic
analysis of law and, more broadly, the economic analysis of public policy
must be comparative institutional.

IV. LAW AROUND THE WORLD

In this book, I have told the story of law and courts mainly in terms of U.S.
law and U.S. courts. But the role of courts and court-made law is a subject
of increasing importance outside the United States. Captured in phrases
like the Rule of Law and constitutionalism, interest in constitutional
rights and constitutional judicial review is surfacing around the globe.
Any nation contemplating constitutional change and an increased role for
courts and rights must understand and deal with both those forces that
create the need for rights and those forces that limit rights – with both
supply and demand.

On the demand side, constitution makers must carefully assess both
the form and the extent of the relevant political malfunctions. Devices
and strategies meant to control the power of the many can create overrepresentation of the few and vice versa. The U.S. Constitution focuses
primarily on the evils of majoritarian bias and the debate that surrounded
its enactment and ratification shows that this focus was hardly uncontro-
versial. As we have seen, that controversy continues today.

Majoritarian bias will not be the dominant fear everywhere. Minoritarian bias – manifested in severe form in the looting of the economy by
the ruling cadre – dominates many political processes. The problems in
Bosnia are not the problems in the Philippines. Effective constitutionalism necessitates a sophisticated but workable vision of the political

process that contemplates the role of varying interests and appreciates the possibility of both the power of the few and the power of the many.

On the supply side, constitution makers and legal analysts must recognize that the adjudicative process, like other institutions, is an intricate system where patterns of participation matter. They cannot simply focus on judges and their independence. The ability of the adjudicative process is constrained not just by the competence or substantive ability of judges, but also by the dynamics of litigation, which can limit or skew what judges see and decide, and by the limited physical capacity of the adjudicative process and its limited ability to grow.

Defining a meaningful role for courts and constitutional rights means jointly analyzing the forces of supply and demand in a serious and sophisticated manner. Judges and other constitutional decision makers must appreciate the manner in which the adjudicative process relates to these various political malfunctions.[22] Courts will inevitably face tough choices that merge the worst instances of political malfunction with the greatest strains on judicial resources. Any constitutional court worth respect will assume responsibility for some of these issues. None can confront all or even most. Courts will have to weigh both their ability to decide and the severity and form of political malfunction. That has been the experience of U.S. courts and, given increasing numbers and complexity, it will be seen more often both in the United States and elsewhere. All areas of constitutional law are, in reality, defined by compromises between supply and demand that are incompatible with the grand rhetoric that accompanies them.[23]

Whether the trajectory of U.S. court activity pictured in this book is equally applicable elsewhere is an issue of central importance. Nations vary in many ways including different levels of numbers and complexity. But some things are universal. Courts and constitutional drafters everywhere must deal with limited judicial resources and make difficult institutional choices.

The institutional dynamics that determine the role of U.S. courts seem to be working elsewhere. Faced with significant need for their services, courts around the world have played substantial roles, while, at the same time, confronting their own limitations. Recent work on the European

---

[22] For example, the dynamics of litigation may mean that courts generally match better with majoritarian bias than with minoritarian bias. See Komesar (1994), 136–8.

[23] See the discussion of Pentagon Papers case, *Korematsu,* and *Hampton* in Komesar (1994), 44–9, 210–13.

Court of Justice shows a court responding with creative judicial activism both to malfunction in the political processes of the states of Europe and to the weakness of the political branches of the European Union. Yet increasing strains on the resources and competence of the European Court of Justice, as well as the increasing ability of the European Union political branches, may be changing the role of the European Court of Justice.[24] Similarly, the highest court of South Africa played an important role in that nation's perilous constitutional transition. Again, however, that role may be changing in the face of shifts in systemic variables.[25] On the international level, the plight of the WTO shows the difficulties and importance of institutional choice in dramatic fashion. Skewed participation in national trade policies has generated the need for intervention in protection of world trade, but complex conflicts such as that between trade and the environment create both substantive difficulties and a concern for the true character of participation in the WTO itself.[26]

V. LAW'S FUTURE

The need to better understand the forces of institutional choice and their impact on law is increasing. All institutions tend to deteriorate in ability as numbers and complexity increase. Numbers and complexity are increasing. Population is growing and a global economy has broadened the relevant populations. Transactions, controversies, and interactions grow increasingly more complex as technologies of all sorts change.

I do not mean to suggest that either increased global interaction or rapid technological innovation are bad. The opposite is true. But growing choices and a growing realization of interconnections confront us with a more complex world or at least with a growing realization of the complexity of the world. The benefits associated with globalization and technology create the possibility of widespread impacts and a more tangled future. There will be an increasing number of real or perceived conflicts.

As we have seen, increased recognition of problems like the beach erosion in issue in *Lucas* or the strains on the environment raised in *Petaluma* and *Mt. Laurel* produce governmental responses that in some instances are socially beneficial, but in others simply cover illicit attempts

---

[24] See Maduro (1998).   [25] See Klug (2000).
[26] See Shaffer (2001a, 2001b).

to exclude. It becomes increasingly difficult for courts to determine which is true. The complexity of these issues – in part produced by innovation and a broadening community – places increasing strains on the alternative decision-making institutions involved. Increasing complexity means an increasing possibility of a skewed pattern of participation that creates problems ranging from misled consumers to apathetic voters.

Determining the role of courts in this world of increasing numbers and complexity and, in particular, determining how the resources of the tiny adjudicative process should be allocated faces legal analysts with a challenge of growing proportions. The challenge is unabashedly one of institutional choice and the choices grow increasingly more difficult. Courts by their nature cannot be expanded nearly as rapidly as the alternative institutions – the political process and the market. As numbers and complexity increase, all these institutions will deteriorate in ability. At the same time that the adjudicative process is deteriorating, however, it will be in greater demand because alternative societal decision makers – the political process and the market – are also deteriorating. Without serious change in the character of institutions, the search will be for the best of increasingly bad alternatives. In order to improve, courts will have to begin by admitting to themselves and to the larger community that they are in the business of institutional choice.

I recognize the risks for the courts in opening a dialogue that reveals the conditional and incomplete nature of revered notions like constitutional judicial review and constitutional rights. Like the Rule of Law with its rhetoric of openness, certainty, and stability, the existing culture of legal discourse depends on a rhetoric of rights phrased in terms of broad principles and important sounding values. I am asking judges and, indeed, the entire legal community to confront problems for which there may not presently be clearcut answers. There is a catch-22 here. These problems cannot be solved without a concerted effort by judges, scholars, and other members of the legal community. But judges and scholars seem reluctant to admit to and, therefore, to confront these challenging issues without the comfort of evident answers.

It is understandable that judges would want to suppress these issues because of the open-ended inquiry they portend and because judges must provide and defend answers in each case they face. It is less understandable for legal scholars who have no such immediate responsibility. Even for judges, however, these issues are increasingly unavoidable. Difficult issues of institutional choice are present in every case and are being decided even if they are not being addressed. The cacophony in judicial opinions and in the pages of the journals already reveals the absence of easy answers. Neither judges nor commentators will agree among themselves on a single picture of institutional choice. But they must begin to consistently speak and think in these terms. All the pretense about original intent[27] and fundamental values and all the reliance on simplistic images of the Rule of Law or of community only get in the way of constructing a meaningful jurisprudence and a meaningful conception of law and rights.

VI. BREAKING THE CYCLE

Recasting legal discourse, analysis, and education in institutional terms provides an opportunity not just a challenge. A focus on institutional choice and the use of comparative institutional analysis clarifies. It enlightens legal doctrine and sharpens both advocacy and planning. We can now see the character of laws, rights, and regulations from a wholly different perspective. Rather than rights and regulations determining the allocation of decision-making responsibility, it is the opposite: Institutional choice determines the character of rights and regulations.

We now have the basic building blocks of law. The true meaning and quality of laws, rights, and regulations lie in understanding the dynamics of participation in political processes, markets, communities, and courts, and the impact of systemic variables like numbers and complexity. Once one sees that institutional choice is present in virtually every major legal issue, it becomes easier to understand and evaluate legal decisions. This is the story of Parts I and II of this book. Focusing legal education on institutional choice and institutional comparison provides a powerful analytical framework to prepare students to represent private clients, governments, the underrepresented, and the public interest, and to assume their roles as judges, government officials, and community leaders.[28]

Comparative institutional analysis also provides a powerful tool of criticism or deconstruction and, in turn, of reconstruction. As I have shown throughout this book, it allows one to go to the heart of seemingly disparate tracts and find common issues and basic flaws. Although often

---

[27] For a sophisticated look at the original intent of the Takings Clause based on institutional considerations, see Treanor (1995).

[28] Institutional choice also provides a natural way to reorganize courses and course materials. For a recent attempt to organize property materials around a comparative institutional theme, see Dwyer and Menell (1998).

unaddressed, central issues of institutional choices are always there. When you spot the issues of institutional choice and the (usually implicit) assumptions the author is making about them, you have the basis for insightful critique. If, as is often the case, the author is assuming a perfect or frictionless alternative, the analysis is largely dead in the water without even the need to critically examine the author's goals or values. If there is a superficial comparative institutional analysis without concern for issues such as participation and numbers and complexity across the alternatives, you can point out and correct this defect, and improve the analysis.

These flaws infect even the most prominent works, and a reader who can identify and diagnose them can then take the best parts of these works and construct newer and better analyses. If, as I suspect, common ideological positions imply not only an affection for a goal but also a strong sense that that goal means the rejection of certain institutional alternatives, then a deeper understanding of comparative institutional analysis will militate against many existing ideological positions and open debate along fronts previously cut off.[29] Analysts extricated from simplistic and mistaken connections between goals and institutions will be free to create new solutions and new allegiances.

Although issues of institutional choice lie at the core of law and rights of all kinds and in all places, constructing a jurisprudence capable of dealing with these issues means addressing many controversial questions. I have asserted that numbers and complexity are growing. But that is hardly incontestable. Technological changes in communication and data processing make information cheaper and more available. Whether even these technological changes decrease complexity, however, depends on the extent to which the decreased cost of information operates to expand opportunities and activities. To the extent that it does, our lives may be better but more complicated. We may in effect know more but be more ignorant because there is simply more to know. Whether and to what extent technological change operates to complicate rather than simplify issues and make us better or worse participants in society's institutional processes will likely vary with the technology, the institution, the issue, and the society.

Similarly, my assertion that courts cannot be increased in size easily or at least as easily as markets and political processes may reflect a lack of

---

[29] Consider the discussion of the ideologies of Margaret Radin and Richard Epstein in Chapter 8.

imagination and my assertion that local governments are subject to majoritarian bias or even that they are more likely to be subject to majoritarian bias is controversial. For reasons I have set out, I believe all these assertions. But they are refutable and may be refuted. What is irrefutable, however, is that these and other issues of institutional choice must be addressed. To refute my assertions, you must focus on systemic forces and on institutional choice and comparison.

The systemic forces that underlie the demand for and supply of law and rights will not go away. Their power grows. The role of courts and the realities of legal rights and of the Rule of Law are dictated by these forces whether we like it or not. Institutional choices are being made everywhere and continuously. The only issue is how well they will be made. That depends on how willing we are to confront the task of institutional comparison.

Legal scholars will have to abandon familiar and comfortable modes of analysis and face the challenging task of employing and even constructing new analytical tools. Failing to do so will leave legal analysis in limbo. I have suggested in this book that, as numbers and complexity increase and the choice is among increasingly less attractive alternative institutions, there will be an unfortunate impetus for cycling among panaceas in general and judicial strategies in particular. This sort of cycling can be found throughout legal scholarship.

A provocative and intriguing example is reflected in recent contrarian examinations of U.S. constitutional judicial review. Two sophisticated works have recently concluded that constitutional judicial review should be jettisoned or at least severely diminished.[30] Given increasing numbers and complexity and the strain they place on all institutions along with the severe constraints facing the adjudicative process, it is hardly surprising that the reality of constitutional judicial review falls far short of the high aspirations of so many constitutional scholars. These contrarian treatments offer a needed antidote to the largely perfectionist images of the courts painted by many constitutional commentators. But these works also reflect the tendency of legal scholarship to constantly look for sweeping and dramatic solutions that first raise an institutional alternative to unrealistic heights and then discard it when it reveals its deeply imperfect character.

---

[30] Rosenberg (1991); Tushnet (1999).

Before we discard constitutional judicial review or any other viable (albeit highly imperfect) alternative, we must confront the reality that the best choices will be highly imperfect and that the relative merits of institutions will vary across different settings. Constitutional judicial review may serve some nations and some societal issues within any nation better than others. That requires confronting the difficult but essential task of dealing more carefully with these distinctions and choices. The comparative institutional framework proposed in this book with its emphasis on the dynamics of participation provides a place to start.

All the easy roads to institutional choice – goal choice, ideology, original intent, simple imagery, and single institutionalism – are dead ends. The real road to the analysis of law and public policy has yet to be explored. Its exploration will require the patience to struggle with the unknown and the imperfect and the willingness to forego the facade of easy answers. Some of us have tried to show that taking institutions seriously can sharpen the understanding of what law is and what it can be. Imagine the insights if the legal community as a whole turned its vast talents to the subject. Much depends on just such an allocation of intellectual resources. To a significant degree, our willingness to explore the limits of the law will determine what those limits will be.

References

Ackerman, Bruce, *The Rise of World Constitutionalism*, 83 VA. L. REV. 771 (1997)

Agresto, John, THE SUPREME COURT AND CONSTITUTIONAL DEMOCRACY (1984)

American Bar Ass'n Section of Litigation, CLASS ACTIONS: IN THE WAKE OF EISEN III & IV (1977)

Anderson, Robert M., *The Board of Zoning Appeals: Villain or Victim*, 13 SYRACUSE L. REV. 353 (1962)

B.N.A., DIRECTORY OF STATE AND FEDERAL COURTS, JUDGES AND CLERKS (2000)

Barzel, Yoram, ECONOMIC ANALYSIS OF PROPERTY RIGHTS (1989)

Been, Vicki, *"Exit" as a Constraint on Land Use Exactions: Rethinking the Unconstitutional Conditions Doctrine*, 91 COLUM. L. REV. 473 (1991)

Been, Vicki & Francis Gupta, *Coming to the Nuisance or Going to the Barrios? A Longitudinal Analysis of Environmental Justice Claims*, 24 ECOLOGY L.Q. 1 (1997)

Berger, Michael M., Lucas v. South Carolina Coastal Council: *Yes, Virginia, There Can Be Partial Takings*, in TAKINGS: LAND-DEVELOPMENT CONDITIONS AND REGLATORY TAKINGS AFTER DOLAN AND LUCAS 148 (David L. Callies, ed., 1996)

Bernstein, Lisa, *The Silicon Valley Lawyer as Transaction Cost Engineer?*, 74 OR. L. REV. 239 (1995)

Bryden, Roderick M., *Zoning: Rigid, Flexible, or Fluid?*, 44 J. URB. L. 287 (1967)

Buzbee, William W., *Sprawl's Dynamics: A Comparative Institutional Analysis Critique*, 35 WAKE FOREST L. REV. 509 (2000)

Calabresi, Guido & A. Douglas Melamed, *Property Rules, Liability Rules and Inalienability: One View of the Cathedral*, 85 Harv. L. Rev. 1089 (1972)

Callies, David L., ed., TAKINGS: LAND-DEVELOPMENT CONDITIONS AND REGULATORY TAKINGS AFTER DOLAN AND LUCAS (1996)

Callies, David L., *Regulatory Takings and the Supreme Court: How Perspectives on Property Rights Have Changed from* Penn Central *to* Dolan, *and What State and Federal Courts are Doing About It*, 28 STETSON L. REV. 523 (1999)

Carrington, Paul D. et al., JUSTICE ON APPEAL (1976)

Carstensen, Peter C. & Paul Olszowka, *Antitrust Law, Student-Athletes, and the*

NCAA: Limiting the Scope and Conduct of Private Economic Regulation, 1995 Wis. L. Rev. 545 (1995)

Coase, Ronald H., *The Nature of the Firm,* 4 Economica 386 (1937)

Coase, Ronald H., *The Problem of Social Cost,* 3 J.L. & Econ. 1 (1960)

Coffee, John C., Jr., *The Regulation of Entrepreneurial Litigation: Balancing Fairness and Efficiency in the Large Class Action,* 54 U. Chi. L. Rev. 877 (1987)

Coffee, John C., Jr., *Class Wars: The Dilemma of the Mass Tort Class Action,* 95 Colum. L. Rev. 1343 (1995a)

Coffee, John C., Jr., *The Corruption of the Class Action: The New Technology of Collusion,* 80 Cornell L. Rev. 851 (1995b)

Cole, Daniel H., *The Importance of Being Comparative,* 33 Ind. L Rev. 921 (2000)

Committee on the Federal Courts of the New York State Bar Ass'n, *Improving Jury Comprehension in Complex Civil Litigation,* 62 St. John's L. Rev. 549 (1988)

Cramton, Roger C., *Individualized Justice, Mass Torts, and "Settlement Class Actions,"* 80 Cornell L. Rev. 811 (1995)

Currie, Daniel P. & Frank I. Goodman, *Judicial Review of Federal Administrative Action: The Quest for the Optimum Forum,* 75 Colum. L. Rev. 1 (1975)

Danzon, Patricia Munch, *An Economic Analysis of Eminent Domain,* 84 J. Pol. Econ. 473 (1976)

Dau-Schmidt, Kenneth G., *Employment Security: A Comparative Institutional Debate,* 74 Tex. L Rev. 1645 (1996)

Demsetz, Harold, *Toward a Theory of Property Rights,* 57 Am. Econ. Rev. Papers & Proceedings 347 (May 1967)

Doherty, Benjamin A., *Creative Advocacy in Defense of Affirmative Action: A Comparative Institutional Analysis of Proposition 209,* 1999 Wis. L. Rev. 91 (1999)

Donohue, John J. III & Peter Siegelman, *The Changing Nature of Employment Discrimination Litigation,* 43 Stan. L. Rev. 983 (1991)

Downs, Anthony, Opening Up The Suburbs (1973)

DuBois, Philip L. & Floyd F. Feeney, Improving the California Initiative Process: Options for Change (1992)

Dukeminer, Jesse, Jr., & Clyde L. Stapleton, *The Zoning Board of Adjustment: A Case Study In Misrule,* 50 Ky. L.J. 273 (1962)

Dukeminier, Jesse & James E. Krier, Property (1988)

Dunoff, Jeffrey L. & Joel P. Trachtman, *Economic Analysis of International Law,* 24 Yale J. Int'l L. (1999)

Dworkin, Ronald, A Matter of Principle (1985)

Dwyer, John P. & Peter S. Menell, Property Law and Policy – A Comparative Institutional Perspective (1998)

Elhauge, Einer R., *Does Interest Group Theory Justify More Intrusive Judicial Review?* 101 Yale L.J. 31 (1991)

Elinor, Ostrom, Governing the Commons – The Evolution of Institutions for Collective Action (1990)

Ellickson, Robert C., Order Without Law: How Neighbors Settle Disputes (1991)

Ellickson, Robert C., *Suburban Growth Controls: An Economic and Legal Analysis,* 86 YALE L.J. 385 (1977)

Ellickson, Robert C., *Property in Land,* 102 YALE L.J. 1315 (1993)

Epstein, Richard A., TAKINGS: PRIVATE PROPERTY AND THE POWER OF EMINENT DOMAIN (1985)

Epstein, Richard A., *Why is this Man A Moderate? Regulatory Takings: Law, Economics and Politics,* 94 MICH. L. REV. 1758 (1996)

Farber, Daniel A., *Public Choice and Just Compensation,* 9 CONST. COMMENT. 279 (1992)

Farnsworth, Ward, *Do Parties to Nuisance Cases Bargain After Judgment? A Glimpse Inside the Cathedral,* 66 U. CHI. L. REV. 373 (1999)

Fisch, Jill E., *The Peculiar Role of the Delaware Courts in the Competition for Corporate Charters,* 68 U. CIN. L. REV. 1061 (2000)

Fischel, William A., REGULATORY TAKINGS (1995)

Fountaine, Cynthia L., Note, *Lousy Law Making: Questioning the Desirability and Constitutionality of Legislating by Initiative,* 61 SO. CAL. L. REV. 733 (1988)

Franck, Thomas M., *The Emerging Right to Democratic Governance,* 86 AM. J. INT'L L. 46 (1992)

Frank, Jerome, LAW AND THE MODERN MIND (1936)

Freilich, Robert H., Elizabeth A. Garvin, & Duane A. Martin, *Regulatory Takings: Factoring Partial Deprivations into the Taking Equation in* TAKINGS: LAND-DEVELOPMENT CONDITIONS AND REGULATORY TAKINGS AFTER DOLAN AND LUCAS 165 (David L. Callies, ed., 1996)

Gilson, Ronald J., *Value Creation by Business Lawyers: Legal Skills and Asset Pricing,* 94 YALE L.J. 239 (1984)

Haar, Charles M., *In Accordance with a Comprehensive Plan,* 68 HARV. L. REV. 1154 (1955a)

Haar, Charles M., *The Master Plan: An Impermanent Constitution,* 20 LAW & CONTEMP. PROBS. 353 (1955b)

Haar, Charles M., SUBURBS UNDER SIEGE – RACE, SPACE, AND AUDACIOUS JUDGES (1996)

Hardin, Garrett, *The Tragedy of the Commons,* 162 SCIENCE 1243 (1968)

Hardin, Russell, ONE FOR ALL – THE LOGIC OF GROUP CONFLICT (1995)

Hayek, F.A., THE ROAD TO SERFDOM (1944)

Henderson, James A., Jr., *Comment: Settlement Class Actions and the Limits of Adjudication,* 80 CORNELL L. REV. 1014 (1995)

Hensler, Deborah, et al., PRELIMINARY RESULTS OF THE RAND STUDY OF CLASS ACTION LITIGATION (1997)

Hetzel, Otto J. & Kimberly A. Gough, *Assessing the Impact of* Dolan v. City of Tigard *on Local Governments' Land-Use Powers, in* PRELIMINARY RESULTS OF THE RAND STUDY OF CLASS ACTION LITIGATION 235 (Deborah Hensler, et. al., 1997)

Horowitz, Donald, THE COURTS AND SOCIAL POLICY (1970)

Houck, Oliver A., *Ending the War: A Strategy to Save America's Coastal Zone,* 47 MD. L. REV. 358 (1988)

Hricik, David, *The 1998 Mass Tort Symposium: Legal Ethical Issues at the Cutting Edge of Substantive and Procedural Law,* 17 REV. LITIG. 419 (1998)

Huber, Peter, *Safety and the Second Best: The Hazards of Public Risk Management in the Courts,* 88 COLUM. L. REV. 277 (1985)

Huber, Peter, LIABILITY: THE LEGAL REVOLUTION AND ITS CONSEQUENCES (1988)

Huffman, James L., *Lucas: A Small Step in the Right Direction,* 23 ENVTL. L. 901 (1993)

Hwang, Dennis J., *Shoreline Setback Regulations and the Takings Analysis,* 13 U. HAW. L. REV. 1 (1991)

Inman, Robert P. & Daniel L. Rubinfeld, *The Judicial Pursuit of Local Fiscal Equity,* 92 HARV. L. REV. 1662 (1979)

Johnson, Judith J., *Rebuilding the Barriers: The Trend in Employment Discrimination Class Actions,* 19 COLUM. HUMAN RTS. L. REV. 1 (1987)

Jordan, Ellen R., *Specialized Courts: A Choice?,* 76 NW. U.L. REV. 745 (1981)

Kaplow, Louis & Steven Shavell, *Property Rules Versus Liability Rules: An Economic Analysis,* 109 HARV. L. REV. 713 (1996)

Kennedy, Duncan, *Form and Substance in Private Law Adjudication,* 89 HARV. L. REV. 1685 (1976)

Kirp, David L., John P. Dwyer, & Larry A. Rosenthal, OUR TOWN (1995)

Klug, Heinz, UNIVERSAL PRINCIPLES, LOCAL PRISM – SOUTH AFRICA'S CONSTITUTIONAL TRANSITION IN GLOBAL PERSPECTIVE (2000)

Kmiec, Douglas W., *At Last, The Supreme Court Solves the Takings Puzzle,* 19 HARV. J.L. & PUB. POL'Y. 147 (1995)

Knauer, Nancy J., *Domestic Partnership and Same-Sex Relationships: A Marketplace Innovation and a Less than Perfect Institutional Choice,* 7 TEMPLE POL. & CIV. RTS. L. REV. 337 (1998)

Komesar, Neil K., *Housing, Zoning, and the Public Interest, in* PUBLIC INTEREST LAW 218 (Burton Weisbrod, Joel Handler, & Neil K. Komesar, eds., 1978)

Komesar, Neil K., IMPERFECT ALTERNATIVES: CHOOSING INSTITUTIONS IN LAW, ECONOMICS AND PUBLIC POLICY (1994)

Komesar, Neil K., *Law's Laws: The Supply and Demand of Rights, in* BEYOND THE REPUBLIC: MEETING THE CHALLENGES TO CONSTITUTIONALISM (2000)

Koniak, Susan P., *Feasting While the Widow Weeps:* Georgine v. Amchem Products, Inc., 80 CORNELL L. REV. 1045 (1995)

Koniak, Susan P. & George M. Cohen, *Under Cloak of Settlement,* 82 VA. L. REV. 1051 (1996)

Krasnowiecki, Jan Z., *Abolish Zoning,* 31 SYRACUSE L. REV. 719 (1980)

Krier, James E. & Steward J. Schwab, *Property Rules and Liability Rules: The Cathedral in Another Light,* 70 N.Y.U. L. REV. 440 (1995)

Krotoszynski, Ronald J., Jr., *Fundamental Property Rights,* 85 GEO. L.J. 555 (1997)

Kunstler, James, *Home From Nowhere,* THE ATLANTIC MONTHLY, September 1996

Laffont, Jean Jacques & Jean Tirole, COMPETITION IN TELECOMMUNICATIONS (THE MUNICH LECTURES) (1999)

Lessig, Lawrence, CODE AND OTHER LAWS OF CYBERSPACE (1999)

Levmore, Saul, *Just Compensation and Just Politics,* 22 CONN. L. REV. 285 (1990)

Levmore, Saul, *Unifying Remedies: Property Rules, Liability Rules, and Startling Rules,* 106 YALE L.J. 2149 (1997)

Luneberg, William J. & Mark Nordenberg, *Specially Qualified Juries and Expert Nonjury Tribunals: Alternative for Coping with the Complexities of Modern Civil Litigation,* 67 VA. L. REV. 887 (1981)

Macaulay, Stewart, *Noncontractual Relations in Business: A Preliminary Study,* 28 AM. SOCIOLOGICAL REV. 55 (1963)

Macey, Jonathan R. & Geoffrey P. Miller, *The Plaintiffs' Attorney's Role in Class Actions and Derivative Litigation: Economic Analysis and Recommendation for Reform,* 58 U. CHI. L. REV. 1 (1991)

MacNeil, Ian R., *Relational Contract: What We Do and Do Not Know,* 1985 WIS. L. REV. 483 (1985)

Maduro, Miguel Poiares, WE THE COURT – THE EUROPEAN COURT OF JUSTICE AND THE EUROPEAN ECONOMIC CONSTITUTION (1998)

Magleby, David B., DIRECT LEGISLATION: VOTING ON BALLOT PROPOSITIONS IN THE UNITED STATES (1984)

Mandelker, Daniel R., *Investment-Backed Expectations in Takings Law, in* TAKINGS: LAND-DEVELOPMENT CONDITIONS AND REGULATORY TAKINGS AFTER DOLAN AND LUCAS 119 (David L. Callies, ed., 1996)

Martin, Douglas, *The Rise and Fall of the Class Action Law Suit,* N.Y. TIMES, Jan. 8, 1988

McDonnell, Brett, *ESOPs' Failures: Fiduciary Duties When Managers of Employee-Owned Companies Vote to Entrench Themselves,* 2000 COLUM. BUS. L. REV. 1999 (2000)

Meador, Daniel J., *An Appellate Court Dilemma and a Solution through Subject Matter Organization,* 16 U. MICH. J.L. REF. 471 (1983)

Meltz, Robert, et. al., THE TAKINGS ISSUE: CONSTITUTIONAL LIMITS ON LAND USE CONTROL AND ENVIRONMENTAL REGULATION (1999)

Menkel-Meadow, Carrie, *Ethics and the Settlement of Mass Torts: When the Rules Meet the Road,* 80 CORNELL L. REV. 1159 (1995)

Merrill, Thomas W., *Trespass, Nuisance, and the Costs of Determining Property Rights,* 14 J. LEGAL STUD. 13 (1985)

Michelman, Frank I., *Property, Utility, and Fairness: Comments on the Ethical Foundations of "Just Compensation" Law,* 80 HARV. L. REV. 1165 (1967)

Mullenix, Linda S., *Mass Tort as Public Law Litigation: Paradigm Misplaced,* 88 NW. U. L. REV. 579 (1994)

Nagel, Robert F., *Liberals and Balancing,* 63 U. COLO. L. REV. 319 (1992)

North, Douglass C., INSTITUTIONS, INSTITUTIONAL CHANGE AND ECONOMIC PERFORMANCE (1990)

Nourse, Victoria, *The Vertical Separation of Powers,* 49 DUKE L.J. 749 (2000)

Olson, Mancur, THE LOGIC OF COLLECTIVE ACTION (1965)

Ostrom, Elinor, GOVERNING THE COMMONS – THE EVOLUTION OF INSTITUTIONS FOR COLLECTIVE ACTION (1990)

Palay, Thomas, *Relational Contracting, Transaction Cost Economics and the Governance of HMOs,* 59 TEMP. L.Q. 927 (1986)

Palmer, Larry I., *Patient Safety, Risk Reduction, and the Law,* 36 Hous. L. Rev. 1609 (1999)

Permut, Michael & Lee Snead, *Coastal Erosion Presents Land Title, Beach Use Issues,* N.Y. Law J., August 24, 1998, § 7, at col.1

Pierce, Richard J., Jr., *Public Utility Regulatory Takings: Should the Judiciary Attempt to Police the Political Institutions?,* 77 Geo. L.J. 2031 (1989)

Polinsky, A. Mitchell, *Resolving Nuisance Disputes: The Simple Economics of Injunctive and Damage Remedies,* 32 Stan. L. Rev. 1075 (1980)

Posner, Eric A., *"The Regulation of Groups: The Influence of Legal and Nonlegal Sanctions on Collective Actions,"* 63 U. Chi. L. Rev. 133 (1996)

Posner, Richard A., The Federal Courts: Crisis and Reform (1985)

Posner, Richard A., Economic Analysis of Law (4th ed. 1992)

Posner, Richard A., Economic Analysis of Law (5th ed. 1998)

Radin, Margaret Jane, *Property and Personhood,* 34 Stan. L. Rev. 957 (1982)

Rai, Arti K., *Intellectual Property Rights in Biotechnology: Addressing New Technology,* 34 Wake Forest L. Rev. 827 (1999)

Raz, Joseph, The Authority of Law – Essays on Law and Morality (1979)

Reps, John W., *Discretionary Powers of the Board of Zoning Appeals,* 20 Law & Contemp. Prob. 280 (1955)

Revesz, Richard L., *Specialized Courts and the Administrative Lawmaking System,* 139 U. Pa. L. Rev. 1111 (1990)

Rose, Carol M., *Planning and Dealing: Piecemeal Land Use Controls as a Problem of Local Legitimacy,* 71 Cal. L. Rev. 837 (1983)

Rose, Carol M., *New Models for Local Land Use Decisions,* 79 Nw. U.L. Rev. 1155 (1984–85)

Rose, Carol M., Property and Persuasion: Essays on the History, Theory and Rhetoric of Ownership (1994)

Rosenberg, Gerald N., The Hollow Hope: Can Courts Bring About Social Change? (1991)

Rosenberg, Ronald H., *Referendum Zoning: Legal Doctrine and Practice,* 53 U. Cinn. L. Rev. 381 (1983)

Rossi, Jim, *Institutional Design and the Lingering Legacy of Antifederalist Separation of Powers Ideals in the States,* 52 Vand. L. Rev. 1167 (1999)

Rubin, Edward L., *Institutional Analysis and the New Legal Process,* 1995 Wis. L. Rev. 463 (1995)

St. Amand, Lisa A., *Sea Level Rise and Coastal Wetlands: Opportunities for a Peaceful Migration,* 19 B.C. Envtl. Aff. L. Rev. 1 (1991)

Scalia, Antonin, *The Rule of Law as a Law of Rules,* 56 U. Chi. L. Rev. 1175 (1989)

Schacter, Jane, *Romer v. Evans and Democracy's Domain,* 50 Vand. L. Rev. 361 (1997)

Scharpf, Fritz, *Judicial Review and the Political Question: A Functional Analysis,* 75 Yale L.J. 517 (1966)

Schneyer, Ted, *Legal Process Scholarship and the Regulation of Lawyers,* 65 Fordham L. Rev. 33 (1996)

Schwartz, David S., *The Case of the Vanishing Protected Class: Reflection on Reverse Discrimination, Affirmative Action, and Racial Balancing,* 2000 Wis. L. Rev. 657 (2000)

Scott, Robert E., *A Relational Theory of Default Rules for Commercial Contracts*, 19 J. LEGAL STUD. 597 (1990)

Shaffer, Gregory, *The World Trade Organization under Challenge, The Law and Politics of the WTO's Treatment of Trade and Environment Matters*, HARV. ENVTL. L. REV. (forthcoming winter 2001a)

Shaffer, Gregory, *The WTO Shrimp-Turtle Case: The Democratic Legitimacy of US Trade Sanctions on Environmental Grounds, A Comparative Institutional Approach*, 2000 Proceedings of the ASIL Annual Meeting (forthcoming 2001b)

Shaffer, Gregory, *Globalization and Social Protection: The Impact of EU and International Rules in the Ratcheting Up of U.S. Privacy Standards*, 25 YALE J. INT'L L. 1 (2000)

Shaklar, Judith N., *Political Theory and the Rule of Law, in* THE RULE OF LAW: IDEAL OR IDEOLOGY 12 (Allan C. Hutchinson & Patrick J. Monahan, eds., 1987)

Sidak, Gregory & Daniel Spulber, DEREGULATORY TAKINGS AND THE REGULATORY CONTRACT: THE COMPETITIVE TRANSFORMATION OF NETWORK INDUSTRIES IN THE UNITED STATES (1997)

Siegen, Bernard H., LAND USE WITHOUT ZONING (1972)

Simon, William H., *Social-Republican Property*, 38 UCLA L. REV. 1335 (1991)

Sterk, Stewart E., *Neighbors in American Land Law*, 87 COLUM. L. REV. 55 (1987)

Sugarman, Stephen, DOING AWAY WITH PERSONAL INJURY LAW (1989)

Sullivan, Kathleen M., *The Justices of Rules and Standards*, 106 HARV. L. REV. 22 (1992)

Sunstein, Cass R., *On Property and Constitutionalism*, 14 CARDOZO L. REV. 907 (1993)

Symposium, *Is the Jury Competent?*, 52 LAW & CONTEMP. PROBS. 1 (1989)

Symposium, *Rule 23: Class Actions at the Crossroads*, 39 ARIZ. L. REV. 407 (1997)

Tarlock, A. Dan, *Consistency with Adopted Land Use Plans as a Standard of Judicial Review: The Case Against*, 9 URB. L. ANN. 69 (1975)

Trachtman, Joel P., *The Theory of the Firm and the Theory of International Economic Organization: Toward Comparative Institutional Analysis*, 17 Nw. J. INT'L L. & BUS. 470 (1996–97)

Treanor, William Michael, *The Original Understanding of the Takings Clause and the Political Process*, 95 COLUM. L. REV. 782 (1995)

Tushnet, Mark V., TAKING THE CONSTITUTION AWAY FROM THE COURTS (1999)

Unger, Roberto M., LAW IN MODERN SOCIETY (1976)

Wagner, Wendy E., *Restoring Polluted Waters with Public Values*, 25 WM. & MARY ENVTL. L & POL'Y REV. 429 (2000)

Washburn, Robert M., *Land Use Control, The Individual, and Society:* Lucas v. South Carolina Coastal Council, 52 MD. L. REV. 162 (1993)

Wiener, Jonathan Baert, *Global Environmental Regulation: Instrument Choice in Legal Context*, 108 YALE L.J. 677 (1999)

Wilkins, David B., *How Should We Determine Who Should Regulate Lawyers? Managing Conflict and Context in Professional Regulation*, 65 FORDHAM L. REV. 465 (1996)

Williams, Robert A., Jr., *Legal Discourse, Social Vision and the Supreme Court's*

Land Use Planning Law: The Genealogy of the Lochnerian Recurrence in First English Lutheran Church *and* Nollan, 59 U. Colo. L. Rev. 427 (1988)

Zalkin, Natasha, Comment, *Shifting Sands and Shifting Doctrines: The Supreme Court's Changing Takings Doctrine and South Carolina's Coastal Zone Statute,* 79 Calif. L. Rev. 205 (1991)

Index